Divine Representations

POSTMODERNISM AND SPIRITUALITY

Ann W. Astell,
Editor

PAULIST PRESS
New York and Mahwah, NJ

Cover photo by Tom McCarthy.
Cover design by Art Jacobs.

Library of Congress Cataloging-in-Publication Data

Divine representations : postmodernism and spirituality / Ann W.
  Astell, editor.
      p.   cm.
  Includes bibliographical references.
  ISBN 0-8091-3528-0
    1. Spirituality—Christianity.   2. Postmodernism—Religious
aspects—Christianity.   3. Religion and culture.   4. Mary, Blessed
Virgin, Saint—Theology.   I. Astell, Ann W.
  BV4510.2.D56   1994
  248—dc20   94-32753
                                                           CIP

Published by Paulist Press
997 Macarthur Boulevard
Mahwah, New Jersey 07430

Printed and bound in the
United States of America

Contents

Acknowledgements   vii

Introduction
   Ann W. Astell   1

PART I
REPRESENTATIONS OF GOD AND SELF

Spirituality as a Stage of Being
   Aldo Tassi, Loyola College in Maryland   21

Overcoming Self: Simone Weil on Beauty
   Ann Pirruccello, University of San Diego   34

Angela of Foligno: Destructuring and Restructuring
of Identity
   Mary Walsh Meany, Siena College   47

The Word Image Opposition: The Apophatic/Cataphatic
and the Iconic/Aniconic Tensions in Spirituality
   Mary Gerhart, Hobart and William Smith Colleges   63

PART II
REPRESENTATIONS OF SPIRIT

Is Spirituality Possible Without Religion?
A Query For the Postmodern Era
  Tom W. Boyd, University of Oklahoma 83

The Marian Counterpoint of Postmodern Spirituality
  Johann G. Roten, S.M., University of Dayton 102

Buddhist and Christian Postmodern Spiritualities
  Donald W. Mitchell, Purdue University 129

Answering to Pluralism: Fr. Kentenich's Concept of a
Secular, Marian Spirituality
  Günther M. Boll, Schoenstatt, Germany 149

PART III
SOCIAL REPRESENTATIONS

Feminism, Deconstructing Hierarchies, and Marian
Coronation
  Ann W. Astell, Purdue University 163

Postmodernism and the Spirituality of the Liberal
Arts: A Neo-Hegelian *Diagnôsis* and an
Augustinian *Pharmakon*
  Thomas Ryba, Purdue University 177

St. Francis and the Environment
  Philibert Hoebing, O.F.M., Quincy University 201

Science and Faith: Is It Possible for a Scientist
To Believe?
  Roberto Colella, Purdue University 216

Spirituality and Contemporary American Medicine:
A Postmodern Perspective
  Valerie Miké, Cornell University Medical College 231

CODA

Reflections on Philosophy, Spirituality, and Mariology
    Elena Lugo, University of Puerto Rico-Mayaguez 248

Contributors 267

Acknowledgements

Most of the papers collected in this volume were given at a conference entitled "Toward a Lay Spirituality For the Postmodern Era," which was held at the International Schoenstatt Center in Waukesha, Wisconsin, in October, 1992. Over a hundred scholars representing a wide range of disciplines travelled from all over the United States to meet at the retreat house there, deliver papers, converse, and pray about a topic of pressing social and personal importance. In the "paradisal atmosphere" of that unique encounter with God and each other, this book was first conceived. It honors the memory and continues the work of Fr. Joseph Kentenich (1885–1968), the Founder of Schoenstatt, who, with characteristic courage and hope, welcomed honest, co-responsible dialogue. With prophetic insight, he saw the advent of postmodernism as a gift, a challenging task, and an opportunity to risk something for God out of an abiding trust in him and concern for the happiness of others.

In his name I wish to thank all the participants in the conference and especially the contributors to this volume for their generous support, cooperation, and encouragement. I am particularly grateful to my colleagues at Purdue, Roberto Colella, Raymond DeCarlo, Donald W. Mitchell, and Thomas Ryba, for the many conversations we have had together about this project and the inspiration that exchange has given me.

I also wish to thank the leaders of the Schoenstatt Movement who graciously hosted the conference, especially Dieter Haas, Jacoba Kesselheim, Elizabeth Dingbaum, Jean Frisk, and Angela Macari. Special thanks go to Homay Valafar, for his help with software; to Thomasine Treese and Marcia Vinje, who read a draft of the entire manuscript; and to Marita Urban and Rita Easterwood, who assisted me in typing. Donald F. Brophy and the staff at Paulist Press have my gratitude for their careful work, kindness, and encouragement. Finally, I owe heartfelt gratitude to Elena Lugo, who first proposed the conference and its postmodern theme.

Since I have offered these expressions of thanks in Fr. Kentenich's name, it is fitting to end with thanksgiving to him and God, a thanksgiving expressed in the dedication of this volume.

Ann W. Astell

IN MEMORIAM

Fr. Joseph Kentenich (1885–1968)
A Prophet at the Turn of Time

ANN W. ASTELL

Introduction

Some are born posthumously.

Nietzsche

Hagiography is "lived forward."

Edith Wyschogrod

The way forward is forward.

Diogenes Allen

Forward then! Into the postmodern era!

Joseph Kentenich

Many studies of spirituality stress its "personal, intimate, and temperamental"[1] quality to such a degree that no classification is possible; others single out certain forms of spirituality as timeless archetypes.[2] A few, such as this one, emphasize the complex interaction between the human spirit, the spirit of the times, and the Spirit of God in order to account for "shifting styles of spirituality"[3] at different historical and cultural intersections. If, as Gordon Wakefield explains, "spirituality concerns the way prayer influences conduct, our behavior and manner of life, our attitude to other people," then this nexus of "praying and living"[4] is necessarily affected in contemporary times by the profound "revolution in consciousness"[5] that we call "postmodernism."[6]

Remembering Ihab Hassan's caveat that "postmodernism . . . requires both historical and theoretical definition"[7]—a caveat that each of the contributors to this volume have heeded, however diverse and provisional their definitions—I propose to open the discussion by naming an historical marker and offering a limited phenomenological description of what is a slowly emerging, whole-scale, cultural transformation.

Referring to developments in architecture, painting, poetry, philosophy, economics or physics, scholars have advanced various twentieth-century dates as birthdates of postmodernism,[8] but few would disagree that the two world wars, taken together as a continuum, mark a decisive break with modernity and its emancipatory beliefs in unlimited human progress. In the words of Jean-François Lyotard, "There is a sort of grief in the *Zeitgeist*,"[9] ever since modernity ended in Auschwitz and the terror that name represents.

As Lyotard explains, Nazism, as a distant mirror of essential elements of French republicanism, brought modernity to an end by exposing its ambiguities. Hitler used the democratic name and the myth of "the people" (*das Volk*) to authorize not only his own totalitarian despotism, but also genocide and the imperialistic conquest of other peoples. "Equality" gained its symbolic expression in the lockstep marching of the troops and the anonymity of deportation and death. "Fraternity" could be found in either the Party or the prison; and "Freedom" was reinscribed in the motto "Arbeit Macht Frei" in the gate at the entrance to Dachau. The triumph of art was the aesthetization of torture and destruction as "beautiful death"; technological advance fed the war machine; and philosophy, reasoning its own unreason, celebrated the Superman, the Will to Power, and the death of God.

"There is no denying," Edith Wyschogrod writes, "that postmodernism is fine-tuned to the apocalyptic dimension of twentieth-century history."[10] Rising from the ashes of the death-camps, the spirit of postmodernism gives new life to the emancipatory impulse associated with modernity: intellectually, in what Lyotard calls "incredulity toward metanarratives";[11] politically, in demands for the empowerment of the marginalized and the deconstruction of hierarchies; socially, in a new respect for plurality and diversity; economically, in the free play of late-capitalist consumerism; technologically, in the valorization of performance; aesthetically, in eclecticism, in strategies of multiple perspective, fragmentation and double-coding, and finally in a penchant for allegory, parody, paranomasia and pastiche.

In each of the cultural expressions, however, the revolutionary impulse again and again threatens to turn into its opposite, into tyranny. As Wyschogrod observes, the insistence on empowerment tends "to endorse a ruthless battle of power in which might determines right."[12] "Difference" itself becomes totalized, and ethics, unmoored; the self-interest of identity politics spawns racism and oppression; the economy consumes the consumer; technology produces the producer; the many are reduced to the one; and "Auschwitz" recurs as a condition of life in what Julia Kristeva calls our "mascara and soap-opera age."[13]

If Lyotard is right in his symbolic focus on Auschwitz, and if the camp experience figures within postmodernity as "recurrence," then, in the context of the present work, we may rightly look to the saints of the World War II era as prophets of a new, postmodern spirituality. The writings of the acknowledged spiritual masters of that time—among them, Dietrich Bonhoeffer, Joseph Kentenich, Chiara Lubich and Simone Weil, all of whom were either incarcerated in concentration camps or endured camp-like conditions— certainly share a sense of prophecy.[14]

Bonhoeffer (1906–45) was executed in Buchenwald before he could complete his visionary reflections on the "religionless Christianity" of the coming age. Kentenich, a prisoner in Dachau from 1942–45, extended there in breadth and depth his vision of the "New Person in a New Community." Lubich began the work of forming a "New Humanity" in 1943 in Trent, while the city was undergoing massive Allied bombing attacks. And Weil (1909–43) at the end of her brief life hailed the advent of "a new type of sanctity" as "a fresh spring, an invention": "Today it is not nearly enough merely to be a saint," she writes; living in "times that have no precedent, . . . we must have the saintliness demanded by the present moment, a new saintliness, itself also without precedent."[15]

While these spiritual leaders all have their own unique charism, greatness and eccentricity, certain common themes are evident in their writings and indicative of a truly postmodern spirituality. Before exploring these common themes in an attempt toward a phenomenological description of postmodern "praying and living," however, we need to discern a common point of departure in their assessment of modern spirituality. As the word itself implies, the "postmodern" entails not only a break with the modern, but also its aftermath.

Postmodern spirituality in the West inevitably confronts the religious heritage of modernity in its related forms. As Wolfhart Pannenberg explains, the split between the Catholic and the Reform Churches in the sixteenth century prompted war and persecution in an attempt to maintain "religious unity as a foundation of social life."[16] The violent rift among believers eventually precipitated the separation of Church and State as a radical measure undertaken to safeguard society against the internal threat posed by sectarian division. While social structures and civil institutions have retained what Bonhoeffer and Weil term an "unconscious Christianity" and what Pannenberg calls "Christian roots," the separation of Church and State has increasingly marginalized the churches from the mainstream of life, making the religious belief and practice of individuals an optional extra, an unnecessary and perhaps irrelevant supplement to their function in society. Commenting on this "displacement of God from the world," Bonhoeffer remarks, "As in the scientific field, so in human affairs generally, 'God' is being pushed more and more out of life, losing more and more ground."[17] Weil speaks similarly of an ever widening "divorce . . . between profane civilization and spirituality in Christian countries."[18]

Believers have tended to internalize this binary opposition of the secular and the sacred in one of three ways. Some have taken an assimilative route of practical agnosticism, perhaps combined with a nominal or purely private religiosity. Some have assumed a pietistic, fundamentalist stance of antagonism and withdrawal that labels the world godless and sinful—a negative image to which the secular order has responded with a corresponding rejection of, and hostility toward, religious influence.[19] As a third option, some have extended the societal division of Church and State in philosophical and theological terms, relegating God to a wholly Other, unknowable, transcendent realm beyond our epistemological and technological limits.

Rejecting both the assimilative route of agnosticism and the fundamentalist stance of withdrawal, the saints of the World War II agon characteristically refuse to let themselves be defined by the modernist secular/sacred binary. Their postmodern spiritualities take the secular order seriously as an indispensable *Lebensraum*, a "living space" for faith and its practice in everyday life. As Bonhoeffer insists, "The church stands, not at the boundaries where human powers give out, but in the middle of the village. . . . God is no stop-gap; he must be recognized at the centre of life, not when we are at the end of our resources" (pp. 282, 312).

This recognition of God "not on the boundaries but at the centre, not in weakness but in strength, and therefore not in death and guilt but in man's life and goodness" (p. 282) entails the obligation, in Weil's words, "to show the public the possibility of a truly incarnated Christianity" (WFG, p. 76). In the Focolare

Movement founded by Lubich, that "incarnation" takes place in practical terms through the daily reflection on and application of the biblical "word of life."[20] In Schoenstatt the members strive for what Kentenich calls "everyday sanctity": "the divinely willed harmony between a loving attachment to God, to work, and to our fellow human beings in every circumstance of life."[21]

In this incarnational Christianity, the absent, wholly Other God of modernism returns, descends, and takes flesh anew. That (Christological) return and (Marian) enfleshment necessarily calls attention to the people, things, places, tasks and events in our lives, and the way they mediate between God and humankind and among the members of a community to represent the Unrepresentable.

The immanence of the transcendent God who is, as Mark C. Taylor puts it, "never present without being absent," reveals itself through the transparency of signs that simultaneously reveal and conceal God.[22] Infinite, and therefore inherently refractory to representation, God bridges the distance between himself and the world through sensible reflections (*Abbilder*) of Christ, the *Logos* and *Urbild* of all creation, who in the fullness of time stripped himself of glory and became human (cf. Phil. 2:6–8; Col. 1:15–20). These creaturely reflections of Christ, precisely because they are not only beautiful and radiantly attractive, but also dark, tangible, imperfect and incomplete, announce their own status as representational and thus occlude idolatry, even as they enable us to come into contact with the Divine. They condition our faith, represent God to us through a kind of transference, allow us to experience his love, capture our hearts, and, finally, allow for the organic transmission of our affections to the God we cannot see.

"How does Christ speak to us today?" Bonhoeffer asks.[23] Perhaps no other concern is more dominant in the writings of these four spiritual leaders, all of whom emphasize the necessity of mediation. Bonhoeffer speaks of Christ as "the Mediator, not only between God and man, but between man and man, between man and reality," whose Incarnation precludes any "immediate relationship" to anything or anyone.[24] Weil also emphasizes Christ as the *Logos* (a word which she translates as "mediation"), and building on that understanding of Christ, she affirms the necessity of creatures as *metaxu* ("bridges" or "intermediaries") to God, the mediative function of beauty and affliction, and the possibility "for us to be mediators between God and the part of creation which is confided to us."[25] Kentenich, unfolding the psychological ramifications of the Thomistic teaching on secondary causes, emphasizes the prophetic function of creation, the "organism of attachments" that binds our hearts to God, and the "transparency function" of the people in whom we encounter and love the divine "You" who loves us. Lubich's spirituality of unity emphasizes the discovery of "Jesus in our midst" and entails an essential mediation of God-Love among people "that all may be one" (John 17:21).

In the postmodern spiritualities we are surveying here, mediation, as a dynamic of exchange between and among persons, has both a vertical and a horizontal dimension. In the vertical dimension, mediation answers to what Pannenberg calls the "long-term effects of the secularization of culture"[26]—including the delegitimation of authority, moral confusion, and personal disorientation— by allowing for an existential meeting with God and an affective dialogue between him and the human person. Confronted by a "world controlled by forces against which reason can do nothing" (p. 298), Bonhoeffer urges the Spirit-filled discovery of the "Thou" disguised in the "It"—a discovery through which "fate" turns into divine "guidance" and invites a free response of human action or submission (p. 218). Similarly, Weil speaks of the transformation of "necessity" into "obedience" when we learn "to love God through everything good and everything evil, without distinction":[27]

> We must love God through the evil that occurs, solely because everything that actually occurs is real, and behind all reality stands God. Some realities are more or less transparent; others are completely opaque, but God is behind them all, without distinction. (SNL, p. 154)

Kentenich, perhaps even more than Bonhoeffer, Lubich and Weil, emphasizes what he calls "practical belief in divine providence," which entails not only the symbolic recognition of God's vestiges and traces, but also the discovery of the living God behind the masks he wears, a freely given "yes" to his wish and will, and a creative coacting with him in the circumstances of life according to the rules of the "Game of Love" and the improvised script of the divine/human comedy.[28] Indeed, Kentenich encourages us "to make it a habit to see all, even the smallest incidents of everyday life as the eternal Father's wish, as his gift of love, as his searching love which requires our answer of love."[29]

Living a faith that discovers God and his love unconditionally in and behind all reality—including the cruellest of experiences and the monstrous deeds of history—necessarily leads, in the vision of Weil and the experience of Kentenich, to what Weil calls "an abiding conception of the divine mercy, a conception that does not change whatever event destiny may send upon me, and which can be communicated to no matter what human being" (GG, p. 168). This radical belief in God's mercy is a peculiarly postmodern charism, as Weil sees it, given the brutality of our own age and our altered perspective on history, which views the past and present more and more from the point of view of the silenced, oppressed and victimized:

> A man whose whole family had died under torture, and who had himself been tortured for a long time in a concentration camp. Or a sixteenth-century Indian, the sole survivor after the total extermination of his people. Such men, if they had previously believed in the mercy of God, would either believe in it no longer, or else they would conceive of it quite differently than before. (GG, p. 168)

Kentenich, who spent four years of his life as a prisoner of the Gestapo, first in a civilian prison and then in the death-camp at Dachau, and who subsequently endured fourteen years of exile, achieved and communicated to others this "different" and "abiding" concept of God's mercy in a remarkable fashion. As a pastor and spiritual director, he himself accepted as "jewels" the fragments and "broken pieces" of the lives entrusted to him, perceived (and thus enlivened) "greatness" in "nothingness," accepted confessed sins as "gifts," and insisted, "We cannot swim enough in the ocean of God's mercies nor be too convinced of his love. . . . Suffering is always a proof of God's love" (p. 79).

The unconditional acceptance of God's will and the entrustment of one's self to his mercy constitute, in the thought of Bonhoeffer, Weil and Kentenich, the achievement of a true freedom, an heroic childlikeness, that enables one to meet and master whatever challenges life may bring. It entails the reception of what Weil calls "grace," the divine "lightness" that triumphs over the pull of "gravity" and the forces of entropy that govern an otherwise self-enclosed system of this-worldly relations. Daring the death leap, freely emptying oneself in obedience to fulfill God's will, thus expresses and results in inner freedom: "Freed of ourselves," Kentenich writes from Dachau, "[we are] free for God and his work. . . . Each new decision [for God] means a corresponding increase of inner freedom" and, with it, the ability to be creative in history, to set into motion a new chain of causes as a creative resultant of an instrumental surrender to God.[30]

Prolonged imprisonment prompted both Bonhoeffer and Kentenich to meditate deeply on freedom. In a beautiful poem, Bonhoeffer identifies discipline, action, suffering and death as "Stations on the Road to Freedom," the "eternal freedom" that is ultimately "revealed in the Lord" (pp. 370–71). Kentenich's own "battle for freedom" had a strongly communal dimension. He aimed at obtaining "perfect inner freedom" for himself and his followers through the "interwovenness of fate" that linked his suffering and striving in prison with theirs on the outside. In the light of faith, he recognized that his very identity was inseparable from that of the community which was joined to him and for which he was ready to sacrifice himself. Rejecting modernist notions of personal autonomy, he and his followers lived out of a deep sense of mutual responsibility in accord with the motto: "What you are, the way you love, affects others, determines their misfortune and increases their happiness."[31]

The vertical dimension of mediation, which links the individual to God through various representations of divine and human love, is thus intimately connected to the horizontal, which helps to secure the presence of God in the midst of people. In its horizontal dimension, as Weil observes, the mediation which is embodied in Christ's "Incarnation . . . implies a harmonious solution of the problem of the relations between the individual and the collective" (WFG, p. 77). Christ's physical body, like his mystical one,[32] is a microcosm joining many members into one—a union that points to the vital interconnectedness of people and the need for, and the possibility of, what Kentenich calls common "points of contact" and "attachment" as the basis for familylike communities characterized by both unity and diversity. Kentenich speaks of the binding power of common tasks, life-experiences, sufferings, symbols and shared ideals, as well as the more fundamental psychological bindings to a common spiritual home and parents—all of which provide a natural basis and presupposition for the working of grace, as well as its outward sign and safeguard.

In the thinking of Kentenich and the spiritual leaders contemporary with him, identifying common points of contact and attachment in an increasingly pluralistic world answers to the root problems posed by the division of Christians in the early modern period, the broader split among the world religions, and the gap between believers and unbelievers, as well as the alienating individualism which remains ours as a modernist inheritance.[33] Bonhoeffer, for example, was an early supporter of the ecumenical movement, which looks, in Pannenberg's words, "toward a plurality of churches which mutually recognize one another within the community of the one Church of Christ."[34] Even more radically, Bonhoeffer experienced that he was often drawn by a " 'Christian instinct' more to the religionless people than to the religious" (p. 281) on the double basis of the "unconscious Christianity" (p. 373) of his unbelieving brothers and sisters and their mutual sharing in this-worldly "duties, problems, successes, failures, experiences, and perplexities" (p. 370).

The cross, however, stands as the most fundamental ground of vertical and horizontal mediation in the spiritualities we are surveying here. In the universality of human suffering, Bonhoeffer finds "the sufferings of God in the secular life" (p. 361), the sufferings of Christ who died for all people without exception and whose cross reconciles Christians and pagans alike. Weil, who stood personally "at the intersection of Christianity and everything that is not Christianity" (WFG, p. 76), speaks in similar terms of the mediation of the cross and the presence of Christ "wherever there is crime and affliction" (LP, p. 17). Echoing St. Paul (Col. 1:24), Kentenich sends a reminder from Dachau that the suffering of the present enables us to share in Christ's ongoing work of redemption and supply "whatever fullness is still lacking in the cross and suffering of Christ."[35] Lubich, too, discovers in human suffering a "oneness with Jesus Forsaken," and thus the basis for the perfect unity that is the special charism and mission of the Focolare Movement, with its emphasis on ecumenism, inter-faith dialogue, and the coming together of believers and unbelievers in mutual love. She advises her fellow Focolarini: "When you find yourself in front of a person, any person at all, remember that in that heart lives God, God who might be abandoned by that same heart."[36]

In all four postmodern spiritualities under discussion here, the idea of divine and human abandonment answers to the much-discussed experiential "absence" of God in our secularized world.[37] Instead of confusing an experiential with a metaphysical absence (as the Death of God theologians did in the sixties), they find in it another form of God's mysterious presence and activity. Kentenich, for instance, speaks of the *Deus absconditus*, "the living Father who hides and even flees from us," in order that we might long and look for him in a game of hide-and-seek (p. 84). He emphasizes that the absolute insecurity of the present day is designed in the plan of God to teach us perfect childlikeness. Similarly, both Weil and

Bonhoeffer speak of modernity's atheism as a providential means of "purification" (GG, p. 168) through which our "false conception of God" (p. 361) is stripped away as a prelude to a new encounter with him. As Bonhoeffer phrases it, "The world that has come of age is more godless, and perhaps for that very reason, nearer to God than the world before its coming of age" (p. 362).

In a stroke of genius, all four spiritual leaders discover in the afflictive experience of God's absence the opportunity to share in Christ's own experience of abandonment on the cross, the moment of agony that marks the divine depth of self-emptying love: "My God, my God, why have you forsaken me?" (Matthew 27:46; Mark 15:34). Lubich calls particular attention to this moment: "We look to Jesus Forsaken. No one is poorer than he; he, having lost all of his disciples, having given his mother away, gives also his life for us and experiences the terrible sensation that his Father has abandoned him" (p. 90). Similarly, Bonhoeffer writes from his prison cell:

> The God who is with us is the God who forsakes us (Mark 15:34). The God who lets us live in the world without the working hypothesis of God is the God before whom we stand continually. Before God and with God we live without God. God lets himself be pushed out of the world on to the cross. He is weak and powerless in the world, and that is precisely the way . . . in which he is with us and helps us. (p. 360)

Weil, writing about the "affliction that causes God to be absent for a time, more absent than a dead man, more absent than light in the utter darkness of a cell" (SNL, p. 172), points to it as a God-given means to reach "the haven of the cross" (WFG, p. 59) where Christ saves the world in the very affliction that "constrained [him] to implore that he might be spared, to seek consolation from man, to believe that he was forsaken by the Father" (SNL, p. 172). In language that points at the same mystery of abandonment, Kentenich asks, "Can the Father show greater love than when he helps his children to become like his only-begotten Son, who hangs on the cross?" (p. 74).

In passages like these, unity with God is seen as paradoxically perfected in the human experience of abandonment by God, when God himself empties himself to such an extent that he endures a kenotic separation from himself in and with us.[38] The reception of this selfless God depends on a correspondent loss of self, dying to self, on the part of the human being undergoing affliction and thus gives meaning to the much-discussed postmodern loss of "self," defined as an autonomous, stable, conscious identity. As Bonhoeffer observes, we experience ourselves as fragmented and incomplete, "but this fragmentariness may, in fact, point towards a fulfillment beyond the limits of human achievement" (p. 215).

The blows of fate; the pace, mobility, and anonymity of contemporary life; the fragility of human relationships; the consumptive materialism that transvalues virtually everything and everyone in late-capitalist culture; and the impact of technology on basic life-processes from conception to death—all teach us, as Simone Weil phrases it, that "the thing we believe to be our self is as ephemeral and automatic a product of external circumstances as the form of a sea-wave" (SNL, p. 188). The loss of this transitory, constructed self is inevitable. The key question is how and to what end this "I" is lost. In biblical terms, the question may be rephrased as follows: Do we, like Christ and with him, freely lay down our life? Or do we allow someone or something else to take our life from us? As Bonhoeffer intimates in a letter from prison, "It is we ourselves, and not outward circumstances, who make death what it can be" (p. 16).

Death in this life, according to Weil, can be one of two things. The experience of affliction—understood as a suffering so intense that it "deprives its victims of their personality and turns them into things" and robs them "of the power to say 'I'" (SNL, p. 175; GG, p. 71)—leads to the death of the self either through destruction (in which something created passes into nothingness) or through decreation (in which the created passes into the Uncreated), into God in whom the "I" is veiled and hidden, even from one's own self (GG, p. 78). As Weil sees it, whether we are destroyed or decreated by the mechanical play of circumstances depends upon the refusal or the free choice to have no "I" but the "I" that is in God, the "I" that belongs to God, and which Kentenich calls the "personal ideal."

Kentenich characterizes the decreative loss of the self as *inscriptio*, as a self-surrender to God that entails a complete exchange of heart, mind, goods and interests with him, so that we are and will to be only what he wills us to be. Lubich, too, speaks of a radical dying to self and forsaking of self in "ego-less" love:

Jesus Forsaken is our style of love. He has taught us to annihilate everything inside us and around us, to "make ourselves one" with God; He teaches us . . . to mortify our senses, to drop even our own inspirations so that we can "make ourselves one" with our neighbors, which means to serve them, to love them. (p. 50)

All four of the spiritual masters, moreover, speak of a paradoxical, new, joyful self-discovery and self-possession that occurs "on the other side" precisely through the attitude and act of self-abandonment. As Lubich phrases it, "This is how you become (by participation) God, who is Love" (p. 71). This discovery of the self-that-is-Love in and through the Other whom we love more than ourselves defines what Edith Wyschogrod has called the "paradox . . . bound up with saintly self-emptying" and its "excessive desire on behalf of the Other."[39] Morality depends on the will and begins with the "I"; saintliness, on the other hand, depends on desire and begins with the Other, putting the interest of the Other first. And, as Weil reminds us, "it is desire that saves": "To long for God and to renounce all the rest, that alone can save us" (WFG, pp. 195–96).

The themes I have briefly sounded in these initial pages find their echo, continuation and rejoinder in the essays that follow. The essays are arranged in three sets. The first set, entitled "Representations of God and Self," consists of four essays. Aldo Tassi uses the image of the mirror, the juxtaposed biblical and Platonic narratives of human origin, and the language of the theater to address the postmodern understanding of the self. Ann Pirruccello places Simone Weil's "decreated self" in dialogue with contemporary theories of the (de)constructed self and reflects on the crucial role that beauty plays in awakening desire in the soul. Mary Walsh Meany brings postmodern theory to bear on the autobiography of Angela of Foligno, a thirteenth-century mystic whose identity was destructured and restructured through the presence of the Other in her life. Finally, Mary Gerhart relates the cataphatic in spirituality to the iconic in church art, the apophatic to the aniconic, the visual to the verbal, and thus probes the intersection between individual and collectives images of the Divine.

The second set of essays, "Representations of Spirit," delineates the broad streams in postmodern spirituality and their particular manifestations in selected contemporary spiritualities. Tom

W. Boyd begins with the cleavage between spirituality and religion in the New Age movement and popular psychology and, extending the position of Paul Tillich, argues for religion as a necessary, but ever incomplete and ultimately transformative "form" of "spirit" in its openness to the Transcendent. Johann G. Roten, S.M., offers a far-ranging descriptive survey of postmodern spirituality and joins to it a Marian counterpoint. Donald W. Mitchell first suggests how postmodern spirituality, both Buddhist and Christian, redresses negative elements of modernism and then proceeds to relate the parallel narratives of two such spiritualities, the F.A.S. Society and the Focolare. Günther M. Boll looks at the challenge to Christianity presented by religious pluralism and argues for the necessity of formative, Marian spiritualities, such as Schoenstatt, which aims at fostering a profoundly elective Christianity in its members.

The third set of essays, "Social Representations," examines specific social concerns and their power to shape postmodern spirituality. Thomas Ryba brings Augustinian sign and learning theory to bear on the late-capitalist commodification of knowledge. I reflect on the cultural symbolism of Marian coronation within the conflictive context of feminism. Philibert Hoebing, O.F.M., highlights the relevance of Franciscan spirituality and Scotistic theology to the urgent questions of the present ecological crisis. Physicist Roberto Colella heralds the death of scientism in the advent of Quantum Mechanics and shows the possibility of, and implies the necessity for, a scientific spirituality. Biostatistician Valerie Miké underscores the importance of a holistic approach to healing and an "ethics of evidence" in contemporary American medicine.

As a coda to the collection, I have included Elena Lugo's reflections on philosophy, spirituality, and Mariology—reflections that she shared in her keynote address at the 1992 Conference at which most of these papers were given.

Although the contributors vary in their respective disciplines and differ in their definitions of the postmodern and their approaches to spirituality, the collection as a whole has a definite shape and sequence. Its imagistic pattern begins with Aldo Tassi's reflections on Genesis and ends with Valerie Miké's commentary on *Final Exit*. While each essay can be read in isolation, each complements thematically the essays that immediately precede and follow it in an approximation of dialogue. Aldo Tassi's essay, for instance, contrasts the Platonic and Hebrew creation stories, and Ann Pirruccello's follows with an exposition of Simone Weil's Platonic response to the beauty of creation. I have, in short, in the spirit of Kentenich and the other "saints" with whom this book began, endeavored to be the instrumental builder of a truly communal collection of essays, "that the many may be one."

Notes

1.   "Preface," in *The Study of Spirituality*, ed. Cheslyn Jones, Geoffrey Wainwright, and Edward Yarnold, S.J. (New York and Oxford: Oxford University Press, 1986), p. xxii.

2.   See, for instance, Geoffrey Wainwright's adaptation of H. Richard Niebuhr's typology in "Types of Spirituality," ibid., pp. 592–605.

3.   Urban T. Holmes, III, *A History of Christian Spirituality: An Analytical Introduction* (New York: Seabury, 1981), p. 8.

4.   Gordon Wakefield, *A Dictionary of Christian Spirituality* (London: Student Christian Movement, 1983), p. v; Geoffrey Wainwright, *Study of Spirituality*, p. 592.

5.   Holmes, *History of Christian Spirituality*, p. 150.

6.   Relatively few studies have approached postmodernism from the perspective of spirituality or religion. See *Spirituality and Society: Postmodern Visions*, ed. David Ray Griffin (Albany: SUNY, 1988); Diogenes Allen, *Christian Belief in a Postmodern World: The Full Wealth of Conviction* (Louisville: John Knox Press, 1989); *Postmodern Theology: Christian Faith in a Pluralist World*, ed. Frederic B. Burnham (San Francisco: Harper, 1989); Edith Wyschogrod, *Saints and Postmodernism: Revisioning Moral Philosophy* (Chicago: The University of Chicago Press, 1990); *Shadow of Spirit: Postmodernism and Religion*, ed. Philippa Berry and Andrew Wernick (London and New York: Routledge, 1992). The latter collection, in particular, "challenges the long-established assumption that contemporary western thought is committed to nihilism" by "illuminating the striking affinity between the most innovative aspects of postmodern thought and religious or mystical discourse."

7.   Ihab Hassan, "The Culture of Postmodernism," in *Theory, Culture, and Society* 2.3 (1985), p. 122.

8. See Andreas Huyssen, "Mapping the Postmodern," in *Feminism/Postmodernism*, ed. Linda J. Nicholson (Routledge: New York and London, 1990), pp. 234–77; Gianni Vattimo, *The End of Modernity: Nihilism in Postmodern Culture*, trans. Jon R. Snyder (Baltimore: Johns Hopkins University Press, 1988); Jean-François Lyotard, *The Postmodern Condition: A Report on Knowledge*, trans. Geoff Bennington and Brian Massumi, Theory and History of Literature #10 (Minneapolis: University of Minnesota Press, 1984); Charles Jencks, *Post-Modernism: The New Classicism in Art and Architecture* (New York: Rizzoli, 1987); Fredric Jameson, *Postmodernism, or, The Cultural Logic of Late Capitalism* (Durham: Duke University Press, 1991).

9. Jean-François Lyotard, *The Postmodern Explained*: *Correspondence 1982–1985*, ed. Julian Pefanis and Morgan Thomas (Minneapolis: University of Minnesota Press, 1992), p. 78. The discussion that follows immediately summarizes and extends Lyotard's observations on pp. 39–59. See especially pp. 52–53.

10. Edith Wyschogrod, *Saints and Postmodernism*, p. xxi.

11. Lyotard, *The Postmodern Condition*, p. xxiv.

12. Wyschogrod, *Saints and Postmodernism*, p. xxi.

13. Julia Kristeva, "Postmodernism?" in *Romanticism, Modernism, Postmodernism*, ed. Harry R. Garvin (Lewisburg: Bucknell University Press, 1980), p. 141; cited by Wyschogrod, p. xv.

14. Among the other spiritual leaders of the time who were profoundly affected by the war years, Martin Buber, Teilhard de Chardin, Etty Hillesum and Edith Stein come readily to mind. There are, of course, many others who could be named.

15. Simone Weil, *Waiting for God*, trans. Emma Crauford (New York: Capricorn, 1959), p. 99. Citations hereafter are parenthetical by abbreviated title (WFG) and page. For a further treatment of Weil's thought, see the essay in this volume by Ann Pirruccello.

16. Wolfhart Pannenberg, *Christianity In a Secularized World* (New York: Crossroad, 1989), p. 13.

17.   Dietrich Bonhoeffer, *Letters and Papers from Prison*, ed. Eberhard Bethge (New York: Macmillan, 1953, repr. 1971), pp. 344, 326. Subsequent citations are parenthetical by page.

18.   Simone Weil, *Letter to a Priest* (New York: Putnam, 1954), p. 19. Citations hereafter are parenthetical by title (LP) and page.

19.   The postmodern rise in religious fundamentalism, on the side of conservatism, and so-called "identity-politics," on the side of radicalism, may both derive from the desire to retain a "self" in the face of an increasingly anonymous, commodified culture. For a comment on the contemporary resurgence of Islamic fundamentalism, see Ernest Gellner, *Postmodernism, Reason, and Religion* (London and New York: Routledge, 1992).

20.   The Focolarini are literally "people of the hearth-fire." For a detailed discussion of the Focolare Movement, see Donald W. Mitchell's essay in this volume.

21.   I quote from a privately published, unauthorized English translation of the German text, *Werktagsheiligkeit*, by M. A. Nailis. For further discussion of Fr. Kentenich and Schoenstatt, see the essays in this volume by Ann W. Astell, Günther M. Boll, and Elena Lugo.

22.   Mark C. Taylor, "Reframing Postmodernisms," in *Shadow of Spirit*, p. 25.

23.   See Dietrich Bonhoeffer, "Preliminary Questions," in *The Cost of Discipleship*, trans. R. H. Fuller (1949; New York: Macmillan, 1963), pp. 249–53.

24.   Bonhoeffer, *Cost of Discipleship*, pp. 106–07.

25.   Simone Weil, *Gravity and Grace*, trans. Arthur Wills (New York: G. P. Putnam, 1952), p. 87. See also pp. 200–02. Subsequent citations are parenthetical by title (GG) and page.

26.   Pannenberg, *Christianity in a Secularized World*, p. 33.

27.   Simone Weil, *On Science, Necessity and the Love of God*, ed. and trans. Richard Rees (Oxford: Oxford University Press, 1968), p. 154. Citations hereafter are parenthetical by title (SNL) and page.

28.   See Aldo Tassi's essay in this volume for further discussion of the theatrical and performative images of play that are so prevalent in postmodern philosophy and spirituality.

29.   Joseph Kentenich, *God My Father* (anonymously translated and privately published at the International Schoenstatt Center in Waukesha, WI, 1977, repr. 1992), p. 80. Subsequent citations are parenthetical by page.

30.   I quote from an unauthorized private translation of *Marian Instrument Piety* by William Brell, privately published by the Schoenstatt Sisters of Mary (Waukesha, WI, 1992).

31.   The motto appears frequently in Kentenich's World War II writings, especially his so-called *Carmel Letters* and *Ceterum Censeo*.

32.   Pope Pius XII issued his encyclical on the Mystical Body of Christ (*Mystici Corporis*) in 1943. Both the Focolare Movement, founded in that same year, and the Schoenstatt Movement find in that document a special confirmation of their own timely experience of and striving for unity. See Judith M. Povilus, *United in His Name: Jesus in Our Midst in the Experience and Thought of Chiara Lubich* (New York: New City Press, 1992).

33.   As Leroy S. Rouner observes, "Community is a key issue for what is often called the "postmodern mind" (*On Community*, ed. Leroy S. Rouner [Notre Dame: University of Notre Dame Press, 1991], p. 2). For a classic study of the problem, see Robert A, Nisbet, *The Quest for Community* (London: Oxford University Press, 1953, repr. 1973).

34.   Pannenberg, *Christianity in a Secularized World*, p. 58.

35.   Joseph Kentenich, *Heavenwards*, trans. Jonathan Niehaus (Waukesha, WI: Schoenstatt Fathers, 1992), p. 53.

36.   Chiara Lubich, *Unity and Jesus Forsaken*, trans. Julian Stead, O.S.B. (New York: New City Press, 1985), pp. 60–61. Subsequent citations are parenthetical.

37.   Umberto Eco, for instance, talks about the God who shows himself "as he who is not," the God approachable through negative

theology, the "secularized and infinitely absent God who has accompanied contemporary thought under various names and . . . has invaded even the thought of the so-called Left" (*Travels in Hyper-Reality*, trans. William Weaver [San Diego: Harcourt Brace Jovanovich, 1986], pp. 93–94). See also *Shadow of Spirit*.

38.   For a recent, excellent study of kenosis, see Donald W. Mitchell, *Spirituality and Emptiness: The Dynamics of Spiritual Life in Buddhism and Christianity* (New York: Paulist, 1991).

39.   Wyschogrod, *Saints and Postmodernism*, pp. 33, xxiv.

PART I

Representations of God and Self

ALDO TASSI

Spirituality as a Stage of Being

The special difficulty that exists with the notion of spirituality comes from the fact that it initially addresses a mode of existence which is essentially problematic: namely, our own conscious existence. Every attempt to fix conceptually the role of humanity in the order of things reinforces the growing apprehension that we are dealing with an elusive reality: with something that does not exist in the normal sense in which the things of the world are said to exist. And, insofar as human existence is the "place" from which being is able to establish itself as "appearing being"—what today, following Heidegger, we would call a "world"[1]—the question of spirituality extends beyond the fact of human existence to being itself.

Traditionally, philosophy has engaged this problem in one of two ways. There is first of all the dualist who, starting with Plato, argues for the presence of a different sort of reality: namely, a reality which is autonomous with respect to material reality and has an existence all its own. The elusive nature of spiritual reality can be explained as arising from the fact that we mistakenly take the experience of material reality to be the norm for our dealings with reality. In opposition to the dualist, we have those who argue for the reverse position: namely, reality is reality and there are no two ways about it. According to this view, the reason why we take the experience of material reality to be the norm is because that is in fact the way reality is. It is understandable that spiritual reality should prove to be so elusive since it is nothing more than a chimera.

Despite the fundamental differences which separate these two positions, both are of one mind in insisting that the ambiguity which we find in our experience of ourselves, and which we extend

21

to reality at large, calls for corrective action. In its "uncorrected" state, such an experience cannot possibly reveal anything that has validity concerning reality, since it would be tantamount to saying that there is something "wrong" with reality. The correct view, we are told, can only be that there is something wrong with our thinking about reality and not with reality itself.

And yet, what are we to make of those moments in our lives— moments we believe to be fundamental—when we experience the fact that there is indeed something wrong: not with our thinking, but with ourselves? Is this not the same wrenching encounter with reality which is enacted in our greatest dramas? What else do *Oedipus Rex*, *King Lear*, *Six Characters in Search of an Author*, *Waiting for Godot*, to only begin the list, have to tell us, if not that there is something "wrong" with reality, beginning with that reality we call ourselves? This reference to the drama is, by no means, a casual one. The theatrical stage, from its earliest days in the Dionysian festivals, has sought to create a space from which to release into our public lives that deeper strata of our existence where we find ourselves connected to reality at large. The twin masks, representing tragedy and comedy, which traditionally serve as emblems of the theater are not only human faces. They are also, in the final analysis, the faces of a reality that has become spiritual.

1. Plato and Genesis: Two Mirrors of the Self

"What does it mean to be human?" Why is this question so intellectually disquieting? Despite the fact that there is no shortage of answers, we find ourselves returning to it again and again. The question itself appears to be no less paradoxical than the reality it inquires after. Let me try to illustrate this. Suppose we use the metaphor of a mirror and describe human existence as the mirror in which nature is able to behold itself. Now, the fact that it is a conscious mirror means that it will be aware that there exists in the world something it does not reflect: namely, itself.[2] It is from this absence that the desire to behold itself takes root. But, as the mirror metaphor clearly illustrates, a mirror cannot reflect itself. Here we begin to feel the element of unease which comes when we ask "What does it mean to be human?" The mirror wants to see its own reflection.

This unease, however, changes very rapidly to dismay when we expand the metaphor and introduce a second mirror whose purpose is to capture and reflect the first. Initially, this solution seems quite satisfying. There, in the second mirror, we do indeed see the first. The latter is, after all, a piece of the world and we would expect to find its reflection in any mirror that we hold up to it. But, the moment we look into that second mirror for a reflection of the first mirror's being-a-reflection-of-the-world, we are drawn into an endless series of reflections which we are literally incapable of bringing to closure. What is useful about the expanded metaphor is that it articulates the unsettling fact that we are unable to identify ourselves with the totality of roles that go into defining what we are at any given moment in our lives. There is, at the core of our existence, an "absence" which generates an endless series of presences. And it is in this "loop," which "de-fines" the absence as it moves endlessly between the two mirrors, that we find the image of the spiritual. Here is that elusive reality we have been on the trail of with that question that endlessly repeats itself: "What does it mean to be human?" The mirror metaphor reveals to us that, despite the fact that there are countless answers, there is no answer which can put this question to rest.

This fact, however, need not reduce us to silence. There is a way of speaking, the language of metaphor, which exhibits the quality of being "in flight" that characterizes the essence of human life. This is the language, for example, Plato uses when he first introduces us to the phenomenon of spirituality in his *Symposium*. You will remember that Socrates recounts a story. It is a story that was told to him by Diotima and which tells of how Eros was born the offspring of Plenty and Poverty. And so it is that through the agency of Eros, the desire that constitutes the dynamic (striving) nature of human existence, the realm of the "intermediate," is brought forth, creating a "place between" heaven and earth.[3] It is in that place that the human takes up its abode. What Plato has done is to give us a myth—a mirror fashioned from metaphors—in which the human is able to behold its elusive nature. In *this* mirror, that part of being which is spiritual beholds its own image.

There is, of course, another story which competes with Plato's as a "root story" shaping Western thinking in its encounter with spirituality. It is the biblical story we find in Genesis which recounts how "in the beginning" God brought forth the world, and how each "day" the world continued to come forth, until creation reached its "final" day—the sixth day—when God fashioned a creature made in his "image and likeness" (Genesis 1:4). It was this creature who would give a "name" to every other creature, and the

world that day came forth as the habitat of man. What we have
here is another myth that serves to "fix," or "de-fine," the place of
humanity in the order of things and with it the nature of spirituality. What is reflected in this second mirror as constituting the elusive nature of the human is the quality of being "in the image and
likeness of God" and, accordingly, an agency which gives a "face" to
the world. In both of these stories, the spiritual nature of man is
brought forward in a manner that corresponds to an extraordinary
feature exhibited by being itself. As the mirror metaphor suggests,
there is a certain "doubleness" to reality, and human existence is
the site from whence this "doubling" comes forth. What I am referring to is the fact that reality not only is, but appears. And this
situation speaks to the corresponding fact that there is a creature
in the world who not only is but is conscious of being. The paradoxical nature of this "doubleness" has caused no end of trouble. How
are we to articulate the ontological significance of a situation
where the appearance of reality is co-terminous with reality itself?
The univocal thinking which characterizes logic is unable to do so
without suggesting that there is a "remainder" which lurks behind
the appearance of things. Plato's story is the first in a succession of
stories to fall victim to this tendency of logical thinking. He has left
us a tradition which speaks of reality as having two distinct parts,
appearance *and* reality or, correspondingly, a tradition which
speaks of ourselves as being two distinct things, body *and* soul.
This is the tradition which has led Western thinking into that series
of blind alleys from which we are only just now beginning to
emerge.[4]

And what of the story we find in Genesis? It has had, to say the
least, a checkered history. All too often it has been confused with
Plato's story and in this capacity it has played a significant role in
guiding us into many of these blind alleys. But, the fact of the
matter is, it tells a very different story from the one we have in
Plato. And, what is more, it has been the failure to keep this difference clearly in view that has hampered the development of an
alternative notion of spirituality. The postmodern era we are living
through today is one which is particularly sensitive to the possibility of alternatives: especially those which, like the notion of spirituality contained in Genesis, have been suppressed by the logocentric
thinking of the Platonic tradition in philosophy.[5] What I want to
do, in the rest of this paper, is to trace the contours of the illusive
image which stares back at us when we peer into the mirror which
Genesis has fashioned for us.

2. The Self in the Beginning

In order to get at the differences contained in the images that are found in the two mirrors, let us begin by taking a look at how the two stories handle the question of the "origination" of being. For Plato, being is eternal. As the *Timaeus* (28c) teaches us, what we call the world, the realm of being which is material, is the result of the demiurge fashioning order out of disorder in accordance with the Forms, which make up the spiritual realm of being. We have, on the one hand, the material realm which is temporal and changing from all eternity; on the other hand, we have the spiritual realm which is non-temporal and unchanging from all eternity. And, inhabiting the realm of the "intermediate," we have the presence of the human which introduces into the world a site for a temporary "visitation" of the spiritual into the material. Whatever it is that may have caused our visit, while we are here in this world we encounter a series of reminders of who we truly are. We find, for example, that we are able to perceive the order in things. The reason for this, according to Plato's *Meno*, is that we come from the same realm of being as the Forms in whose image and likeness material things have been shaped. We have, of course, forgotten this. But each encounter with the orderliness that shapes the things of the world serves to remind us that our true home lies elsewhere. As Plato argues in the *Phaedo*, the cumulative effect of these jolts to our memory results in our awakening to the fact that the trajectory of human life transcribes a circle. The life of the spirit on earth is engaged in what is, in essence, a "return."

Contrast this with what we have in Genesis. There, being is that which is other than God, that which God brings forth. Initially— that is to say, on the "first" day—it is called forth from nothing. Before creation there is no that-which-is-other-than-God. With each succeeding "day" of creation, being continues itself as that which comes forth from that-which-is-other-than-God: that is to say, it comes forth from something, namely, itself. And when we reach the "last" day of creation, we find that the human too, "image and likeness" of God notwithstanding, is brought forth from that-which-is-other-than-God. Man is made from "the dust of the ground" (Genesis 2:7). There is nothing here to suggest that we are temporary "visitors" on earth and that our true home lies elsewhere. God has not fashioned man in his image and likeness "in heaven" and then "placed" him on earth. Man is fashioned *on* earth, *from* earth.[6] A body has become a conscious body, someone's body. And a "self" now walks the earth.

This point is a crucial one. The human is not described in Genesis as a site for the temporary visitation of the spiritual into the material realm. It is, rather, the site for a transformation of being from material to spiritual. With the advent of man, being comes forth as spiritual being. The driving force that constitutes human life does not manifest itself, in this story, as an aspiration to return home. What we find, instead, is an activity, *in that-which-is-other-than-God*, that bears witness to what God has brought forth. Through the agency of human existence being composes itself into a "world," that is to say, into appearing being. The self which walks the earth finds himself, or herself, "in-the-world." These are the terms in which Genesis introduces the spiritual into being, into that-which-is-other-than-God. Spirituality is, in other words, a stage of being.

The tradition of spirituality which traces itself back to Genesis, then, is one which does not reject material reality. Since the human soul has not been fashioned independently of the body and can in no way be understood to pre-exist the body, we must not conceive of ourselves as being engaged in activities which seek to leave the body behind. It is for this reason that the doctrine of the immortality of the soul has never quite been at home in this tradition—certainly not to the degree to which it has been able to fit into the Platonic view of things. Every argument for the immortality of the human soul, in the Christian tradition, must be capable of translating itself into the doctrine of the resurrection of the body.

We see this, for example, in St. Thomas Aquinas who begins by rejecting the Platonic view which speaks of the human soul as having a being other than the being it has as the form of the body and, for which reason, it is able to pursue an existence in separation from the body. He opts, instead, to use Aristotle's notion, articulated in *De anima* 2.1, that the soul's being consists in being the substantial form of the body, which is a view that better conforms to what Genesis has to say about the origin and manner of existence of the human soul. As the form of the body, the soul's activities weave into the fabric of our body the "face" of what we call our identity. We are not a soul, but a "composite" of body and soul. In this context, to say that the human soul is immortal because it is capable of activities which transcend matter is not the same as saying that it is able to pursue an existence in separation from the body. The function of such an argument is to draw our attention to the fact that there are activities of the soul which would be in vain (that is to say, they would lack what would bring them to perfection) if there were no resurrection of the body which would enable them to continue weaving our identity in the hereafter. In a word, St. Thomas finds that the immortal soul is incapable of constituting our identity apart from the body whose form it is.[7]

The image of spirituality which is reflected in Genesis is one that is at odds with the notion of distancing oneself from material reality. A truly spiritual life conducts itself at the "cutting edge" where material being is transforming itself into conscious, spiritual being. The selfhood that constitutes our identity as spiritual issues forth from the same activity that brings being to its appearance. The act of bearing witness to being—to that-which-is-other-than-God— is one that partakes of being *as* the "place" within being (*Dasein*) where being collects itself and "moves" toward consciously being itself. Dasein is, after all, the "there" of Being where "there" signifies a self-appropriation which constitutes the bringing forth of conscious being. We are, if you will, being's own instrument through which it articulates itself as a signifying field. The conduct of our own daily lives takes place in the "already" achieved world that has been brought forth from the ground of being. To speak, in this context, of the spiritual life as a rejection of the world is to signal the necessity for penetrating the "achievedness" of the world in order to retrieve the self whose existence brings forth the appearance of being—*and to make that self one's own*.[8] In a word, the spiritual life to which Genesis calls us is one that requires us to take responsibility for the world.

This way of coupling the self and being is a distinctive feature of the story in Genesis. Spirituality is a "stage" of being. As such, it speaks not only to the present "phase" of being (namely, that it has come forth as conscious being), but also to the "place" which executes its coming forth. It is this latter dimension of spirituality which is reminiscent of the sense which "stage" has in the theater. There, it is a "place" where something is enacted; it functions as a "threshold" across which something is brought forth. At the beginning of this paper, we had occasion to refer to the theatrical stage as creating a space from which it is possible to release that truth which lies hidden at the deepest strata of our existence. Let us now see if this truth corroborates our portrait of spirituality.

3. *The Drama of the Self*

When Aristotle addressed himself in the *Poetics* (VI, 1449b.27) to the question of how the drama differentiated itself from all the other arts—arts which, like poetry for example, it readily incorporated on its stage—his answer was: that the drama imitates an action in the form of action, and not, for example, in the form of narrative. In other words, drama *enacts* what it imitates: it brings it forth. We can still see in this notion the drama's origin in religious ritual. The theatrical stage was originally the place where something is brought forth. *Theatron* means a place for seeing, and in the theatrical production something is "brought to view." The theater, then, was conceived to be a place of "unconcealment." It is one of the misfortunes of Western thinking that *mimesis* has come to mean "duplication" and, as a result, the magical character of the stage has been all but lost. The challenge of the postmodern theater has been to strip the stage bare of all the encrustations that are the legacy of this traditional way of thinking. The stage, we are told, must be returned to itself where it can once again be the "place" where something comes forth.[9]

It is anything but an accident that this way of speaking about the stage should resemble our discourse on human existence. The action which drama imitates—causing it to "cross the threshold" and reveal itself—is the action that shapes and gives identity to human life. We have already seen that such an action *ipso facto* establishes a place into which being collects itself and from whence it comes forth as no longer "hidden," appearing to itself as a "world." As it transpires onstage, the action "continues" this movement of unconcealedness of being and establishes a place where human being collects itself and from whence *it* comes forth as no longer "hidden" from itself. The being-which-discloses-Being now appears to itself and reveals its (human) face. If we can speak, as we did at the beginning of this essay, of human existence as a mirror in which being beholds itself, then, by the same token, we can speak of the theatrical stage as the mirror in which human existence comes to see its own reflection. It is in the "theatrical event" that the human comes forth stripped of all the distractions which, in our daily lives, overlay the essence of our being-in-the-world. And the human which stands forth on-the-stage reveals itself as carrying the full weight of being behind it.

The stage which does this, however, is one that has retrieved its religious roots. Drama, in the final analysis, deals with self-discovery. What comes to pass onstage is a journey that is a "tying back to" (*re-ligere*) and "bringing forth" the truth. It unconceals the "last" concealment, if you will: namely, the act of unconcealment itself.[10] In the contours of the movement by which the characters in a play seek to discover the truth about themselves we discern the lineaments of that very movement by which being attempts to penetrate the veil that shrouds its fateful origin. The tragic denouement which comes to pass on the theater's stage—what Aristotle called the play's final cause and which is supposed to engender "fear and pity" in the audience—enacts the inevitable result of such a movement toward "unconcealedness." In what befalls the tragic hero we behold the fate of being. What has befallen being is that it has become conscious. In taking on his fate and making of it his destiny, the tragic hero enacts/reveals being's assumption of its fate as its own destiny. The journeying of the soul toward its own salvation is staged on the theatrical stage against the backdrop of the journey of being toward its own epiphany. *The human predicament, it turns out, is the predicament of being.*

Tragedy, which couples the self and the world, enacts a coming to presence which reveals the "groundlessness" of being. This groundlessness speaks to the essence of being. Being is an act which is always about to be completed; it is forever "bringing itself to an end." The end to which it brings itself, however, never turns out to be "the end of the matter." This is the ontological dimension of the question with which we began this paper: namely, "What does it mean to be human?" The groundlessness of being speaks to the ceaseless "play of being"— a play which reveals itself "at play" on the theatrical stage. What the enactment on the theatrical stage brings forth is the purified image of the spiritual as the *conscious* movement of being which is ceaselessly "bringing itself to an end." Conscious life "recapitulates," as it were, the life of being.

This is as far as tragedy can bring us. It lays bare the "truth" that we and reality are essentially "incomplete." This is a truth, however, which is not "objective"—it does not "stand before us." It is a truth which we (and being) *are*. The crucial function of theater is that, *for one brief moment, there, onstage*, it makes this truth stand before us. It is for this reason that the theater itself, which brings "the journey of unconcealedness" to an end, is *not* "the end of the matter." The theater is a place of truth to which we return again and again. The mirror which reflects the mirror-which-reflects-being is continually reconstituting itself within this infinite loop.

4. The Self at Play

The truth which we have found in the theater corroborates the picture of the spiritual contained in Genesis. The "word of God" introduces human existence by bringing it forth from *within* the play of being. But Genesis takes this truth a step further than tragedy. What is "at play" in being, we are told, is the act of creation. Being is essentially incomplete by virtue of the fact that it is created. And we, who are the "place" wherein being collects itself in order to be itself "in and from the truth about itself," are incomplete by virtue of the fact that we come forth from a being that has been created, *as* the latter's unconcealment. God created us in order that being—"that-which-is-other-than-God"—might bear witness to itself. This image of the spiritual comes into clearer focus when we recall the tradition that posits angels as co-present with God at creation. Why were angels not sufficient to fulfill the function of "being in the image and likeness of God" and bearing witness with God to the fact that what had been brought forth "was good"? The answer is to be found in the movement of being itself. It is a movement toward "wholeness," not completion. What is created is *ipso facto* incomplete: that is to say, there is no state of affairs which constitutes "the end of the matter" for being. The movement toward wholeness which Genesis describes is toward the "end" where being comes to "realize"—in both senses of the word—its truth. Angels, and the platonic soul, cannot bring this to pass.

The spiritual, then, is indeed a stage of being. The "place" which tragedy has cleared within being for the "final" unconcealment of being has been taken a step further in Genesis. It now reveals itself as a place where the wholeness of being becomes possible. As such, the spiritual must not attempt to bring being to closure. That way lies sin. The "calling" toward wholeness is an invitation to conduct the life of the spirit in a way that leads to an acceptance of the destabilized situation of being as a possible theater for God's creative work.

What is at issue is what we, who have been brought forth "from the earth," shall "put into play" in the play of being. On the one hand, we have Nietzsche's Zarathustra who challenges us to stand on the stage of being and "play with" the play of being as a child would engage in the innocent game of throwing a ball in the air. What comes to pass in such a "game" is the shaping of the "will to power" that ceaselessly takes being beyond itself. It is being that creates its own "otherness." This, according to Nietzsche, is the ancient teaching which is contained in pre-Socratic thinking and in the tragedies of the Greek theater before Euripides.[11]

On the other hand we have the equally ancient teaching in Genesis that presents us with an alternative way of standing on the stage of being. Instead of encountering the stage as a challenge, it offers itself to us as an invitation. Consider the way in which the following words of St. Therese of Lisieux contrast dramatically with the words of Zarathustra:

> For some time I had been accustomed to offer myself as a plaything to the Child Jesus. . . . I was a cheap little ball which He could fling on the ground or kick or pierce or leave neglected in a corner or even press to His heart if it gave Him pleasure. To put it in a nutshell, I longed to amuse the Little Jesus and offer myself to His childish whims.[12]

What we find here is an attitude toward being which holds back from playing with the gift of being that has been given, and instead seeks consciously to be that gift. The words express a response to an "otherness" which being has not created, but which itself has created being. It is by standing on the stage of being in this way that being is brought to a state of "wholeness."

The difference is the difference between pride and humility. For the one, the greatest sin of all is humility. We are exhorted to let our lives show forth the innocence of pride. For the other, the greatest sin is pride, for it cuts us off from "the Other" that is constituting being as that-which-is other-than-itself. Pride and humility: in the last analysis, it is they that make the difference as to how "the play of being" is being played.

In Genesis, then, the spiritual as a stage of being finds itself invited to "put into play" in the play of being the "truth" that being is created. Insofar as it accepts this invitation, the spiritual thereby constitutes the "response" of being itself—the response of that-which-is-other-than-God—to the invitation to collaborate. In other words, according to the story in Genesis, the world on that sixth day was opened to the possibility of reaching out its hand to "the Other." And the life of the spirit is the autobiography of that hand.

Notes

1. See Martin Heidegger, *Being and Time*, trans. John Macquarrie and Edward Robinson (New York: Harper and Row, 1962), pp. 91–148; "Holderlin and the Essence of Poetry," in *Existence and Being*, ed. and trans. Werner Broch (Chicago: Regnery Gateway, 1967).

2. Consider what Aristotle says in his *Metaphysics*, XII.9, 1074b.35–37: "Evidently knowledge and perception and opinion and understanding have always something else as their object, and themselves only by the way."

3. See Plato, *The Symposium*, 202b-211c; *The Republic*, Book X.

4. See Nietzsche, "How the 'True World' Finally Became a Fable," in *Twilight of the Idols*; and Wittgenstein, *Philosophical Investigations*, Part II, xi.

5. Jacques Derrida suggests that there are original heterogeneous elements in the scriptural tradition that "were never completely eradicated by Western metaphysics. They perdure throughout the centuries, threatening and unsettling the assured 'identities' of Western philosophy. So that the surreptitious deconstruction of the Greek *logos* is at work from the very origin of our western culture" (Richard Kearney, *Dialogues with Contemporary Continental Thinkers* [Manchester: Manchester University Press, 1984], p. 117).

6. In Matthew 5:13–16 we read that man is "the salt of the earth," its "flavor." Or, to change the figure, man is "the light *of* the world" (emphasis mine). It is not man, but Jesus, who is "sent into" the world.

7. See St. Thomas' debate with the Averroists in his *De Unitate Intellectus*.

8. See Heidegger's notion of conscience as a call in *Being and Time*, pp. 312–48.

9. See Antonin Artaud, *The Theater and Its Double*, trans. Mary Caroline Richards (New York: Grove Weidenfeld, 1958).

10.   Using the language of the mirror metaphor, we can describe this situation as one where the mirror is reflecting the mirror-reflecting-being.

11.   See Nietzsche, *Thus Spoke Zarathustra*, especially "On the Three Metamorphoses," for his discussion of the child. See also Nietzsche's discussion of the eternal return in his *The Will to Power*, sections 55 and 1066, where he argues against the introduction of an "otherness" which is not of being's own creation. And finally, see *The Birth of Tragedy* for Nietzsche's discussion of Greek tragedy. Following in the tradition of Nietzsche, Jean-François Lyotard, reading Wittgenstein with a Nietzschean lens, characterizes the postmodern person as a child for whom "the observable social bond" is "composed of 'language moves.' " For such a person, "to speak is to fight, in the sense of playing, and speech acts fall within the domain of a general agonistics. This does not mean that one plays in order to win" (*The Postmodern Condition: A Report on Knowledge*, trans. Geoff Bennington and Brian Massumi, Theory and History of Literature 10 [Minneapolis: University of Minnesota Press, 1984], pp. 10–11).

12.   St. Therese of Lisieux, *The Autobiography of St. Therese of Lisieux*, trans. John Reevers (Garden City: Image Books, 1957), p. 85. Joseph Kentenich, the founder of Schoenstatt, reflected on this passage in a series of sermons delivered in Milwaukee, Wisconsin, in 1965. Called the "Game of Love" sermons, they employ both theatrical metaphors and the images of the games of chess, tennis and bowling to characterize the providential play between God and the childlike human co-player.

ANN PIRRUCCELLO

Overcoming Self:
Simone Weil on Beauty

Philosophical postmodernism may be characterized as an attempt to rethink the strong emphasis on rationality characteristic of modern theories of knowledge and self. The French philosopher Simone Weil, whose life was cut short by illness in 1943, did not live to participate in the contemporary debates on modernism, and it is not clear how sympathetic she would be to postmodern philosophical trends. On the other hand, Weil may be seen as something of a transitional figure between modernism and postmodernism on some important issues in philosophy and religion.

Like contemporary postmodern philosophers, Simone Weil rejected what may be called modernist assumptions concerning the human self. Moreover, Weil's rejection of the modernist view of an autonomous, rational and identifiable self is not merely a response to philosophical problems about the meaning of selfhood and human agency. Rather, in the last years before her death, Weil pressed practical religious concerns to the center of her philosophy of self as she attempted to assess the stumbling blocks to human perfection. In a world of pitiless necessity, where perfidy, mass murder and disease were and remain the order of the day, Weil believed that the modernist self-interpretation must be overcome as a matter of philosophical and spiritual necessity. In this essay I will describe how Weil rejects the modern view of the self in a manner similar to that of some postmodern thinkers. The largest portion of the essay, however, will be taken up with demonstrating how Weil thinks the experience of beauty can play a role in freeing the human being from the modern self-interpretation on the plane of the spiritual life.

1. The Modern View of Self and Postmodern Challenges

Charles Taylor has provided a succinct description of the modernist view of the human self that is rejected by some postmodern philosophers. The major "anthropological beliefs" under critique are, first, that the human self is essentially rational and autonomous, and, second, that society is explained adequately by referring to the individual purposes of these free and rational agents.[1]

The first assumption amounts to the claim that, ideally speaking, human beings are wholly rational and as such have the ability to disengage themselves from their social and natural environments. This disengagement takes the form of objectifying the world such that, as Kenneth Gergen puts it, the ideal individual is thought to function "exactly like a mature scientist, observing, categorizing, and testing hypotheses."[2]

The disengagement from the world through rational objectification is crucial to the modern notion of autonomy. As Taylor explains, it is thought that by objectifying the world human beings can act in it as if in a "neutral" environment. This is to suggest that one can neutralize any influence that natural and social forces may have on one in finding and pursuing values and purposes.[3] Human beings are free to make rational choices about their lives, and indeed, that is their virtue.

The second aspect of the modern self reveals the putative nature of human relationships and identities. Since one is free to choose one's purposes from within oneself, and because a human being may pursue ends as his or her largely instrumental reason determines, the social world is explained as a collection of autonomous end-seekers. Human beings are related as so many self-sufficient individuals, the identities of which are independent of one another. Such is the "atomistic" view of society that is embodied by traditional social contract theories.

On the other hand, postmodern challenges to the modern view of the self, of which only a small representation can be offered here, contend that the human self is not isolated and disengaged from the social world, but is in some sense constituted by it. Jean-François Lyotard, for example, rejects the very notion of a socially disengaged self: "Even before he is born, if only by virtue of the name he is given, the human child is already positioned as the referent in the story recounted by those around him, in relation to which he will inevitably chart his course."[4]

Lyotard conceives of the human self as a position in a vast web of communication circuits through which various kinds of messages pass according to the rules of various language games. There is no question of a stable or consistent self; rather, "each exists in a fabric of relations that is now more complex and mobile than ever before" (p. 15).

Postmodern psychologist Kenneth Gergen argues that the technological conditions of today's world have fostered a "postmodern consciousness." Because of the high number, variety, and intensity of social relationships made possible for each person by communication and transportation technologies, our selves become "populated." That is, we acquire multiple selves or character possibilities as we become saturated with social relationships. Gergen writes that

> we are not one, or a few, but like Walt Whitman, we "contain multitudes." We appear to each other as single identities, unified, of whole cloth. However, with social saturation, each of us comes to harbor a vast population of hidden potentials—to be a blues singer, a gypsy, an aristocrat, a criminal. All the selves lie latent, and under the right conditions may spring to life.[5]

Simone Weil also poses a challenge to the modern assumptions about the self. Briefly, her view is that the self is best conceived as an orientation of consciousness that represents a certain way of relating to the world, an habitual way of "reading" (*lecture*) or interpreting the world.[6] Weil's self is not indicative of a disengaged intellect objectifying the environment. Rather, the self signals an inherently contingent and socially constructed network of interpretations and relations. Like postmodern philosophers, Weil believes that the perspective represented by the self is a product of shared views, practices and institutions.[7]

The above does not prevent the self from embodying a self-centric constellation of readings, however. Weil believes that the self may be viewed, on one level of analysis, as a network of psychical energies. And like physical energies, Weil's psychic energies are disposed to spend themselves beyond their own capacity for effectiveness and to become degraded. What this means on the level of meaning is that the human being's interpretations that constitute the self are inherently attempts to buttress the illusion that the self possesses power, being and importance. The social interpretations expressed, consequently, will be those which are most flattering to one's sense of value and strength.[8] The perspective of the self is thus ego-centric in the sense that the way it interprets the world includes a reference to the way these energies of the self interpret themselves as a solid self or being.

The foregoing discussion is meant to convey Weil's belief that there is no firm, thing-like bearer of human identity that may be discovered and understood as the human self. Instead, Weil says of the self that it is "a dead thing, something analogous to matter. [. . .] the thing we believe to be our self is as ephemeral and automatic a product of external circumstances as the form of a seawave" (SNL, p. 188). If the conditions under which a human being lives alter radically enough to render significant aspects of the human being's perspective impossible to maintain, reinterpretations of self and world are forthcoming. What the self happens to "be" at any one time is contingent upon which interpretations social and physical circumstances permit.

2. The Importance of a Postmodern View of Self in Weil's Spirituality

Weil believes that it is important for each of us to realize the conditional, fragile, and ultimately illusory nature of that which we call the self. As I mentioned above, Weil's concern is not merely to elaborate a more acceptable philosophical theory of the self and human agency. Rather, to overcome the modern view of the self as a completely autonomous, responsible entity would be helpful to us on the more concrete level of our spiritual lives. This is because it is the human being's identification with an essentially modern self that prevents a pure desire for the light of God from welling up within the human being: "The self is only the shadow which sin and error cast by stopping the light of God, and I take this shadow for a being" (GG, p. 35).[9] In other words, as long as human beings persist in interpreting themselves as free, sufficient beings who possess both power and the capacity of self-determination, desires and human energies will be directed necessarily toward projects and goods which are seen as valuable to the project of enhancing such a self. The human being will never pursue wholeheartedly what appears to diminish the self's perceived power and independence.

But this is exactly what must be desired, according to Weil, if the human being is to be elevated on the plane of the spiritual life. One must come to desire the kind of goodness which is exclusive of self-referring or personal projects. That is, one must desire God.

The point is that we cannot love what feeds or aggrandizes the sense of self, on the one hand, and God, on the other. They are mutually exclusive. The love of God, which comes from God as well as being directed to God, only manifests itself when the self withdraws or renounces its perceived existence, the barrier to God's love. For as long as the self-oriented loves dominate the human being, there is no opportunity for God's love to enter the human life. Importantly, this suggests that for Weil the coming to desire God is the other side of the coin of coming to shed the illusions of being autonomous selves.

As Weil sees it, the key to throwing off the belief in an independent self is to overcome the ego-centric perspective. But it is not enough merely to recognize that a multiplicity of perspectives exists. The perspective of the self as determiner of value is too firmly installed and requires radical experiences—experiences of a special suffering called affliction or experiences of the astonishing beauty of the world—to overturn the self as that in relation to which all value is measured.

The destruction of the ego-centric perspective is what Weil calls the "decreation" of the self.[10] The self cannot be decreated by an act of human will or by the sheer force of circumstances. Decreation can only occur through the operation of grace. Grace "descends" whenever there is a voiding or emptying of human energies toward some end and that expenditure of energy is not compensated for by some self-enhancing reward or satisfaction. Such compensations can be created either by the imagination or by states-of-affairs brought about by the expenditure. The nature of these compensations is such that they reinforce the value perspective of the ego. For example, if I do some volunteer work while deriving an "ego boost" from it, my work may be helpful, but my spiritual condition is still puffed up. I not only lack true humility, but my attitude will be conveyed to those I help. Without true emptiness of self I treat others as means of self-aggrandizement, and I do not recognize their alterity.

But not only does grace fill the human being who spends without self-flattering compensation; grace is also necessary to prevent the human being from so flattering himself or herself. Yet if grace is the agent of decreation, grace seems to require that one has turned one's attention to a source of grace. Only then can one be caught up in the operation of grace which chips away at the ego-centric perspective. One such source of grace is beauty. The particular beauties of the world and the beauty of the world as a whole hold out a possibility for capturing the human attention and opening the human being to divine love. Indeed, beauty is God's trap for the human soul (WFG, pp. 163–64). The next part of the essay will explore this role of beauty in Weil's spirituality.

3. Beauty and Overcoming Self

Simone Weil believed that a universal sense of beauty, "although mutilated, distorted and soiled" (WFG, p. 162), remains one of the few ways by which the spirit of love and self-detachment may be allowed to penetrate our lives. Endeavoring to interpret the meaning as well as the transformative movement of human desire, Weil thinks that beauty helps to arouse a crucial but often undeveloped longing for goodness. In cultivating one's attention to beauty, this longing for goodness can be heightened and purified, resulting in a self-detached love that enables one to freely consent to the world as it is. Weil regards this consent to suffer the world as the imitation of God's own creative love and beauty.

To begin, Weil believes that all human beings experience a sense of incompleteness and fragmentation. This is attributable, most fundamentally, to the temporal conditions of human existence:

> The thinking being is divided from himself, in his most animal desire and in his highest aspiration, by the distance in time between what he is and what he is tending to be; and if he thinks to have found himself, he at once loses himself again by the disappearance of the past. What he is at any single moment is nothing; what he has been and what he will be do not exist; and the extended world is made up of everything that escapes him, since he is confined to one point, like a chained prisoner, and cannot be anywhere else except at the price of time and effort and of abandoning the point he started from. (SNL, p. 16)

This self-alienation will only be remedied, according to Weil, when the human being has been assimilated in God through the "decreation" of the need-based ego. As we mentioned earlier, Weil thinks the ego or self has been decreated when the ego-centric perspective has been eliminated, and a transcendent center of value has been set up within the human being. As a consequence of decreation, one no longer perceives of goodness in terms of what would give one greater power as an individual or collective self. Moreover, Weil thinks that the human longing for beauty is instrumental to this decreation to the extent that it arouses and intensifies the desire to overcome the fragmentation or incompleteness of human existence.

According to Weil, if we attempt to articulate the deeper meaning of our desire for beauty, an important religious interpretation of this desire becomes available. Whether we are desiring the universal beauty embodied in the order of the world, or the faint echoes of this beauty suggested by particular things and people, what we are longing for is "finality." By "finality" Weil means an end or intrinsic good. Human beings desire ends and not means, however often we confuse them (WFG, p. 166). The important point is that Weil interprets the desire for finality as the desire for what would make us complete. And she thinks that where there is an intention of beauty, phenomenologically speaking, this intention includes a sense of finality. In fact, Weil thinks we could not pursue anything if it did not appear to possess beauty, for it is beauty alone which causes things to appear as ends. In sum, the desire for beauty is a desire for some final good.

But Weil agrees with Kant's view that the finality beauty actually possesses involves no objective beyond itself. That is, the good beauty provides is only the beauty itself and not something additional (WFG, pp. 165–67). The finality of beauty does not bring the good that satisfies the human longing to be complete. Rather, beauty provides an end or finality that is merely beauty itself, a good that appears only from a reverential distance and therefore offers us nothing that we can possess or appropriate without destroying. This kind of good that attracts us without giving us anything tangible ensures that the experience of beauty arouses our feeling of incompleteness, of unfulfilled longing for goodness. While enjoying the good that beauty does provide, we cannot help being referred to an absent goodness, a transcendent goodness of which we possess no idea. We desire this absent good, but without an object on the level of concepts.

When Weil describes our relationship to beauty she says that

> we are drawn toward it without knowing what to ask of it. It offers us its own existence. We do not desire anything else, we possess it, and yet we still desire something. We do not in the least know what it is. We want to get behind beauty, but it is only a surface. It is like a mirror that sends

us back our own desire for goodness. It is a sphinx, an enigma, a mystery which is painfully tantalizing. We should like to feed upon it but it is merely something to look at; it appears only from a certain distance. (WFG, p. 166)

The mention of distance is important in this passage, for a desire for what is and what must remain distant from us has a special character. The desire for beauty inflicts "an exquisite anguish," because an objective good that promises our completion is pointed to, but ultimately is absent.[11] If one does not seek to avoid this anguish by fleeing from beauty or by trying illegitimately to "consume" beauty, such as hoarding beautiful objects or engaging in debauchery, desire is changed. According to Weil, by sustaining the longing for the peculiar, absent finality of beauty "desire is gradually transformed into love; and one begins to acquire the faculty of pure and disinterested attention" (SE, p. 29).

4. Beauty and the Transformation of Desire

To understand this, we may note that Weil joins the Plato of the *Phaedrus* in theorizing about the spiritual effects of beauty. When the exquisite anguish caused by the perception of beauty is endured, one's way of seeing and desiring the beautiful grows ever purer and self-detached. That is, the beautiful is seen and desired less as good for the self and is appreciated and affirmed as something that is simply good.

In the *Phaedrus*, Plato describes the transformation of desire through the soul's encounter with a beautiful person. The initial desire excited by the physical attractiveness of another human being fills the soul with conflict, and Plato describes this in his famous allegory of the charioteer and his horses (253c-254e). The reason the soul becomes divided is because the appearance of the beautiful person arouses, in addition to natural desire for physical contact, a memory of the heavenly beauty the soul perceived when it was "whole" and disincarnate (254b). After a period of struggle the stinging natural desire in the soul is finally tempered by the more potent awe and fear that come from the stirring of memory. The soul comes to revere and love its beautiful partner from a chaste distance, and when love is aroused in the partner the two live in harmony (255a-256b). Their self-controlled way of life, if sustained, will enable them to pursue wisdom with the strictest devotion. At death the chaste love shared by the pair allows them to fly off to a heavenly abode, for their love and pursuit of wisdom will have caused the wings that can carry them aloft to sprout (256b).

Simone Weil takes the story in the *Phaedrus* as an attempt to describe an actual process, a genuine transformation of the regard and consequently the desire in the human soul. This transformation is essentially a change from what Weil feels is naturally selfish desire to the "supernatural" self-detached love that Weil calls "attention" and sometimes "grace." The key to this process, which is essentially the opening of the human being to God's grace, seems to lie in having an object of desire emptied of its promise of future gratification on the level of the ego-self while still being regarded as an object of desire.

In a notebook entry, Weil states that "the beautiful takes our desire captive and empties it of its object, giving it an object which is present and thus forbidding it to fly off towards the future" (GG, p. 58).[12] Weil indicates that when we refrain from clutching at or imagining some future personal benefit to be derived from an attractive object, that object can come to be appreciated as beautiful. The object that comes to be seen as beautiful still exists as an end for us. But, as we saw, Weil assumes that the end beauty possesses is only itself and nothing more, even though it reminds us of some absent good. To see something as beautiful is to see it in an impersonal or self-detached way, insofar as the value of the object is seen to reside in its present beauty and integrity, rather than in some tangible, personal end. This means that the goodness of beauty is not a goodness that is contingent upon the needs of the ego. It is good impersonally, because it is indifferent to the ego's projects. Moreover, the desire is captivated in the present because in order for the beautiful to appear, one must refrain from imagining it as other than what it is presently. To desire the beautiful, Weil thinks, implies a desire that the beautiful exist just as it is.

The struggle in the soul that Plato describes in his allegory of the charioteer and his horses, an allegory that Weil cherishes, demonstrates this. Initially, the chariot is drawn toward the beautiful person by the unruly horse as toward an object of lust that promises future pleasure. But the sight of the person awakens, if only dimly, the memory of transcendent or heavenly Beauty. This motivates the charioteer in a certain manner, and with the help of the obedient horse, he halts the lustful approach to the person. The point I want to emphasize here is that the perception of the other *as beautiful* represents the entrance of the supernatural—some degree of recollection of the divine—into the human life. Plato indicates that the soul continues to attend to the other because through that activity divine beauty is recalled. This means that once the other has been intended as beautiful, has become an object of greater attention, the character of the desire for the person has also changed. The desire is now a desire to attend to and affirm the *divine beauty* and goodness in which the person participates.

For Weil, the beauty to which the human being directs the attention is an object of desire, but *qua* beautiful it is an object that yields nothing but its own existence, as it is attended to, and available under no other conditions. In cultivating attention to beauty, Weil thinks that blind attraction is genuinely transformed into an other-centered, other-affirming love. This is not a natural process, but the occasion in which the human being is opened to God's grace. The love the soul develops for the object as beautiful is necessarily a self-renunciation since to appear, to be *meant* as beautiful, requires the effacement of merely personal desire. In a passage from one of her notebooks, Weil says that

> beauty is a sensual attraction that maintains one at a certain distance and implies a renunciation—including the most intimate form of renunciation, that of the imagination. One wants to devour all other desirable objects. Beauty is something that one desires without wanting to devour it. We simply desire that it should be.[13]

This renunciation is what Weil calls "the price of chaste love" (GG, p. 58). And Weil thinks that what is seen *as beautiful* is also seen in a way that is more revealing of its character as something real. This means that it is discerned as something with its own integrity as an existing thing governed by necessity and it is not veiled by the values and purposes invented by the imagination: "Every desire for enjoyment belongs to the future and the world of illusion, whereas if we desire only that a being should exist, he exists: what more is there to desire? The beloved thing is then naked and real, not veiled by an imaginary future" (GG, p. 58).

To summarize for a moment, the process of coming to see something or someone *as beautiful*—the beginning of what Weil calls supernatural attention—also changes the desire the human being possesses for what or who is seen as beautiful. The desire changes from a desire for the self's own gratification to a self-detached desire for the "naked" existence of the beautiful object. This new desire takes form in attention as love and represents the infusion of grace. And it is more likely to develop than other forms of attention because the human being is already attracted to the object that comes to be seen as beautiful. The regard is captured through natural attraction and held in check by intimations of something fragile and valuable. Supernatural attention is born in the dialectic of passion and intuition.

One further point remains to be made. Weil believed that certain objects functioned as *"metaxu"* or "bridges."[14] She felt that some objects of attention could serve as bridges leading the human being upward by promoting disinterested love. But these are only ladders to a fuller source of grace. In the case of beautiful things, the human being can be led to recognize universal beauty through these intermediaries. The universal beauty is the beauty of the world as an ordered totality.

To see the world *as beautiful* not only is a crucial step to being reconciled with God, since the beauty of the world is essentially the beauty of God perceived through the order of the world, but it also allows the world itself to be loved:

> The world's beauty gives us an intimation of its claim to a place in our heart. In the beauty of the world harsh necessity becomes an object of love. What is more beautiful than the effect of gravity on sea-waves as they flow in ever-changing folds, or the almost eternal folds of the mountains? The sea is not less beautiful in our eyes because we know that ships are sometimes wrecked. On the contrary this adds to its beauty. If it altered the movement of its waves to spare a ship it would be a creature gifted with discernment and choice, and not this fluid perfectly obedient to every external pressure. It is this perfect obedience which makes the sea's beauty. (SNL, p. 178)

Weil says explicitly that "it is because it is beautiful that the universe is a country. It is our only country here below" (WFG, p. 178).

In Weil's view, to love the world just as it is—what beauty is supposed to help us do—is to consent to suffer whatever comes to pass—and that, according to Weil, is the single act of freedom given to human beings. It is the freedom to accept or to not accept the suffering that the necessary order of things inflicts. If we choose to accept this suffering through our love for universal beauty, we are obedient to God's limiting power in a manner that imitates the beauty of the world which is God's own beauty. Human freedom and universal beauty are then seen to coincide: (1) Through beauty, freedom of consent to the harsh necessity that rules the world becomes possible, and (2) Like beauty, human freedom takes the form of consensual obedience to the will of God conceived as the order of the world. We can see, at least theoretically, that it is both through beauty and as beauty that the human freedom that is a relinquishment of the desires of the ego is accomplished. And this is a major step toward overcoming the alienation within and among human beings, and between the human being and God.

In conclusion, Simone Weil, like postmodern philosophers, calls for the end of the modernist view of the self. Unlike more contemporary philosophers, however, Weil does not believe such a self-interpretation can be overcome on the level of human experience without the assistance of grace. Beauty is a source of grace for the human being who is open to it. Regard for the beauty of the world aids the human being in the decreation of the ego, and this leads to a pure acceptance of the world and to the embodiment of God's love.

Notes

1.   Charles Taylor, "Overcoming Epistemology," in *After Philosophy: End or Transformation?* ed. Kenneth Baynes, James Bohman, and Thomas McCarthy (Cambridge: MIT Press, 1987), pp. 471–72.

2.   Kenneth Gergen, *The Saturated Self: Dilemmas of Identity in Contemporary Life* (New York: Basic Books, 1991), pp. 40–41.

3.   Charles Taylor, *Human Agency and Language, Philosophical Papers*, Vol. 1 (Cambridge: Cambridge University Press, 1985), p. 4.

4.   Jean-François Lyotard, *The Postmodern Condition: A Report on Knowledge*, trans. Geoff Bennington and Brian Massumi, Theory and History of Literature 10 (Minneapolis: University of Minnesota Press, 1984), p. 15.

5.   Gergen, *Saturated Self*, p. 71.

6.   See Simone Weil, *Gravity and Grace*, trans. Emma Crauford (London: Routledge and Kegan Paul, 1952; Ark Paperback, 1987),

p. 122. In "On the Love of God and Affliction," Simone Weil speaks of love as a basic "orientation and not a state of soul" or emotional condition. Either the soul has a "right orientation"—that is, "oriented towards God"—or it turns "in the wrong direction." See *On Science, Necessity, and the Love of God*, ed. and trans. Richard Rees (London: Oxford University Press, 1968), pp. 175, 182–83. Note that after the first full citation of a work by Weil, I cite it parenthetically by page and abbreviated title as follows: SNL (*On Science, Necessity, and the Love of God*), GG (*Gravity and Grace*), WFG (*Waiting for God*), and SE (*Selected Essays*).

7. See Simone Weil, *Oppression and Liberty*, trans. Arthur Wills and John Petrie (London: Routledge and Kegan Paul, 1958), pp. 156–68.

8. See Simone Weil, *Waiting for God*, trans. Emma Crauford (1951; New York: Harper and Row, 1973), pp. 158–59.

9. Also in *Gravity and Grace*, see the sections on "The Self" (pp. 23–27) and "Self-Effacement" (pp. 35-37).

10. For definitions of decreation, see *Gravity and Grace*, pp. 28–34.

11. Simone Weil, *Selected Essays*, ed. and trans. Richard Rees (Oxford: Oxford University Press, 1962), p. 29.

12. See also the section on "Beauty" in *Gravity and Grace*, pp. 135–38.

13. Simone Weil, *The Notebooks*, Vol. 2, trans. Arthur Wills (London: Routledge and Kegan Paul, 1956), p. 335.

14. See *Gravity and Grace*, pp. 132–34. For clarification on this point, see Eric Springsted, *Christus Mediator: Platonic Mediation in the Thought of Simone Weil* (Chico: Scholars Press, 1983), pp. 195–219.

MARY WALSH MEANY

Angela of Foligno: Destructuring and Restructuring of Identity

As Edith Wyschogrod has shown, the life of a saint—medieval, modern, or contemporary; factual or fictive—is a narrative that reaches "for what is inherently refractory to representation, a life like that of Jesus," even as it " 'show[s]' unrepresentability itself," displaying through the very imitation of Christ "how impossible it is to bring the divine life into plenary presence."[1] As such, there is something peculiarly postmodern and excessive about hagiography as a narrative form and moral imperative, whether it positions a saint in relation to the divine or human Other. Indeed, the saint's dying to self, selflessness, and altruistic social action continually raise what Wyschogrod calls "the problem of saintly individuation": what is it that constitutes the saint's "self," "singularity," and powerful "difference"?[2]

This essay explores that problem in the disjunctive life-story of Angela of Foligno (d. 1309). Angela's experience of conversion to Christ required separation from her husband and family, and this dislocation caused two levels of tension. First, she had to redefine her identity; second, she had to appropriate new location in the community. What Angela describes in her account of her spiritual journey is the destructuring of the framework of her sense of self, her identity as daughter, wife and mother, and her restructuring a new sense of identity, as her sense of herself was radically altered by her visionary experience of God's presence. Angela's new identity led her, like the later and more famous Dominican tertiary,

Catherine of Siena (d. 1378), to assume a public role, a public voice, within the traditional structure of the thirteenth-century church as a Franciscan tertiary. Indeed, her public role was first supported and guaranteed by the authority of her Franciscan confessor, her relative, Brother Arnoldo, who is also the transcriber and redactor of her description of her experience of God's presence. Later, Angela became the spiritual mother of a circle of disciples which included Ubertino of Casale, a leader of the spiritual Franciscan movement.[3]

I am arguing here that Angela's restructuring of her identity resonates with the postmodern awareness that the self is not autonomous, that the self is formed by being perceived by the Other. In Angela's experience, there is no self of itself or in itself; the self only exists in being loved by the Other. Angela could never have conceptualized the deconstructive critique of the self, but I am suggesting that she experienced a selflessness that is not unlike the deconstructive description of selflessness, according to which the self is formed by the interaction with the Other. In this postmodern understanding, the Other is not simply what (or who) I am not, and thus a counterpart commensurate with myself, "another myself," but is, rather, fundamentally different from my self and thus the object of my desire, even as I am the object of the Other's desire.[4] Desire and difference define Angela's sense of her self. Indeed, recognizing the importance of difference and desire in Angela's unfolding understanding of her self helps us to explicate the violent oscillation between the sense of the presence and the sense of the absence of the Other which are so crucial to her experience. Angela is not postmodern, but postmodernism may illuminate her experience for readers of her text.[5]

Angela of Foligno was born in 1248, probably of well-to-do, maybe even noble, parents. She married young and had several children. Paul LaChance describes Angela as having "led a loose and unconscious life before her conversion."[6] It is not clear just what this meant, but in 1285, when she was thirty seven, she underwent a conversion experience which seems to have begun with a sense of sinfulness and fear of hell (SpJ, p. 85). As a girl and as a married woman, she seems to have lived near Franciscan churches, and it is certain that the Franciscan movement was important in Foligno (SpJ, pp. 81, 73–78). It seems natural, then, that when she began to give serious thought to the state of her soul, she should pray to St. Francis, asking him to send her a suitable confessor, one to whom she would dare confess her sins. St. Francis appeared to her in a dream and guided her to Brother Arnoldo, a relative of hers and chaplain to the bishop (SpJ, p. 86).

For the next five and a half years, Angela made what she described as "small steps" in her spiritual pilgrimage. Meditation on the Cross became central to her devotional life, and she became increasingly serious about detaching herself from material comforts. Her family opposed this tendency, but then her mother, to whom she was very close, her husband, and her children all died suddenly. Angela says:

> And since I had begun the way I have described, and had asked God that they might die, I had great consolation from their deaths. And I said to myself that henceforth, since God had granted me this favor, my heart would always be in God's heart, and God's heart would always be in my heart.[7]

This is an extraordinary statement, not only because of her own attitude but because of her perception of God's love for her.

After the deaths of her family, Angela became increasingly eager to live a life of poverty, of detachment. In June 1291, she went to Rome where she asked St. Peter for "the grace of becoming truly poor," and that summer she seems to have disposed of most of her property. This also seems to have been when she was formally professed as a Franciscan tertiary. The years from 1285 until early 1291 mark a transformation of Angela's life, a process of conversion associated with imitation of the Crucified Christ, an imitation modelled on St. Francis' own meditation on the Cross and consequent dedication to poverty. The pursuit of poverty was also a process of detaching herself from the ordinary sources of identity, the stability and respectability resulting from being located in a family structure.

In the early autumn of 1291, Angela made a pilgrimage to Assisi to pray to St. Francis for the grace "to feel Christ in her soul, to be faithful to the Third Order rule . . . but above all the grace of being and ending up truly poor" (SpJ, p. 90). It was on this pilgrimage, at the crossroads beyond Spello, that Angela had an experience of the presence of the Trinity, an experience which culminated in the upper church of the basilica of St. Francis where Angela was enraptured by the window which shows Francis "in the bosom of Christ."[8] As the experience of the divine presence faded, Angela began to shriek in desolation. Among those whose attention this scene attracted was Brother Arnoldo, her confessor, now living at the basilica. He admonished her never to return to Assisi. Later, however, transferred back to Foligno, he questioned her more closely and, astonished by what she told him of her spiritual journey, on which the actual pilgrimage to Assisi was but a climactic step, he began to write down her account of the steps of that inner journey (SpJ, p. 93).

What we know of Angela is based on a complex book, *The Book of the Experience of the Truly Faithful*, which consists of three sections: first, the *Memorial* or description of her mystical journey as she dictated it to Arnoldo; second, a collection of letters, discourses, instructions, and descriptions of further visions; third, details from Angela's last years, her testament, and the description of her death.[9] Understanding Angela requires that we understand this book, and that project raises not only the problem of sorting out the role of Arnoldo, but also the question of the autobiographical nature of the book. On the face of it, this is a book of spiritual instruction prepared by a friar for the edification of other Christians. I am treating it as an autobiography, Angela's account of her life, setting aside the textual problems and the problems of genre, and arguing that this is "the story of a soul," the self writing her life.

The modern concept of autobiography is of an account of the development of the subject in the context of the circumstances in which that person lives, "interweaving" the outer events of the person's life with the inner evolution or unfolding of the self, and written by the subject.[10] Angela should, thus, have written about her work as a churchwoman, her role in the Franciscan movement. Two elements distinguish Angela's book from the modern autobiography. First, as we have seen, Angela is not simply the author; this text was produced by Angela and Arnoldo, at least—a collaboration which may find some modern parallels in those autobiographies written by a famous person "with" a professional writer.

Second, a more fundamental and substantive difference is the real difference between the medieval and modern understandings of self. Angela's sense of her self is shaped by her relationship with God; her description of her self is a description of this relationship. The modern concept of self assumes an element of autonomy which is missing from Angela's self-consciousness. In the most radical sense, not only is the Creator creating her, but she is also experiencing that creation in her experience of the divine presence. The autobiography has to communicate a sense of what is unique about a life, what makes it significant, what is serious about this life.[11] For Angela what is unique, significant, serious is the divine presence. Encountering this presence is not just a dramatic event (or series of events); it is what makes her who she is.

We might try adapting Mikhail Bakhtin's distinction between single and double voicedness here.[12] The complexities and ambiguities of Angela's discourse are the result of not only its embeddedness in a complex cultural setting and Arnoldo's role in transmitting Angela's experience. They derive more fundamentally from Angela's own experience of self-fashioning as dialogic. As Paul Lehmann insists, autobiography must take the self seriously, revealing its "inner thoughts" and development.[13] Angela's "inner thoughts" are double voiced; her self-consciousness is a consciousness of the presence of God.[14]

This is not the kind of division within the single self that Stephen Greenblatt so brilliantly identifies in Thomas More.[15] It is a much more radical recognition of the insignificance, the unreality, of the self alone. Angela's recognition of her sinfulness is, in the end, this recognition of her own unreality; her fear of hell is a fear of absolute nothingness. If we take her descriptions of nothingness seriously, we can conclude that she is describing the experience that we conceptualize as deconstruction. Indeed, the concept of deconstruction makes it possible for us as postmodern readers to grasp Angela's terms of abandonment in a way the modern and the romantic reader could not.

Angela herself described her spiritual life as a series of steps. From the time of her conversion to the Assisi pilgrimage experience, she described twenty steps. Ten more steps led, in 1296, to a state of mystical union with the Godhead in which she describes her self as being conscious of God in and beyond darkness.[16] Arnoldo, however, found himself unable to keep up with her account of these last ten steps and compressed them into the seven so-called "supplemental" steps. This poses particular problems in understanding the interplay of the experience of God's absence and presence in supplemental steps six and seven. The experience of the last steps is an ultimate transformation of Angela's sense of self as "a two-fold abyss was progressively revealed to her, her own poverty or nothingness and the fathomless depths of the Trinity" (MJ, p. 25). She was so absorbed by this experience of the Divinity, which afforded her a foretaste of the Beatific Vision, that, as LaChance puts it, "her centre of gravity was no longer in herself but in God" (MJ, pp. 23, 25).

The next and last thirteen years, until her death in 1309, were years of public activity as a spiritual director of many disciples, including Ubertino of Casale, for whom she wrote numerous instructions. During this time, or at least up until 1301, she recounts visions of Francis and Christ which consoled her about the welfare of her disciples, but she does not recount further details of her own spiritual life (SpJ, pp. 98–107). In 1308 angels appeared to tell Angela that she was soon to die (she was already bedridden), and she prepared a testament synthesizing her spiritual teachings. She died January 4, 1309. Angela was beatified in 1701, but has not been officially canonized.

Angela provides a clear statement of the tripartite structure of her spiritual life: first, the stage of detachment, characterized by imitation of the works of Jesus Christ, "the passionate God-Man in whom is manifested God's will; second, the stage of cataphatic union: union with God accompanied by powerful feelings and consolations which . . . can find expression in words and thoughts; third, the stage of apophatic union: a most perfect union with God in which the soul feels and tastes God's presence in such a sublime way that it is beyond words and conception."[17] As Angela expresses it, "The transformation of the soul is threefold. In the first place, the soul is transformed in the will of God; in the second place, with God; in the third place, the soul is transformed within God and God within the soul."[18]

The controlling image in Angela's description of her spiritual life is the journey made up of thirty steps, organized in three stages: imitation, union with God, perfect union. This pilgrimage is, however, a progressive transformation of the self. This transformation can be described in terms of Angela's sense of dissolution, of destructuring of her self, and then restructuring of self as self because of the presence of the Other. The restructured self who appears in the stage of cataphatic union is a self who enters into a relationship which, Carole Slade suggests, may be understood as a relationship of alterity in which each experiences self as subject when "even in union, each subject affirms its essential difference from the other . . . a dynamic of irreducible difference which . . . [is] indispensable for providing women the subjectivity they have been denied."[19] The process of destructuring and restructuring is, however, not linear but spiral.[20] The image of the journey, then, is not a simple one; it is not just going from here to there. The journey has to be understood as a visiting and revisiting;[21] the destination is the chamber of the soul which is, not surprisingly, a bridal chamber.[22] What is most significant is not the metaphor of the journey nor of the revisited chamber, but that on this series of steps Angela is restructuring her self as constituted by her experience of God's presence, the presence of the Other.

As she enters on her spiritual journey, as she begins to recognize her self, Angela finds her family, the source of her social identity, of her place in thirteenth-century Foligno, a hindrance, so that she can only take "small steps." Angela describes this problem to Arnoldo in describing the fifth step in her journey, which is self-knowledge. Beginning to know herself, she is aware of her sinfulness, aware of halting at each step.[23] When the members of her family, her external identity markers, are removed by death, she begins to move more rapidly along the spiral path of self-discovery.

In the first part of this journey, she struggles to detach herself from the world, to attain poverty. On one level, this is a simple struggle to put aside material comfort. On another level, it is a stripping away of the sense of self as the center of a matrix of social relationships. The symbolic expression of this experience is, of course, Angela's shocking expression of her joy at her family's death, a joy explicitly connected with being set free to be poor.

During this first stage of her journey, Angela meditates on the Crucifixion and learns to imitate the Crucified, following the example of Francis. She describes this phase as "the first transformation . . . when the soul tries to imitate the works of Christ, since the will of God is manifest in them,"[24] and thus an entrance into "True Love":

> The first sign of true love is that the lover submits her will to the will of the beloved. . . . The first effect of this is that, if the beloved is poor, she will desire to be impoverished, if the beloved is humiliated, she will desire to be humiliated.[25]

At this point, Angela is, thus, very much in the Franciscan tradition of imitation of Christ, expressed as living in radical poverty and acceptance of, and eagerness for, suffering. Paul LaChance describes this process as Angela's being "enabled to reorient her affectivity, strip herself of her possessions, and gradually yield her heart to Christ." It was, he says, "the Crucified Christ who granted Angela . . . knowledge of her false and sinful self and . . . the experience of God's forgiveness and healing" (MJ, pp. 9–10). Angela has attained self-knowledge: knowledge that she is nothing.

Embracing poverty can be read as her embracing the sense of

nothingness on a moral level: she is, but she is worth nothing; she is "false and sinful."[26] The sense of nothingness has, however, another implication for Angela. In her reflection on God's seven gifts to humans, Angela identifies the fourth gift—the first gift that she refers specifically to herself—as the gift of God's having made her a rational creature rather than an irrational beast. Her observation prompts the question: would such a beast have been "Angela"? Angela's sense of identity seems to include the radical ability to admit and imagine that one might not be oneself, might not even be human.

Angela's experience of moral and ontic poverty, of radical nothingness, in union with the Crucified Christ recalls Luce Irigaray's description of the journey of the soul through the slit, down into the cave of abandonment and emptiness, into the darkness which becomes "a transverberating beam of light."[27] The self has been created to desire, and this desire impels her into the darkness of nothingness and self-abandonment:

> [But] if "God," who has thus re-proved the factor of her non-value, still loves her, this means that she exists all the same.... That most female of men, the Son [loves her]. And she never ceases to look upon his nakedness, open for all to see, [on his wounds] as he hangs there [on the cross], in his passion and abandonment.[28]

Looking at the cross is, to use Irigaray's vocabulary, looking into a mirror, the mirror which grants Angela knowledge of her own poverty and nothingness.

The next stage in Angela's pilgrimage, marked by the twentieth step, the dramatic experience at Assisi, has been called Angela's betrothal (SpJ, p. 178). At this point, she was conscious of the presence of the Holy Spirit and began to experience a sweet sense of consolation because of that presence. Angela herself describes this experience as the transformation of the soul: "The second transformation is when the soul is united to God and has deep feeling and great sweetness from God, nevertheless words can express and thought can conceive these feelings and the sweetness."[29] This sense of being transformed *cum Deo* characterizes Angela's cataphatic union with God.[30]

In this second stage, Angela restructures her self by revaluing the cultural categories which first formed her sense of self. God calls Angela "daughter" and "spouse," which is to affirm that God loves her more than she can love God, that God loves her more than anyone else in the world.[31] She responds that this is too much for her, because she is feeble. God consoles her by reminding her that she is God's creature. In that experience of consolation, Angela "[feels] the ineffable divine sweetness" and has a sense of humility greater than any she has experienced before.[32] She begins to feel the presence of the Cross within herself, to feel herself melt, her soul "liquified," in the love of God.[33] One vivid expression of this sense is her description of feeling herself dissolve as she contemplates the dislocation of the limbs of the Crucified.[34]

Angela then enters the third and last stage of her journey, the "most perfect union with God": "The third transformation is when the soul, in a most perfect union, is transformed within God and God within the soul, and from this divine depth feels and tastes that which words cannot express nor thought conceive."[35] In the sixth and seventh of the "supplemental" steps recorded by Arnoldo, Angela's description of her experience of the divine presence reaches its climax in a series of violent oscillations between abandonment and union.

I would suggest that this oscillation is only partly a problem of redaction, of Arnoldo trying to give an intelligible account of Angela's experience. More basically, it is caused by the double or dialogic nature of Angela's sense of being a self who is constituted by the presence of another. As LaChance observes, a "two-fold abyss was progressively revealed to her, her own poverty or nothingness and the fathomless depths of the Trinity" (MJ, p. 25). This is an experience of selflessness which may be described as the deconstructed self. It is Angela's experience of abandonment, not her experience of apophatic union, which is the key to this experience of selflessness. She is no self unless God is present.

This, however, is only one pole in the experience of the abyss. She also experiences the presence of the Other which constitutes her as a self. It is possible to describe Angela as experiencing, being vividly aware of, the presence of the Holy Spirit, which theologians like Karl Rahner describe as the essence of the Christian life:

> Grace is God himself, his communication, in which he gives himself as the divinizing, loving kindness which is himself. Here his work is really *himself*, as the one communicated . . . . Grace also penetrates our conscious life, not

only our essence but our existence too. . . . [Grace as formal object] is the *a priori* "mental horizon," which we are
conscious of in being conscious of ourselves.[36]

This sense of God's presence empowers Angela to assume a
role of leadership, a phenomenon which has received an increasing
amount of attention from feminist scholars.[37] More fundamentally,
however, the sense of God's presence renews Angela's sense of her
own reality, her significance. Describing her experience of inde-
scribable union with God, Angela says, "I felt that I lay or stood in
the midst of the Trinity whom I saw in a great darkness."[38] She
goes on to say:

> When I am in that darkness, I am not aware of any humble
> being, nor of the God-Man, nor of anything which has
> form. Nonetheless, I see everything. . . . I see [Christ] and
> he draws my soul with such gentleness, with such gentle-
> ness he draws it, he draws the soul, that he says, as it were,
> "You are me, I am you."[39]

Angela's sense of being transformed into God who is transformed into Angela is a radical statement of the presence of the
Other, so radical that it has been argued that Angela lost her sense
of her own identity. Carole Slade has argued persuasively and cor-
rectly against this view, citing Angela's own description of her
sense of transformation:

> And now the virtue of love transforms the lover into the
> loved and the loved into the lover. . . . The soul, united to
> God and with God by the perfect fire of divine love, *almost*
> completely gives and releases itself to God and transforms
> itself into God, *but without changing its own substance*; the
> soul transforms its entire life in God's love, and love ren-
> ders it *almost* completely divine.[40]

Angela is once again Angela, but she has become Angela because of
the presence of God. She experiences the Christian doctrine of creation, of creatureliness.

This paper argues, however, that Angela's experience of abandonment should be taken seriously and not just understood as leading to apophatic union. That experience of abandonment is a radical
experience of selflessness from which she is able to reconstruct a

self. Contemporary categories created by deconstructive criticism of self identity help us to take the medieval mystic's experience of abandonment seriously as an ontological rather than a moral category. Angela can imagine not being. She can imagine being but not being as a human being. She can only imagine being Angela in the context of being brought into being by the Other, and she imagines this as the result of desire, her desire for the Other and the Other's desire for her. Her writing of her self, her autobiography, is her story of being brought into existence as a self by the Other.

Notes

1. Edith Wyschogrod, *Saints and Postmodernism: Revisioning Moral Philosophy* (Chicago: The University of Chicago Press, 1990), p. 13.

2. Ibid., p. 252. Wyschogrod focuses on the moral project of saintly altruism, whereas I am concerned with the saint's fundamental sense of self.

3. There are two sets of issues which we might explore as we consider the importance of Angela's visionary experiences. The first set, which I address in this essay, arises from consideration of how this experience affected her sense of self, her identity. The second set of issues, those resulting from the need to find a new location in the community, involves consideration of the public role which Angela assumed in the institutional Church, that is, her relationship to the ecclesiastical community. This relationship was realized in her identity as a Franciscan tertiary, specifically in her relationship with her confessor, Brother Arnoldo, but more notably in her relationship to her spiritual children. This set of issues requires consideration of the framework in which Angela lived out both the private and public dimensions of her life, that is, her role in the controversies over poverty and over the contemplative and active lives. I intend to pursue this second set of issues in further work.

4. See Wyschogrod, pp. 254–55. The ethical implications of Angela's story, the insight it affords into service and compassion, and the radical and potentially disruptive nature of her experience still need exploration.

5.   The question of the intersection of the reader and the text is crucial to understanding Angela, but this complex question is part of what I am setting aside for later work. In her case, there is a further complication introduced by the mediation of Brother Arnoldo.

6.   Paul LaChance, *The Mystical Journey of Angela of Foligno* (Toronto: Peregrina, 1990), p. 7. For a summary of Angela's life, see Paul LaChance, *The Spiritual Journey of Blessed Angela of Foligno According to the Memorial of Frater A.* (Rome: Pontificium Athenaeum Antonianum, 1984), pp. 79–110. I cite these two works by LaChance parenthetically by abbreviated title (MJ and SpJ) and page number.

7.   Angela of Foligno, *Le Livre de L'expérience des vrais fidèles*, ed. M.-J. Ferre (Paris: Editions E. Droz, 1927), I.12, pp. 10/11–12/13. This is a facing page translation of the Latin text into French. For this reason, each citation gives two page numbers, even for the Latin and odd for the French. The Latin reads: "Et quia inceperam viam predictam et rogaveram Deum quod morerentur, magnum consolationem tum habui, scilicet de morte eorum. Et cogitabam quod deinceps, postquam Deum fecerat mihi predicta, quod cor meum semper esset in cor Dei, et cor Dei semper esset in cor meum." (It was this statement which first attracted my attention to Angela. God seems to be acting rather like David when he sent Uriah to his death, but Angela does not make that comparison.) All translations from Angela are mine unless otherwise indicated.

8.   LaChance, *Spiritual Journey*, p. 91. See also Anita Volland, "Where the Road Parted Three Ways: The Mystical Pilgrimage of Angela Foligno," paper presented at the Twenty-seventh International Congress on Medieval Studies, Kalamazoo, MI, May 1992.

9.   The authorship of the book is complex. Angela dictated the *Memorial* to her confessor, Brother Arnoldo, who not only transcribed but also redacted her dictation and translated it from Umbrian Italian into Latin; Part II was dictated to Arnoldo and other secretaries; Part III is the work of secretaries. The book is therefore a compilation formed over a period of years. The more serious problem of authorship is, however, the question of the role of the secretary, specifically of Arnoldo. To what extent was he a secretary, to what extent a redactor, to what extent even an author? See

LaChance, *Spiritual Journey*, p. 13. John Croakey is doing seminal work in this area.

10.   I echo a conversation with John Burkey, August 18, 1992. I have been inspired by his unpublished paper, "Figuring Autobiography," an interesting work-in-progress that focuses on the significance of autobiography in the "philosophical task" of understanding human existence. Paul Lehmann ("Autobiographies of the Middle Ages," *Transactions of the Royal Historical Society*, Series 5, Vol. 3 [1953], pp. 50, 52) distinguishes between *vita* and *gesta* on the basis of attention to this inner development. Lehmann deals only with the Latin works of notable men.

11.   Again I echo my 18 August 1992 conversation with Burkey. Wyschogrod's definition of hagiography is useful here: "a narrative linguistic practice that recounts the lives of saints so that the reader or hearer can experience their imperative power" (*Saints and Postmodernism*, p. 6).

12.   See M. M. Bakhtin, *The Dialogic Imagination*, ed. M. Holquist, trans. C. Emerson and M. Holquist (Austin: University of Texas Press), pp. 263, 324–28, 428.

13.   See Lehmann, "Autobiographies," pp. 50–52.

14.   We can compare this sense of self to Augustine's perception, expressed in the *Confessions* (Books 10; 13.11 and 13.22) and *De Trinitate* (9.4–5, 10.11–12, 15.20-24), that the self is structured in the image of the Trinity and known in encountering the Trinity. Lehmann misses the autobiographical significance of that encounter when he contrasts confession to autobiography (p. 42).

15.   See Stephen Greenblatt, *Renaissance Self-Fashioning: From More to Shakespeare* (Chicago: University of Chicago Press, 1980), pp. 11–73. Greenblatt describes the eventual "shattering of [More's] careful separation of public and private" (pp. 74–76).

16.   Angela, I.105, pp. 208/09: "vidi eum in una tenebra." See LaChance, *Spiritual Journey*, p. 98.

17.   See Angela, I.191, pp. 167/68. I quote LaChance's summary, *Mystical Journey*, p. 8. See Bernard McGinn, *The Foundations of*

Mysticism, Vol. 1 of *The Presence of God*: *A History of Western Christian Mysticism* (New York: Crossroad, 1991), pp. xviii–xix, on the apophatic or negative way and the cataphatic or positive way of being conscious of God's presence, and on the importance of distinguishing between experience and consciousness as appropriate descriptions of mystical experience.

18.   Angela, II.191, p. 466/67: "Est autem triplex anime transformatio. Aliquando enim anima transformatur in voluntate Dei, aliquando cum Deo, aliquando intra Deum et Deus intra animam."

19.   Carole Slade, "Alterity in Union: The Mystical Experience of Angela of Foligno and Margery Kempe," *Religion and Literature* 23 (1991): 111, referring to Luce Irigaray, *Ethique de la différence sexuelle*. As Slade notes, Irigaray herself considers alterity between man and woman utopian and does not think of a mystic's relationship with God as a relationship of alterity.

20.   Ewert Cousins' perception of the spiral rather than linear direction of the spiritual journey is the foundation for my reading of Angela. See Cousins, *Global Spirituality*: *Toward the Meeting of Mystical Paths* (Madras: University of Madras, Radhakrishnan Institute for Advanced Study in Philosophy, 1985).

21.   Reading and rereading might be a convenient image, except that Angela has not chosen to use it. She does refer to Jesus as the Book of Life, but she does not pursue the image of reading.

22.   LaChance comments on this image (p. 25) by providing a summary list of medieval authors who describe the deepest or highest "part" of the soul as the locus for mystical meeting (*Mystical Journey*, p. 31, n. 17).

23.   See Angela, I.8, pp. 6/7–8/9.

24.   Angela, II.191, pp. 466/67: "Arma vero quibus bonus amor debet regi, inveniuntur in anime transformatione. Est autem triplex anime transformatio. Aliquando enim anima transformatur in voluntate Dei, aliquando cum Deo, aliquando intra Deum et Deus intra animam. Prima transformatio est quando anima conatur imitari opera Christi, quia in ipsis manifestatur voluntas Dei."

25. Angela, II.133, pp. 286/87: "Primum signum veri amoris est quod amans submittat voluntatem suam voluntanti amati. . . . Prima operatio est quia si amatus est pauper, studet depauperari, si vilis, studet vilificari."

26. In her so-called "Third Letter," written during the last few years of her life and labeled third because it is the third letter in the third part of the book (pp. 494–98/495–99), Angela describes herself with bitter humor as a hypocrite and a sinner, a lost woman (*illa vilissima mulier*, this vile or ugly woman, translated by Ferre as *femme perdue*).

27. Luce Irigaray, "La mystérique," *Speculum of the Other Woman*, trans. Gillian Gill (Ithaca: Cornell University Press, 1985), p. 193.

28. Ibid., pp. 199–200.

29. Angela, II.191, pp. 466/67: "Secunda transformatio est quando anima unitur Deo et habet magna sentimenta et magnas de Deo dulcedines, sed tamen possunt exprimi verbis et cogitari." This is the transformation "cum Deo."

30. As McGinn notes, "Among the more positive, or cataphatic, mystics, it is primarily a successive experience, as in the coming and going of the Divine Lover" (*Foundations of Mysticism*, p. xviii). This is the way Angela's entire experience, as well as the experience of most mystics who use bridal imagery, is usually described.

31. Wyschogrod refers to the Other's positivity, the Other's "*supra-ontological* or *me-ontic* being in that the Other is always already the object of a desire that exceeds any expectation of fulfillment" (p. 255). When the Other is specifically the Divinity, the sense of the impossibility of fulfillment is a sense of the self's limitation, of finitude.

32. Angela, I.35, pp. 49/50: "et sentiebam dulcedinem divinam ineffabilem."

33. Angela, I.35–36, pp. 54/55–56/57. See LaChance, *Spiritual Journey*, p. 178.

34. Angela, II.135, pp. 290/91–292/93.

35. Angela, III.191, pp. 464/67: "Tertia [transformatio] est quando anima unitione perfectissima est transformata intra Deum et Deus intra ipsam et altissima de Deo sentit et gustat que non possunt verbis exprimi nec cogitari." My translation of *altissima de Deo* is admittedly tendentious.

36. Karl Rahner, *Nature and Grace* (New York: Sheed and Ward, 1964), pp. 128–29.

37. See, for example, Elizabeth Petroff, *The Consolation of the Blessed: Women Saints in Medieval Tuscany* (New York: Alta Gaia, 1980).

38. Angela, I.107, pp. 214/15: "Et in illa Trinitate, quam video cum tanta tenebra, videtur mihi stare et jacere in medio."

39. Angela, I.107, pp. 214/15: "Nec recordor, quando sum in illa, de aliqua humilitate [trans. by Ferre as 'ni d'aucun être humain'] vel de Deo homine nec de aliqua re que formam habeat. Et tamen omnia tunc video. . . . Video Deum hominem, et trahit animam cum tanta mansuetudine, cum tanta mansuetudine trahit, trahit animam, ut dicat aliquando: *Tu es ego et ego sum tu.*"

40. Carole Slade, "Alterity in Union," p. 114. See Angela, II.173, pp. 398/99.

MARY GERHART

The Word Image Opposition: The Apophatic-Cataphatic and the Iconic-Aniconic Tensions in Spirituality

One can find abundant examples of both the apophatic and cataphatic approaches to the spiritual life and to knowledge of God in the Christian tradition. Nevertheless, these two approaches—in scholastic terms, the *via negativa* and the *via affirmata*—have most often been treated as discrete or even opposed possibilities for charting one's demeanor with the Sacred. Similarly, the iconic (or positive rendering of the sacred) and the aniconic (or principled refraining from visual representations of the sacred) attitudes toward images have been understood dichotomously not only within Christianity but as constituting one of the major differences among the three major Western religious traditions.

Conventional wisdom features the primacy of the iconic in the Christian tradition, whereas the aniconic is studied, if at all, in terms of internal protest, with reference to a particular controversy (for example, the iconoclastic controversy in Christianity in the tenth century), or as a general prohibition against images (for example, in some discussions of Islam or Judaism). Conversely, systematic evaluations of mysticism generally privilege the apophatic over the cataphatic as the "higher" form of spirituality. Despite the importance of both the apophatic/cataphatic and the iconic/aniconic distinctions in premodern spirituality, they have not informed one another as much as one might expect.

The purpose of this essay is three-fold: one, to explore the

epistemological assumptions in the cataphatic/apophatic traditions and the iconic/aniconic traditions; two, by taking up the
cataphatic/apophatic in relation to the iconic/aniconic, to bring to
light some complexities not readily visible in separate analyses of
these approaches; and finally, to reassess some of the claims made
about Judaism, Christianity, and Islam regarding these familiar
oppositions. In particular, what comes to the fore in these analyses
is the relationship between word and image—a topic of great contemporary interest.

This essay is exploratory and schematic: it draws upon history
in an attempt to make sense for the present and the future. It
represents a kind of theology in keeping with what I take our current situation to be: namely, one in which the interreligious dialogue will more and more be the context within which the most
fruitful issues will arise. With respect to the three major Western
religions, recent findings have yielded significant evidence that
compels us to revise the view that Christianity is iconic and Judaism and Islam aniconic. The earlier view trivialized important
aniconic tendencies within Christianity and overlooked discoveries
of religious representations in Judaism and Islam. Today it is possible, by means of a better understanding of the forms through
which human beings communicate with the sacred and with other
human beings, to honor a dialectical tension between the need for
knowledge and perceptible representations and the need to transcend them both. We will see later the sense in which these considerations are explicitly postmodern.

1. Definitions

Historians have frequently made the distinction between apophatic and cataphatic as if these two terms refer to two different
paths taken by different persons. In the first volume of his monumental history of Christian mysticism, for example, Bernard McGinn
applies the term "apophatic" initially to persons:

> It would be easy to draw up a lengthy list of texts from the
> mystics . . . that speak of a special consciousness of the
> divine presence as the goal of all their hopes and ef-
> forts. . . . Precisely because of the incommensurability be-
> tween finite and Infinite Subject, Christian mystics . . .
> have never been able to convey their message solely

through the positive language of presence. . . . Sometimes, among the more positive, or cataphatic, mystics, it is primarily a successive experience, as in the coming and going of the Divine Lover. . . . [A]mong the negative or apophatic mystics, presence and absence are more paradoxically and dialectically simultaneous . . . . [T]he real God becomes a possibility only when the many false gods (even the God of religion) have vanished and the frightening abyss of total nothingness is confronted.[1]

Later McGinn confirms that "negative, or apophatic, theology will form a major part of the story" of mysticism in the West (p. 31). Following Stephen Gersh, McGinn distinguishes between subjective and objective apophatic theology. Subjective apophaticism finds negative descriptions of God in which the human mode of perception and expression determine God's unknowability and ineffability. Objective apophaticism, on the other hand, interprets negative descriptions of God "without reference to our mode of conceiving." Subdivisions of objective apophaticism include an absolute form in which "God is unknowable and inexpressible to all humans and in every way" and variations of the latter with respect to group, time, and/or genre. If we distinguish between pre-Enlightenment and contemporary philosophical positions, we can omit the absolute form of apophatic theology in this taxonomy since, as will be reviewed below, the absolute form seems to be based exclusively on formal logic and dismisses without consideration of merit claims based on experience.

In the context of mysticism, the apophatic has received more attention than the cataphatic, whereas in most other discussions the assumption that Christian theology in general is cataphatic goes without saying. McGinn's treatment is typical of the emphasis on the apophatic in mysticism: he refers to the apophatic on forty-seven pages and to the cataphatic on thirteen pages. In contrast to the multiple divisions (such as those just mentioned) to be found within the apophatic, the cataphatic lacks both complexity and distinctions. In his exploration of the tripartite field of cataphatic theology, symbolic theology, and apophatic and mystical theology, for example, McGinn, drawing on the classical distinctions made by Dionysius the Areopagite, characterizes cataphatic theology as the only one functioning solely on the level of reason. Cataphatic theology is thus distinguished from symbolic theology, which depends on sense knowledge. Both cataphatic and symbolic theology are distinguished from modes of apprehension that surpass reason and that appear in both apophatic and mystical theology.

These distinctions are clearly problematic, however. If the cataphatic is aligned exclusively with reason or the *logos* tradition, mysticism of necessity becomes the "other" of reason. If reason is further aligned with logic, the apophatic way is likely to identified with both mysticism and spirituality in general—with the result that the cataphatic way ceases to be a viable possibility.[2] In a different but related way, prophecy—a genre permeated with assertiveness—has also been understood in diametrical opposition to the apophatic.

2. Experiential Basis of the Apophatic and Cataphatic Approaches

Some of the recent literature on spirituality ignores the traditional association of the cataphatic with reason, and of reason with logic, and identifies the cataphatic instead with positive or constructive, primarily psychological experience. Belden C. Lane's "Sinai and Tabor: Apophatic and Kataphatic Symbols in Tension" is a good example of an attempt to relate both the apophatic and the cataphatic to contemporary psychological experience. Lane narrates his own experience of climbing Mt. Sinai and Mt. Tabor when he was on pilgrimage in Israel and Egypt. He expands this narration by referring to two separate early accounts of pilgrimage (from Egeria's travel journal [4th c.] and John Climacus' *The Ladder of Divine Ascent* [6–7th c.]) to the same mountains. Lane uses these experiences to show "how the metaphor of the mountain can be used to speak of God in both constructive and deconstructive ways."[3] He narrates the destructive experience first: Lane's descriptions of the external terrain ("the rough granite slopes of Jebel Mussa . . . in the barren desert") reflect his internal state of suffering the "loneliness of being far from home—stripped of language, bereft of friends . . . . plans having all been ruined." The destructive experience is followed by a constructive one: a description of the external domain as a "lush, green hill rising out of the plains of central Galilee" correlates with an ecstatic experience of discovery in the psychological terrain—"I wandered into the nearby ruins . . . and there I found the stone . . . that I knew belonged to my friend Dana." The author claims that these sequential accounts do more: they show how geography, by "localizing" truth, can assist in grasping the abstract. Geographical locations bring close and open up the apophatic and the cataphatic to the reader's own experience and memory.

Lane also cites previous yokings of the two mountains—from the Scriptures and from the Greek and Latin fathers—and remarks on the coherence of these pairings in iconic representations in Christian art.[4] As "mythic opposites," the two mountains have represented the joining of a "theology of intimate presence with one of elusive majesty" (p. 198). Here the apophatic and the cataphatic are not only complementary but interdependent:

> They need each other. Kataphatic expression without the critique of apophatic prophecy can become dogmatic, abstruse, attaching a truth beyond comprehension to narrow and fixed ways of thinking. Similarly, apophatic criticism, in its effort to challenge all conclusions, can, without a kataphatic willingness to pin itself down, lead to an empty nihilism—never affirming anything. (p. 199)

Here we see Lane making his case for the interdependence of the apophatic and cataphatic approaches in terms of the excesses and defects which result when one or the other is absent. Lane's insight is based on the logic of contrast.

The logic of contrast is especially useful from a psychological point of view. Precisely because it is both formal and static, the categories it opposes can be used to apply to persons according to psychological states, so that some persons are drawn by their personal experience to the apophatic way and others to the cataphatic way. Although Lane does not expand on the psychological implications, he does provide the content for this extension by means of the narrative reconstruction of his own journey. The risks of travel, the taking leave of friends, and the threat to self-identity is followed by finding a place, finding renewed friendship, and the elation of survival.

But the formal logic of excess and defect tends to be inadequate in one important aspect, because it typically focuses on types of experience as distinct from experience as remembered and sometimes changed in recollection.[5] Some well-known psychological approaches to religion do include memory, if only implicitly, in their analyses. In William James' treatment of the "varieties" of religious experience, for instance, and in the description of peak and nadir experiences, gleaned by Abraham Maslow from hundreds of interviews, memory has a definite role in the experiences described. In

James, the distinction between "first-born" and "second-born" implies the ability of the "second-born" to recollect a radical change in experience. In Maslow, the importance of memory is explicit: he notes that as he became more experienced at conducting interviews, his interviewees were more willing and able to remember and to recount both nadir and peak experiences.[6] We will see that, in an epistemological model, memory plays a crucial role not recognized in the logic of excess and defect.

Like the psychological interpretation of human experience, the apophatic and cataphatic approaches to spirituality both provide a sufficiently diverse and common vocabulary and make it possible to compare others' experiences with one's own. This possibility does not mean that the patterning of experience is either entirely intuitive or that it is universally applicable. Like doctrine, psychology and spirituality are partial. Like doctrine, the apophatic and cataphatic can claim only a relative adequacy—which is, nevertheless, a true adequacy—for describing ways to the sacred. Like doctrine, the apophatic and cataphatic may best be understood in tension with some other category. Whereas in premodern theological reflection, doctrine was often treated as an independent category of affirmation, today some theologians argue that doctrine is more adequately understood in tension with some other category.[7] Similarly, the apophatic and cataphatic may best be understood, not just in comparison with each other, but in relation to some other central category. David Tracy points in this direction in his *Dialogue With the Other* (1991), where he argues that the mystico-prophetic trajectory is the one best suited for addressing the challenges currently faced by the major religions.[8]

3. Epistemological Support for Understanding the Apophatic-Cataphatic

As we have seen, the apophatic and cataphatic traditionally tend to be understood as discrete types of spirituality, in association with either persons or "schools." But in the examples which support this analysis, ways of establishing continuities have also been noticed. Most often these continuities have been treated as evidence that the apophatic and cataphatic contain similar elements or that each shares a "basis and moments"[9] with the otherwise quite disparate approach.

In addition, the apophatic as negative theology occupies a very curious position. Detractors of apophatic theology point out its derivative status, suggesting that in its least self-conscious forms it is logically parasitic upon positive theology. Acclaimers of the apophatic sometimes use it, on the other hand, as a hermeneutics of suspicion against a positive theology deemed to have grown positivist and gnostic. Because mystical theology has traditionally been more closely associated with the apophatic than with the cataphatic, part of the strength of the apodictic has been its resistance to those forms of positive theology which have defined knowing in a way that excludes the negative. For these reasons, separate analyses of the apophatic and the cataphatic ways of spirituality are useful as mutual critiques and as means for recognizing the limitations of each taken alone. Harvey D. Egan, for example, notes the following weakness of the apophatic:

> If a person leaves the stabilizing foundation of the explicitly kataphatic Christian mysteries too quickly, the apophatic thrust will collapse. Facile iconoclasm, strain, and a degenerate passivity are seeming dangers in this tradition. . . . Then the contemplative is left with a nothing which is literally nothing. Even in mysticism, nothing is sometimes nothing. (p. 423)

And on the weaknesses of the cataphatic, Egan notices that

> What should be a movement and rhythm towards evergreater purification, illumination, and transformation may harden into an asceticism and recipe-book type of prayer. Thinking about Christ's life, death, and resurrection may be substituted for the genuine entrance into his rhythm, which is basically our own deepest rhythm. The mysteries must not become pious holy cards obscuring instead of rendering transparent the divine-human mystery and drama. (p. 425)

Egan's analysis suggests that the strength of the Christian cataphatic tradition is in its incarnational foundation. The sheer audacity of the claim that God is human generates new possibilities for human beings and "calls into play all [human] dimensions and faculties . . ." (p. 426).

What might an epistemological analysis contribute beyond the usefulness of these analyses on the model of the logic of excess and defect? One reason for an epistemological analysis is to correct some misunderstandings. One might argue that if the definition of knowing were not restricted to logic and if knowledge were understood in terms of thinking processes and understanding, the apophatic and the cataphatic would not be dichotomized—as it is in a tradition dominated by formal logic. Within a larger definition of understanding, knowing is culturally-dominated, but not determined; time- and space-bound, although it can migrate to other times and places. In one sense, hermeneutics is born with the question of how knowledge (as the public part of understanding) can migrate from one person to another and one culture to another. Aquinas must have taken this process for granted in his famous third way, when he wrote that neither truth nor reason reigns supreme alone, but that they continuously inform each other.

In the critique of the formal logic of excess and defect, we saw that memory provides a basis for understanding the apophatic and cataphatic as successive, for it is by means of memory that the subject has some sense of the purposiveness of what is happening—no longer necessarily in the classical sense of divine will, but in the sense that negative experiences do prepare one for a relatively better competence or coherence or relationship with what is sacred than before. We catch glimpses of this in our responses to others—responses we have reason to believe would not be as adequate had the negative experience not occurred. This experience suggests that an "other"—the other as experienced in personal relationships, in the oppressed and suffering people of our era, in the marginalized in our society—may play a vital role in sustaining what is authentic in either mystical way. Egan speaks of the focus of the mystic as "God-with-us as the way to the ever-greater God and the Giver of God-in-us." In the added light of the combined mystico-prophetic trajectory, the pronoun is plural in number: God-with-us is present to us not only as individuals but as members of various human communities.

In his *Method in Theology*, Bernard Lonergan creates a space and offers an epistemological basis for seeing a processual continuity between the apophatic and the cataphatic by treating religious development as dialectical. Whatever one calls the dynamic state reached in the goal of this development, it involves "self-transcendence . . . which is ever precarious."[10] In epistemological terms, "self-transcendence involves tension between the self as transcending and the self as transcended" (p. 110).

What is the significance of an epistemological analysis for understanding the relatedness of the apophatic and the cataphatic? Lonergan's epistemology distinguishes operations of consciousness: experience, understanding of experience, affirmations or negations of our understanding of experience, decisive action based on our affirmations or negations of our understanding of experience. When in motion, these operations are transcendentals—that is, they are contained in the questions which are prior to any answers or categories we give. The transcendentals are

> the radical intending that moves us from ignorance to knowledge. They are a priori because they go beyond what we know to seek what we do not know yet. They are unrestricted because answers are never complete and so only give rise to still further questions. They are comprehensive because they intend the unknown whole or totality of which our answers reveal only part. (p. 11)

In Lonergan's epistemology, knowing and not knowing are part of a single development. Rather than being only the result of a process of inquiry, the desire to know is dynamic materially, "just as a dance is a pattern of bodily movements, or a melody is a pattern of sounds." The image suggests that both the pattern of the dance and the space enclosing the pattern of the movements are vital. Second, the desire to know is also dynamic formally, as "a growing organism puts forth its own organs and lives by their functioning." The image emphasizes equally rootedness and change. And third, the desire to know is open-eyed in negative as well as positive experiences; it is, in Lonergan's words, "a conscious intending, ever going beyond what happens to be given or known, ever striving for a fuller and richer apprehension of the yet unknown or incompletely known totality, whole, universe" (p. 13). With this description of knowing as a basis for what is the cataphatic, can it not be said that spiritual development, viewed over a lifetime, includes both negative and positive "ways"?

In some of the most memorable examples which incorporate both the cataphatic and the apophatic as related parts of an individual's spiritual journey—Teresa's interior castle, John of the Cross' spiritual canticle—the narrative structure of discourse both gives the images a temporal dimension and orders them within a life process. Even more emblematic images, such as the visions of mystical bodies recorded in Hildegard's *Scivias*—visions that simultaneously showed souls in torment alongside souls in glory—

are best interpreted as part of a narrative structure. Traditional depictions of heaven and hell as places, moreover, gain new implications when interpreted in the context of stages in a spiritual journey. Teresa's descriptions of the First Mansion, for example, incorporate many aspects of traditional visions of hell. Similarly, her descriptions of the Seventh Mansion are informed with traditional images of heaven. Such comparisons invite an interpretation that frees the images from an exclusive association with place or a typological obsession with kinds of persons and allows them to be interpreted within any person's life-long struggle for authenticity. The best premodern example of such an integration of these images is, of course, Dante's *Divine Comedy*, where both the text and others' illustrations of it combine individual scenes in a continuity from the middle of life (time of crisis and beginning of the spiritual journey) to its culmination (a spiritual maturity that is experienced as a gift, but not a guaranteed nor permanent possession). Epistemology, then, emphasizes that both knowing and not-knowing are regular and expected elements of the spiritual life—a continuous process of moving through and beyond what is known and what has been affirmed.

4. The Iconic-Aniconic Tension: More Evidence of Continuity and Incommensurability between Knowing and Not Knowing

In all three of the major Western religious traditions, the tension between the iconic and the aniconic, taken alone, has revolved about the issue of misplaced worship. Until recently, both Judaism and Islam were perceived as being primarily (if not exclusively) aniconic, whereas the popular perception of Christianity is of a religion wherein the iconic stance has been victorious. Recent scholarship has shown this assessment to be too simple on two counts: (1) within any given period several different positions on the issue of the use of icons can be found; (2) different kinds of images, together with the possibility of displacement from one to another genre, need to be taken into account. As a third point of consideration, I am suggesting here that the apophatic-cataphatic controversy may be related to the iconic-aniconic dispute in several interesting ways.

Might it not indeed be productive to correlate the aniconic tendency with emphasis (or lack thereof) on the apophatic in a specific historical situation—in other words, to study how doctrine is conceived in relation to images and to determine its status at a particular time and place in the tradition; to ask which genres of knowledge were being affirmed and which were proscribed? In the Byzantine iconoclastic movement (724 C.E.-843 C.E.), for example, there initially was a direct relationship between iconoclasm and apophatic theology: iconoclastic theologians held that to represent Christ was improperly to limit Christ's nature—that to represent God was to violate God's essential indescribability. Here, not-knowing is understood as visually *beyond* knowing something about God; resisting the imaging of Christ was not therefore necessarily an objection to knowing something about God, but an objection to *the inadequacy of describing Christ in a particular way*—in this case, visually. Other forms of knowing and describing God—for example, certain abstractions about God as all knowing, all good, etc., and many non-realist modes of representing Christ became acceptable.

Another historical example suggests a most promising test-case for postmodern spirituality and the questions it raises about divine representation. Pope Gregory the Great (540–604 C.E.) was faced with the iconoclastic undertakings of Serenus of Marseilles, one of his bishops, who, it was reported, was destroying statues on the grounds that they tempted people to worship them. Gregory wrote two letters to Serenus in which he granted that worship of idols was only one of the possible uses of statues and argued that their positive use, that is, their contribution to knowledge for those who could not read, outweighed the possible negative use.[11]

By calling art the "books and writings" of those who cannot read verbal texts, Gregory left the way open for an emphasis on the interpretation of these visual and verbal teaching strategies. This shift of focus from an opposition of word to image to an interpretation of strategies and their effects on readers has helped to remove many of the traditional fears of and objections to the iconic and the cataphatic in the Christian tradition. The shift has also permitted the iconic to become more complex. Today we do not hesitate to attribute to the iconic that which was traditionally reserved to the aniconic—as can be seen in Mark C. Taylor's statement about Ad Reinhardt's paintings, one of which is entitled "Black": "These paintings are, in my judgment, the most powerful statement of negative theology ever developed in the twentieth century."[12]

What did not come up in either Gregory's letters to Serenus or the Hebrew Bible's treatment of idol worship was the precise function of images in religious instruction, particularly their function with respect to major historical figures or events formative of the tradition. Why was the positive function of images not elaborated? Probably because there was no adequate way of expressing both their ambiguity and their complexity—a task for which we are hardly much better equipped today, because word and image are traditionally studied in two separate realms. If we ask, for example, why it is permissible in Islam to represent Muhammad's sandal but not his face; why, during the iconoclastic controversy within Christianity, Christ could not be imaged; and why the proscription against images in Islam does not preclude the words of revelation in the Qur-an being reproduced on the walls of mosques, we see that in each case, the tension is not between visual representation and no representation, but between some kinds of visual representation and other kinds.

Even in the case of Judaism, the Old Testament passages pertaining to the prohibition of idol worship do not offer a clear-cut aniconic stance. Whereas formerly such language was taken as implicit evidence that the Hebrew religion was monotheistic, today such passages reveal more than a vehement attempt to extirpate the worship of idols. The language also gives us a glimpse into the pervasiveness of the desires and actions called idol worship— else why the strong protest against it? The very strength of the prohibition may conceal a troubled and conflicted treatment of images of the sacred. At the same time the discovery of Dura Europas and other ancient synagogues constitutes evidence that some Jewish communities were so untroubled about the use of images that they adorned their spaces for prayer and worship with murals representing scenes from the Old Testament. Here imaging of the sacred went beyond liturgical vessels to the building itself.

We might well suspect that in many instances the tension between the iconic and the aniconic has its buried root in the tacit opposition of word to image and vice versa—an opposition postmodern culture and thought opposes in various ways. Mieke Bal is one theorist who has pointed out that this opposition is "medium-bound"; that is to say, the "terms of spectatorship, story telling, rhetoric, reading, discursivity and visuality"[13] are used to interpret either verbal or visual art—but not both. In her *Reading Rembrandt: Beyond the Word Image Opposition*, Bal proposes to ask questions of each medium, using both verbal and visual works as objects of interpretation. She shows how narrative is operative in visual art, in spite of our expectation that narrativity is an aspect only of verbal language, and concludes that the word-image opposition as traditionally posed does not point to two different essences, but is instead a matter of "specific strategies" used by each art.

Contemporary artists frequently combine the visual and the verbal in their art.[14] The practice in some ways recalls the book art of the Middle Ages and has contributed to a rediscovery of the epistemological, rhetorical and pedagogical assumptions underlying the visualization of texts in premodern culture. As Mary J. Carruthers has shown, prior to the eighteenth century "reading was considered to be essentially a visual act," dependent on the formation and recall of "mental images" or "pictures."[15] This rediscovery of the visual element in reading resonates in many ways with the emphasis of postmodern literary theory on both the "framing" of discourse and the opacity and slipperiness of language itself in its capacity to yield multiple interpretations. This open-endedness, which characterizes every kind of sign, likens words to pictures, the verbal to the visual image.[16]

Indeed, one of the most promising fruits of postmodernity comes from its ability to see language as more than a tool. Whereas the modernist assumed control over language, the postmodernist is both playfully and painfully aware of the effects of language on human beings, on action and understanding. The modernist confidence in using traditional language in many cases has given way to a heightened consciousness and disciplined gaiety in listening, speaking, and writing. Theologically, the panentheistic understanding of God has provided new opportunities to speak of God in relation to human beings. This welcome change in philosophical theology should bring about changes in the ways we speak about, understand and perhaps experience God, knowing, as we do, that relational language about God is not exempt from the ambiguity that postmodernism has taught us to recognize in other language.

What, then, does "going beyond the word-image opposition" mean for our understanding of the apophatic and cataphatic approaches to spirituality? First of all, in the important field of interfaith dialogue, the old platitudes about which religions are iconic, which aniconic, about which theological traditions are cataphatic, which apophatic, need no longer be the starting point of intertheological discourse, for the margins and the intersections of the apophatic/cataphatic and the iconic/aniconic will have become the most fruitful sites of inquiry. We can already say that all three religions—Christianity, Judaism, and Islam—affirm some kind of material images as vehicles of the sacred. They differ in the type and strategies of representation employed and approved.[17]

Recognizing an iconic "common ground" among believers will enrich the doctrinal discussions among the world religions and help us to understand better the ambiguous role that doctrine has played in the galaxy of genres that pertain to the spiritual life. It could be argued that doctrine was originally derived from liturgy: the use of formulaic expressions in the liturgy gave rise to doctrinal affirmations. (The kind of knowledge represented by liturgy and doctrine is, of course, a complicated epistemological issue.) It could be argued, as a complementary proposition, that icons were also originally derived from liturgy. Given that today we expect and allow much more latitude in the visual than in the linguistic expression, it is interesting to wonder what a difference might have been made had the pluralism of the iconic tradition (as represented in visual art) been supported as strongly in the cataphatic tradition (as represented by doctrine).

Allowing the visual representation of God to complement the verbal, doctrinal representation answers in many ways to the apophatic postmodern critique of the false pretensions and overestimates of rationality and its power to know. Postmodernism leads contemporary thinkers to eschew the expectation that what the text says and what it means coincides on some obvious level, even as it calls attention to the ease with which human beings can be deceived with respect to the claim of possessing "unified selves."

Joining the visual to the verbal, moreover, allows for a fuller, more inclusive, divine and human representation. The best of postmodernism rebukes those who systematically exclude some voices—the poor, the mad, the prophetic, the marginalized, racial or gender minorities—from consideration and the need for interpretation.[18] At the same time it welcomes and attends to multiple sources of inspiration: the experience of lay and religious, secular and cloistered, gay/lesbian and heterosexual, married and single people; the memories and imaginations of men and women who have encountered God in light and darkness, in fullness and emptiness, on the mountain heights and in the abyss, as they travelled the cataphatic and apophatic "ways."

Throughout this essay, we have discovered several reasons why the tension between the apophatic and the cataphatic is appropriate: the tension correlates with the epistemological experience of knowing that is always already relatively adequate in itself (judged to be virtually unconditioned) and on its way to being relatively inadequate in new circumstances (judged to be in need of being transcended).[19] Likewise, the tension between the iconic and the aniconic is appropriate: it correlates with the sensual experience of being affected by place and time and others—experience that is always already sufficient and always already going beyond itself in memory and desire. Augustine's often quoted adage, "Our hearts are restless, O Lord, until they rest in you," gains new meaning in the light of these tensions taken together and further related to the prophetic in our postmodern times.

Notes

1.   Bernard McGinn, *The Foundations of Mysticism*, Vol. 1 of *The Presence of God: A History of Western Christian Mysticism* (New York: Crossroad, 1991), p. xviii. Subsequent citations are parenthetical.

2.   See Saint Thomas Aquinas' attempt to unite the two kinds of spirituality in *Quaestiones disputatae*, VII,5. See also Vladimir Lossky's summary of Aquinas' attempt in *The Mystical Theology of the Eastern Church* (Crestwood, NY: St. Vladimir's Press, 1976): "In attributing to God the perfections which we find in created beings, we must deny the mode according to which we understand these finite perfections, but we may affirm them in relation to God *modo sublimiori*" (p. 21). Thomas' solution was ingenious for his time. Today we would find it overly dependent upon logic and lacking in an experiential basis. Lossky finds Aquinas' attempt unsuccessful, but his skepticism stems from a suspicion of the cataphatic way in general.

3.   Belden Lane, "Sinai and Tabor: Apophatic and Kataphatic Symbols in Tension," *Studies in Formative Spirituality* 14.2 (1993), p. 189. Subsequent citations are parenthetical. Lane uses the notion of the "deconstructive" in a commonsensical way—not in the technical sense of deconstructionist theory. The deconstructive philosophy of Jacques Derrida has, however, inspired some interesting approaches from the perspective of mysticism, Buddhism, negative theology, and Jewish Kabbalism. See also Julia Kristeva's semiotic/deconstructionist analysis of writings by several mystics in *Tales of Love* (New York: Columbia University Press, 1987).

4.   For example, Lane finds Andrei Rublev's icon of the Transfiguration in the monastery church at the foot of Mt. Sinai eminently

expressive and inductive of both the apophatic and cataphatic spiritual ways.

5.   Memory also implies forgetting. In *The Drowned and the Saved* (New York: Vintage, 1988), Primo Levi writes that "human memory is a marvelous but fallacious instrument" (p. 23).

6.   In a hermeneutics of suspicion, one would suspect the influence of the interviewer and dismiss the text as unauthentic. In a hermeneutics of retrieval, one would take into account the effect of the interviewer and also pay attention to what is disclosed in the interview.

7.   For example, in *The Analogical Imagination: Christian Theology and the Culture of Pluralism* (New York: Crossroad, 1981), David Tracy suggests that the New Testament presents the genre "doctrine" as being in tension with the genre "apocalypse."

8.   See David Tracy, *Dialogue With the Other: The Interreligious Dialogue* (Grand Rapids, MI: Eerdmans, 1991).

9.   I borrow the phrase from Harvey D. Egan's excellent treatment of the religious interdependence of the apophatic and cataphatic, "Christian Apophatic and Kataphatic Mysticisms," *Theological Studies* (September, 1978): 399–426. See especially pp. 409–10. Subsequent citations are parenthetical.

10.   Bernard Lonergan, *Method in Theology* (Toronto: University of Toronto Press, 1972), p. 110. Subsequent citations are parenthetical.

11.   For a fine treatment of this episode, see Celia M. Chazelle, "Pictures, Books, and the Illiterate: Pope Gregory I's Letters to Serenus of Marseilles," *Word and Image* 6 (April-June, 1990): 138–53. See also Robert A. Markus, "The Cult of Icons in Sixth-Century Gaul," in his *From Augustine to Gregory the Great* (Inductive Reprints, 1983), pp. 151–57.

12.   Mark C. Taylor, in Robert Scharlemann, ed., *Negation and Theology* (Charlottesville: University Press of Virginia, 1992), p. 27.

13.   Mieke Bal, *Reading Rembrandt: Beyond the Word Image Opposition* (Cambridge: Cambridge University Press, 1991), p. 4.

14. For a study that emphasizes the eclecticism of postmodern art in general, see Charles Jencks, *Post-Modernism: The New Classicism in Art and Architecture* (New York: Rizzoli, 1987).

15. See Mary J. Carruthers, *The Book of Memory: A Study of Memory in Medieval Culture* (Cambridge: Cambridge University Press, 1990), p. 17. See also V. A. Kolve's brilliant treatment of memorial images, faculty psychology and iconography in *Chaucer and the Imagery of Narrative: The First Five Canterbury Tales* (Stanford: Stanford University Press, 1984).

16. See the special issue with a combined focus on Literary and Art History in *New Literary History* 3 (1972).

17. It seems reasonable to presume that the development of technological skills and political considerations had a small part to play in the type of representations that become representative of each religion (e.g., calligraphy in Islam, painting and sculpture in Christianity, vessels and murals in Judaism).

18. Some deconstructionist theology has been criticized for giving inadequate attention to social issues. See, for example, reviews of Mark C. Taylor's *Erring: A Postmodern A/Theology* (Chicago: University of Chicago Press, 1984).

19. The terms of Goethe's Faust's wager with Mephistopheles is interesting in this regard: "If ever I say to any moment, 'Do stay with me; you are so good,' you may take my soul."

PART II

Representations of Spirit

TOM W. BOYD

Is Spirituality Possible Without Religion? A Query for the Postmodern Era

When a therapist friend, teaching an adult church school class, was asked recently what he was teaching, he responded, "I am trying to help these people move beyond religion into spirituality." Not long before that a student confessed after a university class, "I am a spiritual person, but I am not religious. I don't even like religion." These two comments represent a common attitude among contemporary devotees to spirituality. They drive a wedge between spirituality and religion and depreciate or dismiss religion in the process.

Whether this bifurcation between spirituality and religion is acceptable, or even coherent, will be the query of this study. The claim here is twofold: that the current attempt to split spirituality away from religion is an expression of postmodern thinking and that spirituality and religion, while distinguishable, cannot be separated.

The terms "postmodern" and "postmodernism" are running loose across the intellectual landscape and are being employed to cover a multifarious range of expressions. With respect to religion, however, and specifically with respect to the breach between spirituality and religion, the version of postmodernism most pertinent is the popular movement commonly called "New Age." This movement, along with popular psychology which increasingly ties itself to elements of the New Age, is responsible for the remarkable currency of the terms "spiritual" and "spirituality."[1] For the most part they identify spirituality with a process of achieving the highest degree of psychological integration. As important as such integration surely is, it is not the sole, or even the specific, aim of spirituality. To think otherwise is to deny to humanity its most profound liberation through the encounter with self-transcending mystery.

On the contrary, the argument to follow holds that spirituality thrives in dialectical tension with religion, one calling for the other. To prosecute this claim I will maintain that spirituality is not exhausted in self-realization or actualization, but that spirituality also entails the encounter with *self-transcendence*. Once this is understood, the inevitability of religion as a concomitant of spiritual life becomes evident.

The succeeding discussion proceeds in five movements. First, I will examine the phenomenon of postmodernism and particularly the New Age movement as an expression of it, to discover the conceptual milieu for current attempts to separate spirituality from religion and to elevate the former at the expense of the latter. Second, I will offer a representative formulation and analysis of the popular distinction between spirituality and religion. In this context attention will be given to an adequate conception of "spirit," "spiritual" and "spirituality." Third, I will employ Paul Tillich's conception of "spirit," wherein he shows that spirit, as the singular feature of human being, necessarily includes the encounter with self-transcendence and thus renders religion ingredient to the spiritual life. Fourth, I will argue, following Tillich, that religion is to spirituality as form is to dynamic and that, given the essential structure of human finitude, dynamics is not possible without formative articulation. Finally, I will examine the use of "religion" as form and offer a suggestive phenomenological analysis of it in relation to spiritual dynamics.

1. New Age as a Postmodern Spirituality

Postmodernism is not so much a movement as a collection of intellectual, and increasingly popular, responses to the failure of modernity. The unity of the phenomenon lies in its attempt to fill the lacuna left by that failure. More specifically, the unity is two-fold. First, postmodernism is united against modernism. That is, the worldview fomented by the eighteenth-century Enlightenment and its nineteenth-century flowering is under interrogation and in profound doubt. Second, postmodernism is united against modernity, that is, against the prescriptions and excesses in the lifestyle aligned with the modernist worldview.

Beyond these two unifying interests postmodernism splinters in myriad directions, largely along lines of intellectual specifications. Until quite recently postmodern thought was rather confined to intellectual enclaves, beginning with literature and the arts and eventually filtering into other disciplines. Theology, it seems, has been one of the last to take up the challenge.[2]

Eventually, however, the concerns of postmodernism were bound to enter the public, even the popular, sphere. One such popular outbreak can be seen in the New Age movement. While New Age appears to be past its prime as a newsworthy phenomenon, it has by no means disappeared. Rather, its discourse is now integrated into a surprisingly broad spectrum of American culture. This includes the discourse of religious communities and even of theology.[3]

To understand New Age at least two qualifications are in order. First, "New Age" covers a range as multifarious as postmodernism itself. Plotting its boundaries is well nigh impossible, though its center of gravity in relation to spirituality readily yields to investigation. Second, New Age includes groups more nearly associated with premodern than with postmodern thinking. That is, some are drawn to the spiritual expressions found among primal and ancient peoples. For this reason New Age has been described by some as "neo-paganism."[4] (Of course, the appeal to premodern alternatives against modernism is one way of expressing the postmodern situation.[5]) Granting this, much of the New Age discourse remains indeed quite contemporary and is allied closely with certain perspectives in psychology, especially in the psychoanalytic tradition.

In order not to fall into the labyrinth of the New Age, the present discussion is limited to the notion of New Age spirituality. People wishing a more general introduction to New Age thinking can do no better than read Marilyn Ferguson's 1978 work, *The Aquarian Conspiracy*.[6] Although she later became quite critical of what she considered New Age excesses and distortions and separated herself from the label "New Age," her work is considered a primary stimulus to the movement and a definitive description of its cultural shape.

With respect to its understanding of spirituality, the New Age is deeply indebted to two twentieth-century thinkers: Carl Jung and Joseph Campbell. For the sake of brevity, Campbell will not be discussed. Suffice to note, though he focuses on world mythology rather than psychoanalysis, his view is quite in accord with Jung's conception of spirit.[7]

Jung's attention to concepts related to spirituality is far too voluminous to survey here. The specific question of his understanding of spirituality in relation to religion will suffice.

In an essay entitled "The Phenomenology of Spirit in Fairy Tales" Jung addresses the relation of spirituality to religion.[8] After tracing the etymology of the uses of "spirit," he acknowledges that its modern use has altered fundamentally. After discussing the impact of materialism on the modern notion of spirit, he observes:

> Even though the materialistic view did not prevail everywhere, the conception of spirit nevertheless remained outside the religious sphere, caught in the realm of conscious phenomena. Spirit as 'subjective spirit' came to mean a purely endopsychic phenomenon, while 'objective spirit' did not mean the universal spirit, or God, but merely the sum-total of intellectual and cultural possessions which make up our human institutions and the content of our libraries. (p. 7)

He adds that, outside religion, "spirit had forfeited its original nature, its autonomy over a very wide area." Jung then proceeds to make his critical point that spirit has, as it were, descended and become purely a feature of the psyche. He says:

> This spiritual entity approaches primitive man from outside; but with increasing development it gets lodged in man's consciousness and becomes a subordinate function, thus apparently forfeiting its original character of autonomy. That character is now retained only in the most conservative views, namely, in religion. (p. 8)

The key description, "lodged in man's consciousness," lays the groundwork for driving the wedge between spirituality and religion. Indeed, Jung symbolically strikes the first blow.

Religion retains a role for Jung. It is to remind people that they are not originators of their spirits nor ever fully in control of spirit within them. Thus, Jung acknowledges some mode of self-transcendence associated with spirit and spirituality. Nevertheless, he concludes, "As can readily be seen, the common modern idea of spirit ill accords with the Christian view, which regards it as the *summum bonum*, as God himself" (p. 9). In other words, his notion of self-transcendence remains bound to intra-psychic life.

Jung warns that in the realm of spirit much power, for good and evil, lurks. He says, "Spirit threatens the naive-minded man with inflation, of which our own times have given us the most horribly instructive examples" (p. 9). Jung's warning has not been heeded by most New Age exponents. A plethora of overreaching claims have been made. One of the most celebrated voices is that of Shirley MacLaine who made the phrase "the God within" and even "I am God" commonplace in wide circles of the movement. According to Harold Bloom, even the relatively moderate voices of the movement, such as that of Matthew Fox, collapse God into a radical immanence:

> To render justice unto Fox and most followers of the New Age, he and they hedge the obsessive immanence of God with a touch of transcendence. There is thus a heavenly or archetypal (divinity) somewhere, as well as the enveloping cosmic (divinity). But this difference makes so little difference, on a daily basis, as not to survive the pragmatic test. Fox has a nostalgia for the Church's sacraments but he, like all newagers, doesn't really need them.[9]

If Jung is right to insist on at least a minimal role for religion as reminder of the "otherness" and power of spirit, then the New Age emphasis on the radical immanence of divinity becomes dangerous indeed. Further, by cutting a cleavage between spirituality and religion the danger is accentuated. In other words, if spirituality without religion is inevitably self-inflating, then the split is treacherous both for the human psyche and for the prospects of modesty within our social and political schemes.

2. The Spirituality-Religion Cleavage

The notion of the separation between spirituality and religion has been variously stated, but for the present purpose one formulation will suffice. Cultural historian William Irwin Thompson asserts in *The Time Falling Bodies Take to Light*:

> Religion is not identical with spirituality; rather religion is the form spirituality takes in a civilization; it is not so much

the opiate of the masses as it is the antidote for the poisons
of civilization. (Of course, an overdose of an antidote becomes a poison in itself.) Because religion is a response to
the conditions of alienation in a civilization, religion is unnecessary in a culture of hunters and gatherers. The culture
of hunters and gatherers is spirituality personified; every
event is part of a story, every part is connected to the whole,
every act is flooded with the sacred.[10]

While it is readily agreed that spirituality and religion are not
identical, Thompson draws too sharp a line between them.

Thompson goes on to assert that moderns are so alienated that
their only recourse in recovering the sacred may be through art. He
makes no appeal for a recovery of religion but implicitly treats it
more nearly as symptom than as an antidote to the modern dilemma. He appeals to primal peoples (a premodern appeal) as
having a sort of pristine spirituality uncontaminated by religion. Is
this an accurate portrayal of primal peoples? Certainly they seem
to be far less differentiating than we regarding any distinction
between spirituality and religion.

Writing about Native American tribal peoples, Joseph Epes
Brown notes:

It has not become abundantly clear that it is a fundamental and universal characteristic of Native American cultures, as indeed of all primal or primitive cultures, that
"religion"—there is no equivalent word for this in any
American Indian language—is not a separate category of
activity or experience that is divorced from culture or
society. Rather, religion is pervasively present and is in
complex interrelationship with all aspects of the peoples'
life-ways.[11]

At first blush Brown's statement seems to corroborate Thompson's, but on closer reading Brown is not saying there is a split
between spiritual life and religion among Native Americans, but
that they do not **differentiate** between them.

Even Brown's assessment, however, may not be quite accurate.
Bronislaw Malinowski closely observed the Trobriand tribes and
found that they made rather subtle distinctions at least between
magic, science, and religion.[12] This suggests that some tribal peoples do make quite precise differentiations.

Reading back into primal peoples a pristine or pure spirituality unmediated, and uncontaminated, by religion is dubious in the extreme. In the eighteenth century such an idealization of primal peoples was common, but David Hume presented a telling challenge to the notion in his work, *The Natural History of Religion*.[13] Indeed, Hume recognized that religion, as with other dimensions of human life, unfolds through historical process.

At least this much may be asserted with confidence: there was never a time when human beings enjoyed a pure spirituality unexpressed as what can best be described as religion. Even if primal peoples had no word for it, this only means that they did not distinguish religion in the way we now do. In any case, it is inadequate to leave the impression, as Thompson does, that religion is reducible to a **corruption** of spirituality and a symptom of cultural alienation.

A more adequate understanding of the relation between spirituality and religion requires a clarification of how we use the terms "spirit," "spiritual," and "spirituality" as well as how we use "religion." Both will be described more fully as the discussion proceeds, but a preliminary characterization of "spirit" and its cognates is fitting. Most discussions of *spirit* as it applies to human beings hark to its etymological grounding in "breath" or "wind." On this basis, along with an assessment of ancient and classical usage, spirit is widely construed as an immaterial, hence invisible, force which is experienced as "presence," that is, as making claims upon one. This is the case even in speaking of one's own spirit. Spirit is not simply at the disposal of the Self but is that which calls the Self both to itself and beyond itself.[14] Paul Tillich, whose understanding of spirit will shortly be examined more fully, defines it this way: "Spirit as a dimension of life unites the power of being with the meaning of being. Spirit can be defined as the actualization of power and meaning in unity."[15]

A further qualification of "spirit" may be useful in applying it to human being. A distinction may be made between spirit and soul. Spirit is more nearly an event than an entity, while soul is more nearly an entity, albeit not in any tangible sense, than an event. Soul has locus in relation to Self as itself. Spirit happens to the soul/self, blowing where it will, at once within but grasped as something granted and even invasive. Spirit is the union of meaning and power, but the power is never simply in our power. For this reason occasions of high spiritual intensity are described as *ekstasis*. One is more than simply a fully realized Self, whatever that might be. One is beyond Self without losing Self.

Granting this general description of spirit, when persons behave in a "spiritual" way, that is, express their "spirituality," they
are nurturing the possibilities that inhere in spirit. They are opening themselves to power and meaning of their being. The question
before us is this: how is spirituality, thus described, related to
religion?

3. Spirit and Self-Transcendence

In responding to this question, the work of Paul Tillich in his
Systematic Theology (3:21–110) offers guidance. Tillich begins the
volume with a discussion of *life* as a general concept. He notes how
life moves from its simplest to its most complex forms. Human
beings alone, as the most complex mode of life, possess the dimension of *spirit*. This is evident from his understanding of spirit as the
unity of power and meaning.

According to Tillich's analysis of spirit, it has three manifestations in human existence. First, spirit manifests as *self-integration*,
and this accounts for *morality* as the constitution of the personal
self. Second, spirit is expressed in *self-creativity* as *culture*. All creativity in the arts and in science is a disclosure of spirit. Finally,
spirit is expressed in *self-transcendence*, taking the form of *religion*.

Tillich spends almost eighty pages expositing what he means
by these three aspects of spirit in relation to the ambiguities (that
is, finitude) of life. For the purposes of this study, his overall position need not be elaborated. Two features of his analysis of spirit
are important for this discussion. First, spirit, as a unique dimension of human life, is more inclusive than religion. The very stuff of
personality, morality, and culture also belong to spirit and fully
interact with the religious expression of spirit. Second, the full and
adequate, although always ambiguous, expression of spirit necessarily includes self-transcendence and therefore religion. That is,
religion is an inherent feature of the human spirit as such.

Tillich's position places him squarely in the tradition of liberal
Potestantism. Its "father" Friedrich Schleiermacher sounds the message to the detractors from religion in his 1799 classic, *Speeches on
Religion to Its Cultured Despisers*.[16] He insists that religion is *sui
generis* belonging to the very nature of human being, and that it is
expressed in the "feeling of absolute dependence." Although Tillich
rejects the identification of religion with "feeling," he uses "self-
transcendence" to designate the same sense of the encounter of

finitude with the infinite as Schleiermacher is describing. Whatever differences these two may have otherwise, both agree that religion is an inherent and fundamental aspect of being human.

Numerous criticisms might be made of Tillich's analysis of spirit, but one is especially pertinent to this study. Tillich conflates morality and what he calls "the constitution of the personal self" under one category, namely, self-integration. He would have done better to designate a fourth category such as *self-consciousness* and/or *self-realization* to describe personhood as a quality of spirit. Then the category of self-integration and/or self-regulation could characterize morality as a separate aspect of spirit.

My reason for suggesting personhood as a separate and fourth category is that much of the current popular discussion of spirituality in New Age thinking, as described in the first section of this study, isolates the personal aspect of spirit and limits the discussion of spirituality to self-conscious self-realization. While this is surely a feature of human life in the dimension of spirit, it hardly exhausts the range of spirituality, and this is where the thought of Carl Jung and the New Age deserve faulting. Even where popular discussion of spirituality acknowledges an element of self-transcendence, as Jung does, it tends to dissolve the notion into "the God within" and thereby scuttle any serious grasp of *otherness* as an essential feature of self-transcendence.

An adequate conception of self-transcendence is crucial to Tillich's view that religion is ingredient to the dimension of human spirit and, by implication, to spirituality. When the word "self" prefixes "transcendence," it can still mean a number of things. For instance, Sartre means by transcendence of the self that the self is always more than its given actuality at any moment. Human freedom, Sartre contends, allows the self to be always beyond itself and more than its sheer givenness. This is existential self-transcendence. Again, Jung also acknowledges psychological self-transcendence through notions of "archetypes" and "the collective unconscious." Still another can be found in thinkers like Martin Buber and Gabriel Marcel. For them self-transcendence refers to the experience of other persons as having a claim upon the self. The other person is a "Thou" and in this sense transcends the self.

When Tillich speaks of spiritual self-transcendence, he is not speaking existentially, psychologically, or interpersonally, though he does not necessarily reject these aspects of self-transcendence. He is speaking ontologically. The Self is "grasped and shaped" from beyond the Self. The essential finitude of human existence entails that the Self is never contained within itself and that the Self can discern this. Herein lies his strong tie to Schleiermacher and liberal Protestantism. Put another way, the Self is never the source of itself. This ontological understanding comes clear as one moves from Tillich's discussion of human spirit to his treatment of Holy Spirit which he denominates "Spiritual Presence." The human spirit is the point of engagement with Divine Spirit. Herein Tillich is acknowledging St. Paul's understanding: "It is that very Spirit bearing witness with our spirit that we are children of God. . . ." (Rom 8:16). Human recognition and response to this condition is the beginning of religion and constitutes a primary religious expression of spirit.

At this point a notable difference between Protestant and Catholic thought deserves mention. In Protestant thought the polarity of the finite and the infinite is essentially unmediated. In their finitude humans can be aware of the infinite, be open to it, and long for it, but the infinite remains essentially *other*. Søren Kierkegaard, a maverick Protestant, declares that human being "is a synthesis of the infinite and the finite," but he characterizes the synthesis as "the torment of contradiction." In *The Concluding Unscientific Postscript* he makes his most radical claim against Hegelian mediation by asserting "the infinite qualitative difference between the finite and the infinite."[17]

Karl Barth, this century's Protestant theologian *extra ordinare*, early in his work takes up Kierkegaard's "infinite qualitative difference" as a battle cry against any "natural" mediation between the finite and the infinite. To mediate this cleavage requires a radical act, an "intrusion" of the infinite, as in Christ, and a "leap of faith" toward the (Kierkegaardian) infinite in response.

Given the unmediated—or only mediated through intrusion—relation between human finitude and the infinite, both Kierkegaard and Barth struggle with religion. It seems to be, at best, a necessary concession to human finitude. Hence, Kierkegaard's scathing attack on "Christendom" and Barth's description of religion as "unbelief."[18] Popular evangelical Christians have taken up the Bartian criticism of religion to defend Christianity, holding that it is not a religion. This spurious claim allows them the convenience of not having to deal with Christianity in relation to other religions.

This more radical Protestant view of religion contrasts sharply with Tillich's perspective on mediation. He stands closer to Catholic thought, which holds to an essential mediation between the finite and infinite. For instance, Karl Rahner in *Foundations of*

Christian Faith states in a section entitled "Transcendental Knowledge of God as Experience of Mystery":

> By its very nature subjectivity is always a transcendence which listens, which does not control, which is overwhelmed by mystery and opened up by mystery. In the midst of its absolute infinity transcendence experiences itself as empty, as merely formal, as necessarily mediated to itself by finiteness, and hence a finite infinity.[19]

The telling phrase is "finite infinity." In a significant sense, however formal and empty, the finite self includes something of the infinite, but only as mystery. Thus, for Catholicism formal religion is more decisively necessary to spiritual life than it is for the more strident Protestant interpreters. Tillich represents a middle ground which renders him more compatible to Catholic thought. Still, even the more radical Protestant thinkers acknowledge the inevitability of religion, albeit grudgingly.

4. Spirituality as Dynamic, Religion as Form

If spiritual self-transcendence issues in religion, this implies something about the nature of religion. To explain this, another distinction made by Tillich may prove fruitful. In a section of his *Systematic Theology* entitled "The Basic Ontological Structure, Self and World," Tillich describes three sets of polarities: "Individuation and Participation," "Freedom and Destiny," "Dynamics and Form." These are ontological categories which characterize all human existence.

The polarity most directly revealing of the relation between spirituality and religion is "Dynamics and Form." Tillich holds that, " 'Being something' means having a form." Form without dynamics, however, becomes empty formalism. Thus, "Every form forms something." That "something" is what he calls *dynamics*, an ontological potentiality which cannot articulate itself except as form. In human experience this polarity expresses itself in the relation between *vitality* and *intentionality*: "The dynamic element in man is open in all directions; it is bound by no a priori limiting structure." Yet, it cannot be manifested in human beings apart from intentionality, namely, "living in tension with (and toward) something objectively valid." This intentionality is the form of the dynamic vitality. Because of dynamics, human form is always open to new form or being re-formed, and this makes *becoming* possible (1:178–182).

Using Tillich's analysis of form and dynamics, we propose that dynamics is manifest in humans as spirit. Spirit as dynamics, however, cannot be separated from formation. Because spirit has at least three, and I suggest four, expressions, it also has as many corresponding formations: in personality, morality, culture, and religion. The formation of the dynamic of spirit in the encounter with self-transcendence is religion. As Tillich says, " . . . spirituality means the unity of dynamics and form in man's moral and cultural acts" (1:180). He does not mention religion in this passage, but adding it is fully consistent with his later discussion of spirit in the third volume. We conclude, therefore, that spirit is to religion as dynamic is to form. Since the two cannot be separated in actual existence, it follows that spirituality without religion is inadequate to the very nature of spirit.

If spirituality is not fully realized without religion, some account of religion as a fundamental *form* of spirituality is in order. Tillich's own formal conception of religion is rather general. He defines religion as "a state of being ultimately concerned" (1:11–14). On this view virtually any orientation to anything can serve as one's religion. In other words, the form is endlessly open. Yet, Tillich is fully aware that many religious forms fail to meet the demands inherent in self-transcendence and that no form can be fully adequate. Nevertheless, the most adequate forms of religion are those that actually serve the demands of self-transcendence.

A minimal expression of an adequate religion, on Tillich's account, may be illustrated from one of Bertrand Russell's personal letters. He says:

> I must before I die, find some way to say the essential thing that is in me, that I have never said yet—a thing that is not love or hate or pity or scorn, but the very breath of life, fierce and coming from far away, bringing into human life the vastness and fearful passionless force of non-human things . . . . [20]

Commenting on Russell's confession, Colin Wilson describes it as "a statement of the essence of religious belief." Given Tillich's definition of religion as "ultimate concern," he would likely agree that Russell's confession is fundamentally, and properly, religious.

5. Religious Formation

Our question here is whether Tillich's view of the fundamental form of religion is adequate. Although it may be a necessary feature within the formation of religion, religion as "ultimate concern" lacks the concreteness and comprehensiveness necessary to account for and explain religion.

Accordingly, a certain progression in the formation of religion might be offered. First, Tillich may be said to represent *foundational* religion. That is, the one necessary condition for any religious formation is the orientation of the self to the unconditional, to ultimacy. Religion as form has its birthing where one embraces, and is embraced by, the very givenness of spiritual, that is, ontological, self-transcendence.

Second, foundational religion becomes explicit in *formal* religion. As Schleiermacher would say, religion is always particular, taking on specific identifiable formation. It can be, as it were, "handled," because human beings are immersed in concrete particularity. This theme is sounded brilliantly in the sacramental theology of Edward Schillebeeckx. In *Christ: the Sacrament of the Encounter with God*, he contends that sacramentality makes it possible for the Divine Presence to be mediated to materially conditioned human existence.[21] Thus, the way is opened for the formal structures of religion. Religious conviction and conduct are brought to expression through story, symbol, and ritual, and these are orchestrated to bind its practitioners to the very process of human life. As Ernesto Buonaiuti puts it, "Human religiosity is nothing other than the performance of a number of 'transitional rites' which serve to carry man unharmed through the most difficult and critical periods of transition."[22] While this description is not sufficient, it acknowledges a necessary feature of religion. In this sense formal religion is indeed the concrete particular articulation of "the encounter with God" of which Schillebeeckx speaks.

In quite another context psychotherapist Rollo May, a student of Tillich's, describes creativity as the "passion for form." He goes on to comment: "This passion for form is a way of trying to find and constitute meaning in life." This is quite close to Tillich's definition of spirit as the unity of power and meaning. May realizes that passion (that is, spiritual dynamics) is dangerous. Without formation, "it can destroy meaning and produce chaos again."[23] If this is true of the creative process in general, it is pointedly true of religion as an expression of spiritual self-transcendence. Formal religion, therefore, while it provides stability within the dynamics of spirit, can also imprison and crush spirit with its formalism. Thus, there can be no final formal religion.

In other words, spirit and spiritual life can not be *reduced* to religion. That is, religion as form can never circumscribe or contain the spirit which in-forms it. The element of *ekstasis*, if nothing else, resists the bondage of spirit to form. When psychiatrist Robert Coles worked with a child of eight who was devoutly Roman Catholic, he found that she could also be strikingly critical of the church. In this context he noted, ". . . there was a personal *spiritual* life in her that was by no means to be equated with her *religious* life."[24] This distinction is quite proper so long as it doesn't entail the idea that religion is thus superfluous to spiritual life.

While there is no one formal religion, life under the dimension of spirit yields a religious structure and process by which self-transcendence can be consistently attended. This religious formation, however, dare not harden but must participate in its own becoming. Otherwise, it violates the spiritual dynamics on which it relies.

Finally, because the dynamic of spirit also manifests itself in the forms of morality, culture, and personality, these features of spirit also participate in the way self-transcendence takes form in religion. Thus, formal religion always takes shape within the moral, cultural—and I believe, personal—structures which disclose the human spirit. Hence, the great variety and perpetual mutation within formal religion.

Third, in mature states of life under the dimension of spirit, dynamics may fuse with form to such an extent that they are virtually one. This is *trans-formative* religion. In this context "transformative" refers to the capacity to remain oriented to one's own formal religion while seriously participating in, and being shaped by, other forms. This is a highly cultivated level of religion and is correspondingly rare.

One twentieth-century exemplar of transformative religion is Thomas Merton. Edward Rice, writing in his biography of Merton, describes Merton's later years: "Merton was searching not for a religion—which he had—but a discipline of a different color and intensity from the Trappists'. He turned to Zen Buddhism." Rice reports that, while Merton was travelling in India, "He expressed the belief that there was a real possibility of contact on a deep level between the contemplative and monastic tradition of the West and the various contemplative traditions in the East."[25] Merton is not guilty of "losing" his formal religion but of transforming it through a more inclusive appreciation for the form of religion as such.

This third level in the formation of religion can be, and often is, misunderstood. It is taken to mean that one can outgrow religion and live only by the dynamics of spirituality. This is a gross misconstrual of the situation. Because of the essential relation between dynamics and form within human finitude, the form can never be dismissed. It furnishes the particularity which binds it to moral, cultural, and personal life and to the continuity necessary for sustained meaning in life. This is why Merton remains intensely faithful to his particular formal religion, while liberating the form from formalism—and most certainly from absolutism—through transformative consciousness. Those who glibly dismiss formal religion in the name of spirituality have not reached the state described as transformative religion. They more often flounder on those treacherous shoals where dynamic spirituality seeks to avoid form in favor of sheer subjective freedom or to treat religion arbitrarily. This is the sort of spirituality which can be found among some exponents of New Age and which this study challenges.

Conclusion

Having exposited a view of spirituality and religion which shows them to be mutually entailed, I acknowledge a heavy, albeit critical, reliance on Tillich's ontology. Further, I have laid out a position without mounting a defense of it, choosing to rest my case on the coherence of the position and its general explanatory power. To flesh out this position and lend it appropriate support is a larger program than could be undertaken in this presentation.

In this project I have claimed (1) that spirituality and religion cannot finally be separated, (2) that because spirit and spiritual life entail engagement with self-transcendence, religion becomes an inevitable expression of spirit, and (3) that the proper relation between spirituality and religion is that of the relation between dynamic and form. Spirit is the dynamic of which religion is the formation. Furthermore, dynamics and form do not exist apart from each other.

The importance of this topic lies in the urgency it represents. The forces of secularization have dismissed all but intra-mundane forms of self-transcendence. As a consequence, spirituality has shrunk and become increasingly shallow, indeed, self-serving. This dwarfed spirituality is further aggravated by a propensity to Promethean arrogance in which people are urged to delusional grandeur regarding self-mastery. Only by a new depth and sobriety in the understanding of religion as a bearer of spirit, along with a liberation of religion from its propensity toward hardened exclusivism, can we wend our way into a future worthy of embrace.

Some general conclusions may be drawn from this analysis:

1. Religion is an inevitable expression of the human spirit. Only where the spirit is suppressed and dwarfed by forces inhibiting its full expression is the existence of religion significantly threatened.

2. Religion may take on an endless array of forms as it participates in other forms of the dimension of spirit: morality, culture, and personality.

3. Some religions are more adequate than others in giving form to the encounter with self-transcendence. The criteria for adequacy are best explored in a comprehensive phenomenology of religion.

4. No form of religion can ever be fully adequate, let alone final. All religions fail in the attempt to give form to the infinite. In short, any form of religion, which does not acknowledge its formal limits before the mystery of what it seeks to articulate, distorts itself. The biblical name for this distortion is "idolatry."

5. Finally, any form of religion can lose its bond to the spiritual dynamic which vitalizes it. Indeed, a constant danger in religion, along with its claim to finality, is its loss of vitality and urgency. In such cases formal religion degenerates into hollow formalism. Religions can and do die, and spiritual vitality is a necessary antidote to moribund religion.

Notes

1. One example of this phenomenon will suffice to illustrate the point. The journal *Common Boundary Between Spirituality and Psychotherapy* (published at 4304 East-West Highway, Bethesda, Maryland 20814) is informative. A review of back issues reveals a progression of interest in New Age themes integrated with those of modern psychology. (The popular Twelve-Step programs provide a

further example of the current briding between psycho-centric self-help programs and a type of spiritual direction.)

2. This judgment must be qualified. In Catholicism the Second Vatican Council may have been a precursor to the church's own version of postmodern theological thinking. In Protestantism "secularization theology," and especially its most radical expression in the "death of God" movement, telegraphed postmodern concerns. This can be seen in the fact that some current voices in postmodern theology are those which also articulated "the death of God." See Thomas J. J. Altizer, et al., *Deconstruction and Theology* (New York: Crossroad, 1982).

3. The infiltration into mainstream American religion of ideas now common among New Age exponents, notably neo-gnosticism, predates the movement itself and indeed runs deep in the ethos of American Protestantism. See Philip J. Lee, *Against the Protestant Gnostics* (New York: Oxford University Press, 1987).

4. See, for example, Thomas Molnar, *The Pagan Temptation* (Grand Rapids: William B. Eerdmans, 1987).

5. See David Ray Griffin, et al., *Varieties of Postmodern Theology* (Albany: State University of New York Press, 1989), pp. 5–7. The authors are speaking here of certain Roman Catholic trends being "premodern" versions of postmodernism. The same can be said of some viewpoints in the New Age movement.

6. See Marilyn Ferguson, *The Aquarian Conspiracy* (Los Angeles: J. P. Tarcher, 1980).

7. See Joseph Campbell, *The Power of Myth* (New York: Bantam Double Dell, 1988); *The Inner Reaches of Outer Space* (New York: Alfred Van Der Marck, 1985).

8. Jung's essay appears in *Spirit and Nature*, ed. Joseph Campbell, Bollingen Series 30 (Princeton: Princeton University Press, 1982), pp. 3–48. Subsequent citations are parenthetical.

9. Harold Bloom, *The American Religion* (New York: Simon and Schuster, 1992), p. 186.

10. William Irwin Thompson, *The Time Falling Bodies Take to Light* (New York: St. Martin's Press, 1981), p. 103.

11. Joseph Epes Brown, *The Spiritual Legacy of the American Indian* (New York: Crossroad, 1985), p. x.

12. Bronislaw Malinowski, *Magic, Science, and Religion* (Garden City: Doubleday, 1954), pp. 17-92.

13. See David Hume, *The Natural History of Religion* (New York: Macmillan, 1992).

14. See Campbell, *Spirit and Nature*, pp. 4–10.

15. Paul Tillich, *Systematic Theology*, Vol. 3 (Chicago: The University of Chicago Press, 1967), p. 111. Subsequent citations of Tillich are parenthetical by volume and page.

16. See Friedrich Schleiermacher, *On Religion: Speeches on Religion to Its Cultured Despisers* (New York: Harper and Row, 1958). See especially the second speech, "The Nature of Religion."

17. See Søren Kierkegaard, *The Sickness Unto Death* (Princeton: Princeton University Press, 1980), p. 13; *The Concluding Unscientific Postscript* (Princeton: Princeton University Press, 1953), Chapter 3.

18. Karl Barth, *Church Dogmatics*, Vol. 1, Part 2 (Edinburgh: T. and T. Clark, 1963), pp. 297–325.

19. Karl Rahner, *Foundations of Christian Faith* (New York: Seabury, 1978), p. 58.

20. Quoted by Colin Wilson in *C. J. Jung, Lord of the Underworld* (North Hamptonshire, England: The Aquarian Press, 1988), p. 14.

21. Edward Schillebeeckx, *Christ: the Sacrament of the Encounter with God* (New York: Sheed and Ward, 1963), pp. 43–45.

22. In Joseph Campbell, *Spirit and Nature*, p. 214.

23. Rollo May, *The Courage to Create* (New York: Bantam, 1976), pp. 149–69.

24. Robert Coles, *The Spiritual Life of Children* (Boston: Houghton Mifflin, 1990), p. 14.

25. Edward Rice, *The Man in the Sycamore Tree* (Garden City: Doubleday, 1972), pp. 125, 175.

JOHANN G. ROTEN, S.M.

The Marian Counterpoint
of Postmodern Spirituality

The surge of contemporary spirituality is multi-faceted and all-pervasive. It speaks in many and discordant voices, beckons to colorful gurus and worships in chapels of all sizes. Yet, its various forms share at least two strongly marked features: (1) Contemporary spirituality advocates unity and wholeness on all levels of human life; it rejects whatever separates, particularizes and isolates. (2) Emotional density and strong personal involvement are paramount to this age of spirituality. The inner experience is decisive, not the actual presence of a personal God.[1]

I. VARIATIONS IN POSTMODERN SPIRITUALITY

These two pillars of sacred interconnectedness and radical inner experience on which the temple of contemporary spirituality seems to be founded are key elements of the much cited and advocated grammar of postmodernism.[2] Or so it would seem.

Postmodernism leans toward philosophical and spiritual irenism at all levels of the construction of human and non-human reality. It rejects what smacks of purely external, accidental and derivative connections, and in its place decrees internal, essential and constitutive relations, where body and soul, the natural environment, family and culture constitute but one close-knit fabric of the same life substance. This new world unity and view is called "Mystical Cosmology" by some (Matthew Fox), and "Creative Communion" by others (Joe Holland). Postmodern spirituality in many

ways constitutes a revival of romanticism, and its profession of
faith in organicism. It attempts to stem and turn the tide of modern dualism by declaring the world again home to the human species in its kinship with all other species.

In Matthew Fox's words: "A dualism that haunts spirituality to
this day is that between individual and society, or the personal and
the communitarian. A living spirituality, one built on experience,
power, and cosmology, would never acquiesce to even the naming
of such a dualism."[3] In similar fashion, dualism between nature
and the supernatural is overcome by panentheism, that is, the assessment that all things are in God and God in all things (Mechtild
of Magdeburg). Postmodern spirituality understands itself as holo-
graphic, following suit to holonomy as it applies to the theory of
information (Bateson), social sciences (Ferguson), and physics
(Capra). God is seen as an eminently "sociable God" (K. Wilber).[4] A
perfect state, no longer the expression of longing and striving, God
is the supreme level and crowning of our collective individuality.

The other high visibility feature of postmodern spirituality is
radical inner experience. Experience comes in many different
shades; it stresses right brain over left brain, mystical over rational
activity, and feminist over patriarchal attitude. Experience leads to
wisdom rather than knowledge, to the "Divinity of Mother Earth
Crucified" rather than "Divinity in the Sky." At the heart of radical
inner experience is a backward movement which evolves in four
stages: from the dichotomy of the personal level of consciousness
(that is, the experience of two beings in one: body-soul; public-
private) to the experience of the I-level, where to be oneself is actualized mainly in body awareness; to the longing for unity with the
"total organism" of reality, and finally on to "transpersonal awareness," when in the depth of the person's soul the soul of humanity as
divine, transcendent soul is discovered.[5] It is at this level of experience that postmodern spirituality comes full circle: in radical inner
experience all dualisms are vanquished, since this kind of experience leads to the capture of the innermost reality of human being
which happens to be—as the one "ultimate equation"—the principle of the universe.

A considerable number of other features of postmodern spirituality could be spelled out. They deal mostly with the unity of space
and time, the co-creativity of deity and creatures, and the extraordinary capacity of human beings for self-determination. However, it
would seem fair and useful to further assess *analytically* the expressions and potentialities of contemporary spirituality in order to

surface more adequately, because more concretely and specifically, the numerous facets of postmodern spirituality. An analysis of writings on spirituality published in the 1980s and early 1990s yields the following observations.

In the present, *spirituality* has become a "proliferation term" operating with a "clutter" definition, good for ambivalent use and, alas, sometimes for poignant ridicule of true spirituality. Springfellow, in his *Politics of Spirituality*, attempted to bundle contemporary meanings of spirituality in the following almost classical German sentence:

> "Spirituality" may indicate stoic attitudes, occult phenomena, the practice of so-called mind control, yoga discipline, escapist fantasies, interior journeys, an appreciation of Eastern religions, multifarious pietistic exercises, superstitious imaginations, intensive journals, cults, monastic rigors, mortification of the flesh, wilderness sojourns, political resistance, contemplation, abstinence, hospitality, a vocation of poverty, nonviolence, silence, the efforts of prayer, obedience, generosity, exhibiting stigmata, entering solitude, or, I suppose, among these and many other things, squatting on top of a pillar.[6]

In the face of much confusion and disarray, but at the same time of much vital and committed interest and genuine creativity in the area of spirituality, there is need for clarification and reassessment.

1. *"Common Property" Spirituality*

Spirituality until recently, and to a great extent, reflected and meant the spirituality of religious or of religious life. It was sometimes highly specialized (for instance, atonement spirituality), highly structured (timetables, spiritual accounting, formalized prayer), and oftentimes esoteric. Nowadays, spirituality tends to be *secular*. Considered common property, it concentrates on everyday life and sustains special causes, such as women's spirituality and liberation spirituality. It rejects dogmatism, especially clerical and theological, and puts forward the quest of self-actualization for people from all walks of life. It declares itself "lay," because "ordinary people can and do inspire others into healthier, more mature choices and behaviors," as Marsha Sinetar explains in *Ordinary People as Monks and Mystics*.[7]

2. Levelling or Bonding?

There is, further, a certain tendency toward syncretism and its varied expressions. Spiritual masters of the past are adapted to the needs of the present (for instance, Meister Eckhart cited as witness to panentheistic religiosity), contemporary figures identified with classical saints (for instance, President Corazon Aquino compared with Catherine of Siena), spiritualities of different religious traditions reduced to a common denominator (for instance, the affirmation that Buddha's, Muhammed's and Ramakrishna's religious experiences "can be authentic encounters like the God and Father of Jesus Christ").[8] While there is ample space for commonality and complementarity, contemporary spirituality sometimes denotes a tendency to squeeze rightful differences into a fictitious harmony or identity.

3. Spirituality for a Broken Age

One of the characteristic aspects of contemporary spirituality deals with its *therapeutic* thrust. Much of contemporary spirituality is convalescence spirituality, stressing healing and compassion, empathy and affirmation.[9] It wants to be, on the social level, a corrective of past "sinful" history by proposing, for instance, a justice-and-peace or an ecological spirituality. The quest for a new wholeness of the person (for instance, becoming centered or engaging in harmonious and reflective living), the transcending of dualism, and the pursuit of unity with the universe also belong to this category.[10] Some of these aspects call for caution, such as latent pantheism and the belittling of sin, fall and redemption.[11]

4. A Spirituality of the Visual

Contemporary spirituality retrieves the importance of the symbolic dimension of religious life. It rediscovers the significance of the imagination for Christian faith—the place of dreams, colors, images, artists and poets. One of its most rewarding consequences lies in the realization that reason and imagination need no longer be pitted against one another as rivals. One of its most practical applications has resulted in the rediscovery of the spiritual significance of the icons.[12] Thanks to the symbolic, spirituality becomes visual, concrete and aesthetic. It reflects the rootedness of Christian spirituality in the grammar of Incarnation.

5. The Rediscovery of Ritual

Surprisingly enough, contemporary spirituality can be highly *ritualistic*. We note a proliferation of spiritual methods and techniques, fromcrystals and "I Ching" to centering prayer and non-verbal expressions of spiritual experience and attitudes such as dancing or miming. There exists a variety of group rituals, from witchcraft and goddess-cults to prayer group patterns and mourningsessions.[13] Last but not least, there exists a re-evaluation of spiritual programs and spiritual accountability (for example, in journaling).[14] This ritualistic aspect of contemporary spirituality sometimes conveys magic tendencies (anti–intellectualism) and the need for self-invented structures; it expresses a do-it-yourself attitudeand, to some degree, a-liturgical tendencies. For certain, it reflects the ambition of all ritualisms to produce spiritual experience.

6. The Imperative of the Experiential

Most prominent for contemporary spirituality is its *experiential* character. This is the attempt to relocate God in the sphere of the experiential, a quest for meaning and relevance, the need to discover God with all the senses, to strive for a permanent experience of the presence of God in a so-called mystical continuum. Spiritual experience is mainly directed toward self, bodiliness and nature, attempting to reach God in and through one or all three of these dimensions of reality.[15] The experiential often leads to the experimental, where different sources and possibilities of spiritual experience (from the religion of North American Indians to Celtic mythology) are sampled, tested, tried and often rejected, in view of finding a new and more permanent peak of spiritual experience.

7. The Temptation of Hedonism

Contemporary spirituality stands for different groups of persons, for different needs and problems. It is therefore *pluralistic*: an instant spirituality (need-centered) and an adaptive spirituality (leaning toward particularization).[16] Finally, contemporary spirituality is strongly subject-centered. Spirituality is *for* the individual, and, likewise, spiritual experience of God, through nature and in community, is directed toward the satisfaction *of* the individual— God, nature and community often serving as mere vehicles and opportunities toward satisfaction. There are features in this spiritual way which bear unmistakably *hedonistic* aspects; like consumerism, it voraciously pursues spiritual fulfillment here, now and totally.[17]

8. Action-Oriented Spirituality

Action-oriented spirituality is in itself a "clutter" definition and draws its impetus from many different sources: the social gospel, pastoral therapeutics, the self-consciously religious left of the sixties and the various social justice movements. Its mainstream contemporary expression is social spirituality, the working toward justice and peace. It directs itself against escapist religion where the fatally poor are eventually rewarded in heaven. Social spirituality is sustained by a triple conversion: political (accurate understanding of how society functions), moral (openness to others and practical commitment) and religious (rejection of false gods, quest for the true God). This broad action-orientation branches out into more specific movements, such as liberation spirituality, ecological spirituality, spirituality of empowerment and mysticism in action.[18]

9. The Appeal of Eastern Mysticism

No doubt one of the most enthralling and mystifying spiritual forces of the present, Eastern spirituality has generated in the West countless groups inspired by Advaita Vedanta, Sikhism, Theravada Buddhism, Aikido, the Lotus Sutra or, more broadly, ethnic Asian religions. There exist—for serious students who go beyond the purely exotic encounter and a simplistic syncretism—ways and means of achieving convergence between Eastern and Western spirituality on more than one point: for example, on behalf of the human condition as such, the ideal and practice of following a spiritual path, the awakening to the true self, the quest for and the existence of a mystical center and the importance of action.[19]

10. Retrieval of the Spirit

A more typically Catholic movement of spirituality, the Catholic charismatic renewal had and still has a powerful impact on the life of the Church. It has revived prayer in its various expressions (for example, prayer of praise), emphasized the scriptural basis of the spiritual and pastoral discourse (shared prayer, homilies), restored healing as one of the most tangible expressions of the Spirit's action, and rekindled the fire of evangelization (the awakening to the need of proclaiming God's presence). The Catholic charismatic renewal presents challenges that are typical of an alternative spirituality. It understands itself as a renewal force, based on faith in the full power of the Spirit operative in the Church. Its basic traits reflect important aspects of contemporary spirituality: 1) experience (dialogical notion of faith); 2) wholesomeness (in the experience of God's Spirit, wholesomeness of prayer); 3) God-centeredness (the centrality of prayer and, thus, the importance of the prayer of praise).[20]

11. The Psychological Focus

There may be no such thing as a "psychological spirituality," but there are a number of spiritual attitudes coined, or at least suggested and promoted, by various trends in psychology, mainly personality psychologies such as Ego-psychology, personality typologies, developmental psychology and transpersonal psychology. Some of their more salient features are: the positive and optimistic outlook on the self, the experience of creative power toward self-transformation, the experience of God as call to growth (within oneself and in interaction); self-discovery through psychology, individualization of the spiritual life, application of the "scientific" approach to the spiritual life (combination of psychology and spirituality); the understanding of spiritual life as a process, the dynamic reinterpretation of perfection, and the suggestion that the spiritual life can be managed with appropriate psychological techniques. Also, transpersonal psychology emphasizes the experience of the self's depth, the experience of "unity" between microcosm (psyche) and macrocosm (nature), as well as the attempt for self-transcendence into totality.

Some of these "attitudes" absorb spirituality into psychology; they are typical examples of spiritual pelagianism based on programs of psychological utopia. On the other hand, psychology has its rightful place in the spiritual life. Its major functions should be to highlight 1) the total human involvement in the spiritual quest, 2) the congruence between grace and human psychology, and 3) the clear distinction to be maintained, at all cost, between the human person and God.[21]

12. Feminist Imprint

Women's and/or feminist spiritualities present a variety of facets, reaching from matriarchal revival spirituality to political feminist spirituality.[22] In a very broad sense, feminist spirituality is and wants to be a challenge to the whole Church. It understands its spiritual vision as derived from the Christian message itself and sets out in search for liberating and empowering impulses in an otherwise patriarchal tradition. Although proximately concentrating on the experience of women, feminist spirituality promotes and implements the demand of the Christian Gospel that impels both feminist women and men today to call for Church renewal.

This spiritual orientation has integrated the main elements of feminist critique with regard to patriarchal tradition. It affirms feminist sisterhood; encourages autonomy, self-actualization and self-transcendence; it focuses on the human person as the integrating factor of the full range of human possibilities; combats all types of oppressor-oppressed relationships; promotes the spiritual experience of joy and new images of God (friend, sister, mother), and understands itself as the vehicle of a genuinely mystical tradition based on God-experience, liberation and empowerment. Church-related women's spirituality focuses on the de-masculinizing of religious experience with regard to ministries, spiritual socialization and God-representations.

13. "Esoteric" Options

Of lesser overall importance and visibility, but of no little appeal to millions of people in quest of meaning and spiritual power are the various tendencies, currents and options of esoterism. According to some, esoterism is to prepare the transition from the age of Pisces (the violent age of Christianity) to the age of Aquarius (the "soft" age of post-Christianity). For others, it is linked to parapsychological realities such as telepathy, psychokinesis, and the life-after-death movement.[23]

More specifically, there are four esoteric currents attempting to reach beyond rationalism and positivism in order to appropriate the secret powers of the spiritual world. 1) Esoterism pursues the discovery of the "secret world formula" and its use for improvement and fulfillment of B-values. At stake is the secret of perpetual self-renewal. The Enneagram—with its nine personality types—represents a simplified version of this age-old quest for the ultimate key to reality. 2) A second current concentrates not on a secret formula, but promotes the initiation into an age-old secret wisdom tradition and the participation in it. An example thereof is Tarot, based on hermeticism (*Hermes trismegistos*). 3) Still another expression of esoterism are those techniques or rites which explore and communicate with the forces of nature. The contemporary witchcraft movement fits this description. It blends medieval witchcraft beliefs and practices with modern views of the power of the goddess. The goddess is earth herself; women are part of her being and share in her cycle of birth, maturing, death and regeneration (changing of seasons; waxing, full and waning moon). 4) Beyond the quest for the "secret world formula," the initiation into age-old wisdom traditions and the communication with the hidden energies of nature, there lies still another source of secret power: black magic or the communication with the powers of evil, as, for example, in satanism. It rests on hedonism, devil worship (inversionary sects), magic rituals (spells and curses), iconoclastic tendencies, and millenarianist beliefs.

II. THE LEITMOTIV OF MODERNITY[24]

In an attempt to allay some of the misgivings of previous spiritualities, contemporary versions of the "spiritual way" have initiated a new consciousness and some important new perspectives: a wholesome approach to human reality and activity, the reactualization of the spiritual as such, and a new alliance between the physical and the spiritual, the natural and the supernatural, creation and God. Are these new perspectives a mere declaration of intent or do they have the weight of solid foundations upon which to build the spirituality of the future?

At closer inspection, the majority of features of postmodern spirituality seem to suggest that its focal point is and remains the human subject.[25] Our basic assumption is that postmodern spirituality, although in apparent contradiction and rejection of modernity, shares and participates in its underlying structure of knowledge and essential thought patterns. Whether we are dealing with the mythic mind of postmodernity or the more literal mind of modernity, the common denominator always refers to the mind. Self-preservation and amalgamization, that is, the exclusivist tendencies of modern dualism and the inclusivist tendencies of postmodern interconnectedness, are both the result of an authoritative decision made by the same human subject. Similarly, the modern monad of self lives in splendid rational isolation, while the postmodern ego is opening the doors to its own non-rational dimensions of self, existential situations and history.

There exist a variety of assessments about modernity, from Max Weber, Romano Guardini and Arnold Gehlen to Jürgen Habermas and Jean-François Lyotard.[26] Among its most salient characteristics we would like to pinpoint the following: the gnoseological dualism, the idea of freedom as emancipation, the "metanarrative" of necessary and unlimited progress and its program of progressive dominion over nature. Most of these characteristics have to be read against the backdrop of science as the dominant modern ideology.

Thus it became a part of the program of science to institute in human knowledge the ontological chasm between subject and object. With Descartes, the symbiotic relationship of *fieri aliud inquantum aliud* is severed and the ontological link between *res cogitans* and *res extensa* shattered and broken. Knowledge now means "to know what we can do with it when we have it" (Hobbes). Modern consciousness considers knowledge as power (*Herrschaftswissen*), the rightful tool for progressive domination of nature. Simultaneously, modern consciousness emancipates the human person (formerly also *animal rationale*!) from its nature-context and opposes both: person and nature. This is in part also what modernity understands by freedom. Freedom is characterized as auto-determination through emancipation, as freedom *from* and not as freedom *for*. Freedom is a *process* of emancipation, where the continual augmentation of possible options (Hobbes) constitutes the ultimate goal. Finally, the idea of necessary and unlimited progress was copied from biological models, where progress is considered as pre-programmed (although not necessary). Progress according to the creed of modernity is necessary and therefore without prize, but it is also universal and therefore, ironically, without a specific content.

Modernity failed—at least superficially—not so much because of the fallacy of its theoretical program (gnoseological dualism and objectivism; freedom as emancipation), but because of the failure of its practical program: the emancipation from and domination of nature, as well as the idea of necessary and unlimited progress.[27] Modernity as metanarrative came to a standstill because the project of progressive dominion over nature failed. By the same token, the myth of necessary and unlimited progress was demystified. Not only did the political program of modernity collapse, but far from being a universal narrative, the creed of modernity was also demasked as the typical story of North Atlantic civilization, essentially. Simultaneously, the crisis of modernity, as epitomized in ecological consciousness, documents beyond doubt the utopian character of the Marxist paradigm of justice for all in and through the (super) abundance of goods.

On the other hand, and unfortunately, the theoretical program of modernity, that is, its dualism of knowledge, objectivism, and— to a certain degree—freedom as emancipation, is still alive and well and as such it undergirds postmodern spirituality. Western Christian culture and civilization is subliminally impregnated and permeated by the *Cartesian-Kantian Syndrome*.[28] Condensed and translated into modern thinking and language, its meaning can be formulated in the following three points:

1. True and absolute human identity exists only in one's own self, specifically in the act of freedom understood as emancipation;
2. Nothing coming from the outside of the realm of subjectivity can root the human person in the absolute; freedom alone is able to achieve this;
3. The divine—to some extent—is identified in the human act of freedom.

The *Cartesian-Kantian Syndrome* as spelled out here constitutes the mental structure of postmodern spirituality. It can be traced in major characteristics of postmodern spirituality. The self-actualization for people of all walks of life, the dictate of radical inner experience, the core of self as core of both the divine and the universe, heightened consciousness as bridge to wholeness: the sub-

ject as constant point of reference can be detected in most of the
variations presented.

There is no real contradiction between this and the other major aspect of postmodern spirituality, namely its tendency to reject
whatever separates, particularizes and isolates. The claim of unity
and wholeness is mediated in and through the subject. Internal,
essential and constitutive relations are determined, defined and
orchestrated by the self. The self in postmodern spirituality is not
altogether a rejection of the universal subject of modernity.[29] As in
and for modernity, the postmodern self is the universal subject of
meaning, even if meaning is no longer articulated in terms of
power and dominion.

The postmodern self as found in spirituality garners meaning
from inner experience and growing consciousness. Experience and
consciousness indicate two complementary psycho-spiritual movements: the centripetal movement of hedonist self-appropriation (experience) and the centrifugal movement of mythic expansion of self
(consciousness). In both instances the center of direction remains
what we called the postmodern self. It is thus that the reaction of
postmodern spirituality with regard to metanarratives and history
remains ambiguous. By reactionary choice, postmodernism rejects
(universalist) narratives and the concept of history as progressive
movement toward an ultimate goal; in point of fact, however, the
ideas of progress and metanarrative are deeply engrained in the
postmodern self, and take on the significance of a narrative of progressive self-realization.

If therefore the *Cartesian-Kantian Syndrome* constitutes the
mental structure of postmodern spirituality, the various and typical
expressions of this mental structure should be termed the *Stoic-
Romantic Syndrome*.[30] The self-sufficient feeling individual, as it
appears in many facets of postmodern spirituality, shows a high
degree of resemblance with the personality profile of the Stoa. Even
its quest for sacred interconnectedness recalls Marcus Aurelius'
holy bond between all things and their implication with one another. However, with even greater resemblance postmodern spirituality reproduces typical thought patterns of romanticism.

Both inner experience and mythic expansion of consciousness
set the stage for what we would like to call the *chaotic self*. The
chaotic self is the child of the Stoic-Romantic Syndrome, or, at
least, the potentially negative pole on the parameter of postmodern spirituality. The postmodern subject opens itself to the non-
rational depth of its psyche—a reaction against modernity—and

consents to dissolve itself in the numinous so as to recuperate the mythic and cosmic memory of its personal and collective past. Its centrifugal psychic outburst attempts to tear down the walls of the mechanistic modes of separateness and thus to flood all dimensions of human and non-human reality with its own contents. However, the already raised questions remain: Is centrifugal postmodern spirituality more than the unrelenting *conquista* of "reality" by the postmodern self? Is mythic consciousness more than the self-appropriation of the non-rational dimension of self? Is "alterity" (that which lies beyond the walls of rational subjectiveness) more than the self-projection of the postmodern self into ever new and other states of consciousness? In an attempt to overcome the separation and isolation of the subject of modernity, the chaotic self of postmodernity engages in spiritual amalgamization at any cost. Where the subject of modernity tends to evolve to ever heightened reflexivity and concentration of the subject on itself, the chaotic self celebrates heightened states of consciousness.

The subject of modernity imperceptibly tends to evolve toward what we would like to call the *empty self*, for, by progressively eliminating the extrinsic and impure elements of non-subjectivity, it isolates itself in the rarefied atmosphere of reflexive reflexivity and ultimate emptiness of self. The chaotic self, on the contrary, attempts to absorb "alterity" in all its forms to overcome separation and isolation, only to find itself in the end in a state of spiritual chaos. Yet, as mentioned earlier, the *empty self* and the *chaotic self* are children of the same father, they are both offsprings of what we call modernity.

III. THE MARIAN COUNTERPOINT

After the variations in postmodern spirituality and the assessment of the leitmotiv of modernity, we now turn to the Marian counterpoint. Indeed, we pointed out so far that postmodern spirituality is thoroughly steeped in the philosophical program of modernity—so much so that contemporary spirituality is permeated by the ideological characteristics of both the Cartesian-Kantian (modernity) and the Stoic-Romantic Syndromes (postmodernity). The Cartesian-Kantian Syndrome ultimately leads to the empty self, whereas the Stoic-Romantic Syndrome suggests and—*nolens volens*—promotes what we have called the chaotic self. In both situations, postmodern spirituality reaches a dead end. The empty self is the result of radical separation between subject and object. The chaotic self is the result of obsession with connection. Radical separation leads to emptiness, whereas compulsive amalgamization creates chaos. It is in order to correct the potential or real shortcomings of postmodern spirituality that we would like to suggest the Marian counterpoint. Where contemporary spirituality presented us with the principle of separation, the Marian counterpoint proposes active receptiveness (the Marian principle); and where contemporary spirituality established the principle of connection or connectedness, the Marian counterpoint invites us to the apprenticeship of the *right* connection (the Marian way of individuation). Thus, we would like to replace the two pillars of postmodern spirituality: radical inner experience and sacred interconnectedness, with what we call the Marian principle and the Marian way of individuation. They are both grounded in the Marian structure of the religious personality. The Marian counterpoint further develops various practical consequences for contemporary spirituality.

1. The Marian Principle[31]

The Cartesian-Kantian syndrome tends to destroy authentic spirituality, because it puts the cart before the horses. Spiritual life exists only *because* of the Spirit; human spiritual initiative can be understood only as an answer and response to God's revelation and call. That is why, in our understanding of things, the best antidote against the Cartesian-Kantian syndrome lies with the Marian principle in theology and spirituality. For indeed, the Marian principle is most efficacious in counteracting the spiritual shortcomings rooted in the Cartesian-Kantian syndrome. The freedom to listen to God's word (faith sustained by reason), the translation of God's self-revelation into one's personal life where meaning becomes value, and fidelity reflects the continued answer to God's ongoing self-revelation—all these attitudes are personally and archetypically represented in Mary.

A spirituality centered on the attitude exemplified by Mary is not just one spirituality among others. For this reason, although Mary is an individual believer and, as such, the prototype and model of all response in faith, she resolves all particular spiritualities into the one spirituality of the Bride of Christ, the Church. What is special in Mary's spirituality is the radical renunciation of any particular spirituality other than the overshadowing of the Most High and the indwelling of the divine Word. Only thus could Mary's response be made, through grace, so complete and perfect as to become the perfect response of the bride, the Church, and the form of all the responses made by individual believers.

Whoever reflects on the spiritual journey of Mary will, without doubt, notice the tremendous discrepancy between the historical (epochal) significance of her mission and the overall, less-than-extraordinary, almost banal lifestyle, the humble social and cultural settings, of her historical figure. The example of Mary sharpens our awareness of the intimate presence of God in the world of daily life and the reality of divine immanence in the "secular city." Reality, as a whole, has—for the faith-trained life—sacramental character. While experience may not be a necessary guarantee for truth, God's truth certainly reveals itself in human experience. This is reflected in the Magnificat: great things are done to God's servant in her lowliness. The temporary dryness of our hearts, the dreariness of our everyday concerns, even our own secularized habits or those of our environment, luckily, are no foolproof screen against God's creative and recreative spirit.

Such is the Marian principle that will supersede the Cartesian-Kantian syndrome. But this principle is a she, a concrete person. She is the Marian way. Without it, without her, Christianity threatens imperceptibly to become inhuman. The Church becomes functionalistic, soulless, a hectic enterprise without any point of rest. With her, with Mary, the Church and each one of its believers have light, warmth, and protection.

2. The Marian Way of Individuation[32]

The Marian way is an antidote against the Stoic-Romantic Syndrome. Only true individuation will overcome the obsession of postmodern spirituality with interconnectedness and the tendency toward amalgamation. You do not have to be Jungian to believe in individuation. Is it not one of our most cherished ambitions to find our true self, to have identity, to be one and whole? We attempt to overcome the chaotic tendencies of our self. We oppose our true self to the forces of dissipation and destruction. However, individuation holds an insidious promise: to be oneself, is one not in a very real sense on top of the situation and, therefore, the master of at least a small world? To be master of self is the fruit not of an instantaneous achievement, but of a lengthy and always painful process. The self emerges gradually from the magma of psychic life, takes shape through interaction and confrontation and reaches the peak of its consciousness only to discover that the true self blossoms in the *gift* of self and in communion with others.

There is such a thing as the Marian version of individuation. It corresponds to those aspects of Christian spirituality which represent a transformation module, a sequence of steps or phases taking us through the process of individuation.

The Marian way of individuation prompts our understanding that authentic selfhood can be achieved only in mission. This understanding dawns on us as we are drawn into a process of transformation in the Spirit. The powers that shape our spiritual personality are not self-imposed moral imperatives, a system of intellectual guidelines or a self-induced emotional thrust. The spiritual personality grows in encounter and interaction with persons. For the committed member of the Christian family this means the experience of the Spirit, the encounter with Jesus Christ, the interaction with Mary and the companionship with brothers and sisters.

There exists a certain sequence or psycho-spiritual logic in the Marian way of individuation. Worded in psychological language, the individuation process leads from the experience of being loved for what I am and what I am to be to the quest of self, in the course of which a new consciousness gradually emerges. This new consciousness transforms the spiritual person in his/her attitude toward the self. The quest for self is no longer inner-directed, an odyssey to the depths of subjectivity, but outer-directed and re-centered on mission. It is intimately linked to the experience of being needed. The Marian way of individuation is a labor of love according to the triple acceptation of this expression. 1) We are guided and sustained in our own process of spiritual growth by the inspiring and patient love with which the Spirit, Jesus Christ, his and our mother, and our brothers and sisters gradually inform and form our quest of self. 2) To mature in the Spirit also means to lovingly suffer through the woes and throes of our innermost re-centering in the Spirit. 3) Finally, our new self will be engaged in a labor of love, sharing in the mission of Christ together with our brothers and sisters.

Specific articulations, of course, exist in this way of individuation. These are stages which punctuate our maturing in the Spirit. They are indicated hereafter not as fully developed contents

but as developmental rhythms directed toward a final goal. These
are the major articulations of the Marian way of individuation:

1) THE AWAKENING TO THE SPIRIT

We progressively awake to the intimate realization that our
existence is no accident, that there is goodness in our life. Scrutiniz-
ing our life story we reach a point where only gratuitous love
stands reason for our being. Our reaction to this discovery is one of
gratitude, security and quest or search. Feeling ourselves loved we
go in search of the source of this love. This is the awakening to the
Spirit and the beginning of our pursuit of individuation.

2) THE QUEST FOR SELF

The pursuit of knowledge about the sources of love that hold us
and generate us raises the question of our identity. What does it
mean to be loved? What or who reflects who or what we are? The
quest for self takes us through a gallery of idols, ideals, and role
models to the one living portrait in whom we recognize ourselves
as the *imago Dei*. We discover in Jesus Christ our super-ego, but we
discover him as in a broken mirror. We intuitively sense that he is
the ultimate answer to our quest for self: In him is not only the love
that holds us, he is also the true image of our self. But again, as we
measure and compare, he seems too big for us, and to see him in a
broken mirror means that my own projection of self stands in the
way between myself and him. The ultimate answer to our quest of
self is at hand, yet not quite within reach.

3) THE APPRENTICESHIP OF THE FEMININE

Sensing the dichotomy and ambiguity in our relationship with
him, Jesus Christ takes us to his mother. He introduces us to the
apprenticeship of the feminine. It represents the typical human
way to God (Jesus Christ), and expresses the most typical articulation of the Marian way of individuation.

We are entrusted to Mary in whom we discover the memory of
Jesus' ways and her own, shaped in the company of Jesus. She
teaches us her ways which are in fact the ways of the Father, of the
Spirit and of Jesus. Yet, these ways are very definitely feminine
ways. Mary prepares the second encounter with Jesus Christ, our
super-ego.

She teaches and forms us in the Spirit to active receptiveness,
to "relationality" and fruitfulness. In full autonomy she gives her-

self over to God's plans, carries, ponders, births and educates God's Word, and is herself educated and made fruitful by God's Word. Mary makes us receptive and sensitive to the laws of incarnation. Adopting these laws we progressively assimilate the ways and dispositions of Jesus, Son of the Father, Son of Mary. Mary, the woman, is the great facilitator. She teaches "relationality," because everything in her is in reference to the Father, the Spirit, and Jesus, but also to the Church and to the world. In Christianity, the word for success is fruitfulness. Mary teaches us the sense of Christian kenosis, which is nothing else but our becoming fruitful in the service of Christ's mission.

4) IN THE COMPANY OF SAINTS

Marian individuation reaches its ultimate concretization in our own Pentecost experience. The Church's final Marian memory is that of Pentecost, where Mary in a way "channels" and shares the Paraclete with the whole Church. The Spirit of Christ is given to the first community of disciples and thus constitutes the communion of Saints. Mary's Son is no longer hers, but given for the salvation of all. Paradoxical as this may seem, the ultimate encounter and nearness with Jesus coincides with our ability, thanks to the Marian individuation process, to receive him in others and to share him with them. Jesus Christ is no longer the image of our way to imagine him, but the icon of God's crucified love and the icon of our own human kenosis in him. It is when we lose him for others and in others that we are closest to Jesus. Our personal Pentecost experience signifies the second and real encounter with Jesus Christ as our "super-ego." In the christoform habits and ways of our brothers and sisters, we recognize our own ways and are encouraged to ever greater christoformity. More important, with like-minded brothers and sisters we are committed to Christ's mission. This leads to our second encounter with Christ: in our brothers and sisters and as active participants in his mission.

"Marian principle" and "Marian individuation" thus constitute two major antidotes against what we called the empty self and the chaotic self, or, in different terms, spirituality as modern and postmodern expressions. Based on the Marian principle and following the path of Marian individuation, we are now able to articulate and to formulate the foundational features of the Marian structure of religious personality.

3. The Marian Structure of Religious Personality

Mary's life articulates the basic structure of religious personality, and, since Mary is the first disciple of Christ and simultaneously our mother in faith, the structure of her religious personality takes on the character and meaning of the Rahnerian "Existential" for the constitution and development of our own religious personality.

Based on the foundational premise of God's free divine self-giving, religious personality is constituted in the Annunciation Event which signifies free acceptance as a "lasting readiness to accept the Transcendent."[33] This implies the readiness to accept in one's concrete life situation that which is experienced as God's will and the lasting faith in the ultimate yet mysterious benevolence of the incarnate transcendent God. Mary's fundamental decision at the Annunciation is one of acceptance of God's self-communication and not the human construction of pseudo-religious reality.

The fundamental attitude of acceptance in the Marian personality unfolds and is further articulated in what Van Kaam calls self-actualizing surrender, fidelity and creative care.[34] (1) It is of paramount importance to understand that Mary's education through her Son in the various rejection scenes and in her implication in his redemptive ministry (Cana and Cross) is both self-surrender and self-actualizing. This is based on the fundamental anthropological principle undergirding *Mulieris Dignitatem* according to which self-realization can only be achieved "through a sincere gift of self."[35] Growth in maturity implies the kenotic experience, the readiness to change gradually or to be changed into the constant participation in the dynamically developing presence of the Transcendent in us. Thus, the religious mode gradually takes over and eventually becomes the dominant mode in one's existential project.

(2) As in Mary's existence, the initial Yes will have to grow into a permanent Fiat-structure which corresponds to the attitude of fidelity. Without this "all-pervading attitude of unconditional loyalty the religious mode of life is psychologically impossible."[36] True religious commitment, because it is my acceptance of God's project for me, needs continuity and duration. It has to become my personal life story. Fidelity expresses the readiness for every and any effort and sacrifice necessary to preserve the original commitment.

(3) And again as in Mary's attitude at Cana, under the Cross and at Pentecost, the total acceptance of the Divine necessarily promotes and assures the attitude of creative care. The gift of one-

self leads to the gift for others, patterned ultimately on the very self-emptying of Christ himself and reactualized in the human mode by Mary's being given to John and to the whole Church. Consequently, creative care is not the pelagian backlash of the initial fiat, but an integral part of the original commitment, and its creative dimension is as much a part of God's initiative as the result of our own involvement. According to Van Kaam the attitude of creative care is "the readiness to care for the reality in which the Transcendent is revealed within the world of the religious person."[37] The famous de-centering of oneself and re-centering in somebody else, the de-privatizing of one's life in order to be re-socialized within the parameter of a God-received mission bring the true meaning of "creative care" into focus. Ultimately, true creative care is the powerful vehicle of Incarnation because in its fundamental gesture there is the need to pass on and to let go.

The dimensions of the Marian personality have traditionally been highlighted in Mary's titles as Servant of the Lord, Helpmate of Christ, and Mother of the Church. Their epochal significance may be evident to the Church in her memory of the past (*Memoria Domini*). They need to be translated into categories of contemporary mentality and existential concerns. Unless we succeed in pointing out its actuality for this period in history, there will be, at least in our conciousness, no epochal significance attached to Mary's life and characteristic way of life—its fundamental attitudes; its characteristic process of individuation; its self-actualizing self-surrender, fidelity, and creative caring.

John Macquarrie has undertaken such a task in dialectically opposing one of the key concepts of the Enlightenment with Marian values. Modernity in its practical political formulation is based on the French Revolution's summary of enlightened virtues: liberty, equality, fraternity. Mary in turn represents the personification of the theological virtues of faith, hope and love.[38] The development and result of this study does not really import in this context. Yet it is interesting to note how much the threefold mystery of the Incarnation, the Passion and the Resurrection undergirds the revolutionary motto of political enlightenment.

The paschal mystery is the connecting and interweaving force which makes freedom to be freedom for the pursuit of equality in view of fraternity. Enlightenment philosophy is based on dissociative reason stressing rights, privacy (individualism) and romantic socialism. Love alone can overcome disruptive and mutually exclusive values; it is grounded in the grace and strength flowing from

God's crucified and glorified love. A rather forgotten Church tradition entrusts this deepest of Christian mysteries to the three Mary's and their feminine care: Mary of Bethany, Mary the Mother of Jesus and Mary Magdalene. The three Mary's constitute the ecclesial acceptance of the fundamental moments of the Christ event: the Incarnation, the Passion and the Resurrection.[39]

The epochal significance of the "Memoria Domini" and its Marian dimension has to be retrieved for each age and every generation anew. What we have called "the Marian counterpoint" not only pinpoints some of the basic structures of authentic Christian spirituality; the various features of Marian spirituality here outlined attempted to counterbalance some of the more questionable aspects of modern and postmodern spirituality.

Postmodern spirituality lives, acts and reacts in the still looming shadows of the Cartesian-Kantian syndrome. Postmodern spirituality in many ways reminds of "The Cry," the famous painting, by E. Munch. Although mute, this cry of postmodern spirituality has a piercing quality. It articulates the need for liberation, but at the same time expresses confusion and disorientation. In times like this, a solid point of reference is needed for a self that is neither "empty" nor "chaotic." We believe that such a point of reference can be found in the Marian counterpoint.

Notes

1.   The range of contemporary spirituality, movements and contents, is enormous. It reaches from constituted or labeled movements such as "New Age" to specific techniques, behavioral patterns and life styles, that is, e.g., from I Ching to ecology-oriented ways of conducting one's life. The two strong and common feelings here mentioned are all pervasive and omnipresent. If they are postmodern in character, they only seldom expressly refer to the label of postmodern spirituality. However, this is what they in fact are. The following pages attempt to point out not only this fact but also the difficulty in making a clear and final distinction between these two characteristics and what is commonly considered as Catholic spirituality. The "Marian counterpoint" tries to fulfill the purpose of pointing out the authentic Christian dimension of spirituality.

2.   See D. R. Griffin, ed., *Sacred Interconnections: Postmodern Spirituality, Political Economy and Art*, SUNY series in Constructive Post-

modern Thought (Albany: State University of New York, 1990). This and other writings of the SUNY series deal with constructive postmodern thought in theology and spirituality. Simultaneously, we find a number of writings of negative critical stance. To mention only some: Aldo N. Terrin, *La religiosità del postmoderno* (Bologna: Edizione Dehoniane, 1992); J. Demetrio Jiménez Sánchez Mariscal, "Posmodernidad ¿Encanto desilusionado o ilusion del desencanto?" in *Religion y Cultura* 182 (1992): 367–388. Postmodernism is a polymorphous cultural movement of many and often contradictory facets whose time and definite identity is yet too close to call. Thus, the use of the term postmodernism and its contents remain fuzzy. It comes as no surprise that the favorite and somehow typical allegory used by postmodernist writers remains Borges' famous fable of the Chinese encyclopedia mentioned by M. Foucault in his introduction to *The Order of Things* (1966).

3. M. Fox, "A Mystical Cosmology: Toward a Postmodern Spirituality," in D. R. Griffin, ed., *Sacred Interconnections*, p. 18.

4. K. Wilber, *A Sociable God: Toward a New Understanding of Religion* (Boulder: New Science Library, 1984).

5. This train of thought again is multifaceted and can be situated anywhere between F. Capra's *The Turning Point* (1982) and St. Grof's *The Adventure of Self-Discovery* (1988).

6. W. Springfellow, *The Politics of Spirituality* (Philadelphia: Westminster Press, 1984), p. 19.

7. See M. Sinetar, *Ordinary People as Monks and Mystics* (New York: Paulist Press, 1986), esp. pp. 1–10; E. Dreyer, "A Spirituality of the Laity: Yes or No?" *Spirituality Today* (2/38/1986): 197–207. The fragmentation of spirituality, as such a modern rather than postmodern phenomenon, results in spiritualities for specific groups and special occasions ranging from the spirituality of elderly and single persons, respectively, to a spirituality for apocalyptic times. For examples, survey the articles in recent issues of *Spirituality Today*.

8. For examples of these kinds of syncretic couplings, see M. Fox, "Medieval Spirituality Revisited," *Spirituality Today* (3/31/1979): 258–69; M. A. Fatula, "Truth that Transforms the World," *Spirituality Today* (1/38/1986): 167 ff.; R. Drummond, "Experience of God

Outside the Judeo-Christian Context," *Spirituality Today* 30 (1978): 138–52.

9.   G. Leach, *Hope for Healing: An Invitation to Hope and Healing through Personal and Social Relationships*, n.d.; M. Fox, *A Spirituality Named Compassion and the Healing of the Global Village: Humpty Dumpty and Us* (Minneapolis: Winston Press, 1979).

10.   See C. M. Brissette, *Reflective Living: A Spiritual Approach to Everyday Living* (Whitinsville, MA: Affirmation Books, 1983); S. Muto, *Meditation in Motion* (Garden City, NY: Image Books, 1986); J. Carmody, *Holistic Spirituality* (New York: Paulist Press, 1983).

11.   M. Fox, *Original Blessing: A Primer in Creation Spirituality Presented in Four Paths, Twenty-six Themes, and Two Questions* (Santa Fe: Bear, 1983).

12.   See J. Braggley, *Doors of Perception: Icons and Their Spiritual Significance* (London: Mowbray, 1987); K. Fischer, *The Inner Rainbow: The Imagination of Christian Life* (New York: Paulist Press, 1983); Ph. St. Romain, "Dreams and Christian Growth," *Spirituality Today* (2/36/1984): 123–34; Beesing, Nogosek, O'Leary, *The Enneagram: A Journey of Self-Discovery* (Denville, NJ: Dimension Books, 1984), pp. 210–18.

13.   P. Brennan, *A Spirituality for an Anxious Age* (1985), pp. 113–30; J. Sauro, "Dancing: A Symbol of Reconciliation in the Four Quartets," *Spiritual Life* (3/21/1975): 184–88; W. Johnston, *The Inner Eye of Love: Mysticism and Religion* (San Francisco: Harper & Row, 1978), pp. 182–95.

14.   M. L. Santa-Maria, *Growth through Meditation and Journal Writing: A Jungian Perspective on Christian Spirituality* (New York: Paulist Press, 1983).

15.   Cf. Th. Stratman's assertion: "There is no spiritual experience in this life that is not bodily and sensate. We are each a body-soul, a psychosomatic unity" ("The Boy and the Hen: An Instance of Experiential Spirituality," *Spirituality Today* [3/33/1981], p. 210). See also Ch. M. Magsam, *The Experience of God: Outlines for a Contemporary Spirituality* (Maryknoll, NY: Orbis Books, 1975); J. Wijngaards, *Expe-*

riencing Jesus (Notre Dame, IN: Ave Maria Press, 1983); B. Bush, "Experience of God," *The Way* (4/13/1973): 259–70.

16. L. P. Carroll and K. M. Dyckman, *Chaos or Creation: Spirituality in Mid-Life* (New York: Paulist Press, 1986); M. W. Pable, O.F.M.Cap., *A Man and His God: Contemporary Male Spirituality* (Notre Dame, IN: Ave Maria Press, 1988).

17. R. Bellah, *et al., Habits of the Heart* (Berkeley: University of California Press, 1985); W. Au, S.J., *By Way of the Heart: Towards a Holistic Christian Spirituality* (New York: Paulist Press, 1989); A. B. Ulanov, *Carl Jung and Christian Spirituality* (New York: Paulist Press, 1988), pp. 38–65; P. Vitz, *Psychology as Religion: The Cult of Self Worship* (Grand Rapids, MI: Eerdmans, 1977).

18. D. Dorr, *Spirituality and Justice* (Maryknoll, NY: Orbis Books, 1984); R. Haight, "Spirituality and Social Justice: A Christological Perspective," *Spirituality Today* (4/34/1982): 312–26; J. Risley, "Liberation Spirituality," *Spirituality Today* (2/35/1983): 127–40; W. Granberg-Michaelson, *A Worldly Spirituality: The Call to Redeem Life on Earth* (San Francisco: Harper & Row, 1984); U. King, *Towards a New Mysticism: Teilhard de Chardin and Eastern Religions* (London: Collins, 1980); W. Johnston, *The Inner Eye of Love* (1979), esp. chap. 18: "Mysticism in Action," pp. 173–78; W. M. Cunningham, "Power: Finding It and Using It," *Spirituality Today* (1/31/1979): 55–62.

19. The following famous names are to be mentioned among the pioneers of a future spiritual "marriage" between East and West: Aelred Graham, O.S.B.; Bede Griffith, O.S.B.; Henri le Saux, O.S.B.; Jules Monchanin, S.J.; William Johnston, S.J.; Thomas Merton, O.C.S.O.; Raymundo Panikkar; Anthony de Mello, S.J.; Thomas Keating, O.C.S.O.; John Main, O.S.B., and Georges Maloney, S.J. About the potential convergence between Eastern and Western Spirituality, see, for example, W. Teasdale, "The Meeting of East and West: Elements of a Relationship," *Spirituality Today* (1/38/1986): 111–24.

20. F. Sullivan, *Charisms and Charismatic Renewal: A Biblical and Theological Study* (Ann Arbor, MI: Servant Books, 1982); D. Roth, "Confused by the Spirit," *Spirituality Today* (3/38/1986): 209–20.

21.   Aside from the classical authors such as S. Freud, C. G. Jung, E. Erikson, E. Berne, aside also from psychological typologists such as A. Roldan, I. Briggs Myers and Don R. Riso (Enneagram-Theory), see Ch. J. Keating, *Who We Are Is How We Pray: Matching Personality and Spirituality* (Mystic, CN: Twenty-third Publications, 1987); R. Burke, "Psychology and the Christian Faith," *Spirituality Today* 30 (1978): 334–47; J. S. Main, "Self-Knowledge and Prayer," *The Way* (3/14/1977): 229–38; B. J. Groeschel, *Spiritual Passages: The Psychology of Spiritual Development "For Those Who Seek"* (New York: Crossroad, 1984).

22.   See Sandra M. Schneiders' article, "Feminist Spirituality," in M. Downey, *The New Dictionary of Catholic Spirituality* (Collegeville, MN: The Liturgical Press, 1993), pp. 394–405, concerning the basic terminology, the phenomenology of feminist spirituality and the characteristics of Catholic feminism and feminist Catholicism; also S. M. Schneiders, "The Effects of Women's Experience on Their Spirituality," *Spirituality Today* (2/35/1983): 100–16; M. E. Giles, *The Feminist Mystic and Other Essays on Women and Spirituality* (New York: Crossroad, 1982); J. Wolski Conn, ed., *Women's Spirituality: Resources for Christian Development* (New York: Paulist Press, 1986); A. C. Carr, *Transforming Grace: Christian Tradition and Women's Experience* (San Francisco: Harper & Row, 1988).

23.   Esoterism of the recent past is linked to such names as Helen P. Blavatsky, Rudolf Steiner and George I. Gurdjew; the gnostic roots thereof are pinpointed by K. Rudolph (1977). The four examples of esoterism chosen here correspond to some of the more common contemporary practices. For the Enneagram, see Don R. Riso, *Personality Types: Using the Enneagram for Self-Discovery* (Boston: Houghton Mifflin, 1987); for the Tarot, Anonymous, *Meditations on the Tarot: A Journey into Christian Hermeticism* (Amity, NY: Amity House, 1985); for witchcraft, D. Stein, *The Women's Spirituality Book* (St. Paul, MN: Llewellyn Publications, 1987); Starhawk, *The Spiral Dance: A Rebirth of the Ancient Religion of the Great Goddess* (San Francisco: Harper & Row, 1979); for Satanism, see Glock/ Bellah, *The New Religious Consciousness* (Berkeley: University of California Press, 1976), pp. 187–93; LaVey, *The Satanic Rituals* (New York: Avon, 1972).

24.   The allusion to musicological terminology (variations, leitmotiv and counterpoint) should underscore three things: (1) the diffi-

culty to bind into simple and univocal description what goes by the name or label of postmodern spirituality (variations); (2) the underlying and active presence of modernity in postmodern discourse on spirituality (*leitmotiv*), and (3) the need for a critical counterpoint, not with the intent to reject the contribution of postmodern spirituality but in order to refocus it and to put it in perspective.

25.   The following reflections have been inspired in part by such authors as Robert Spaemann, Peter Koslowski, Heinz-Günter Vester, Odo Marquard and Charles Jencks. See especially P. Koslowski *et al., Moderne oder Postmoderne? Zur Signatur des gegenwärtigen Zeitalters* (Weinheim: Acta Humaniora, VCH, 1986).

26.   Weber's "disenchantment" theory, Gehlen's "Posthistoire" (a final a-historical state based on consumerism), Guardini's "Ende der Neuzeit" dealing with the "desacralization" of the world, Jürgen Haberman's "neue Unübersichtlichkeit" and J.-F. Lyotard's "condition postmoderne": all of them are dealing with the dialectical relationship of modernity and postmodernity. See, for example, A. Wellmer, *Zur Dialektik von Moderne und Postmoderne* (Frankfurt: Suhrkamp, 1985).

27.   See R. Spaemann, "Ende der Modernität," in P. Koslowski *et al., Moderne oder Postmoderne* (1986), pp. 19 ff.

28.   See J. Sudbrack, *Neue Religiosität: Herausforderung für die Christen* (Mainz: Matthias Grünewald Verlag, 1987), pp. 84 ff.

29.   See R. Kearns, "L'imagination herméneutique et le postmoderne," in Jean Greisch et Richard Kearney, *Paul Ricoeur: Les métamorphoses de la raison herméneutique* (Paris, 1991), p. 357.

30.   The formulation of the Stoic-Romantic Syndrome, as well as the expressions *chaotic self* and *empty self,* is a personal attempt to differentiate and articulate some of the more salient aspects of modern and postmodern ideology and their relationship to spirituality.

31.   The expression was coined by Hans Urs von Balthasar and published in various contexts. See, for example, "The Marian Principle," *Communio International Catholic Review* (Spring 1988), p. 12. The "Marian principle" as used here reflects some of the basic aspects of the Balthasarian understanding.

32. The expression "individuation" here suggests true spiritual identity as a result of a personal transformation in and through the Spirit of God.

33. See A. van Kaam on the lasting readiness and the unifying "surrenders" to the transcendent in "Dynamics of Spiritual Self-direction," *Spiritual Life* 21.4 (1975): 261–82.

34. For more specific information on self-actualizing surrender, fidelity and creative care, see A. van Kaam's early and foundational book *Religion and Personality* (Englewood Cliffs, NJ: Prentice-Hall, 1964), esp. 139–41.

35. *Mulieris Dignitatem* 7, citing *Gaudium et Spes*, 24.

36. Van Kaam, *Religion and Personality*, 140.

37. Ibid., 141.

38. John Macquarrie, *Mary for All Christians* (Grand Rapids, MI: W.B. Eerdmans, 1991), 127.

39. A well-known topos in medieval mystery plays and in iconography, the figure of the three Marys was recently used in the above-mentioned sense by such noted authors as R. Laurentin, H. U. v. Balthasar and R. Spaemann.

DONALD W. MITCHELL

Buddhist and Christian
Postmodern Spiritualities

Postmodernism claims that our modern culture has come to an endpoint and that human history has now reached a major turning point. In the words of Diogenes Allen, "A massive intellectual revolution is taking place that is perhaps as great as that which marked off the modern world from the Middle Ages. The foundations of the modern world are collapsing, and we are entering a postmodern world."[1] In other words, the principles, values and ideals that were formed during the Enlightenment and laid the foundations of our modern way of thinking about ourselves and our world are being seriously questioned. This questioning has arisen because of particular negative effects, resulting from this modern mode of thought, on our personal lives, our societies and our planet. Many people are beginning to doubt whether our modern presuppositions can really contribute to building the kind of future in which we would want to live.

These questions and doubts about modernity are being addressed in the East as well as in the West. One of the places in which the challenge to modernity is voiced the loudest is in the context of religious communities. Many leaders in the major religions of the world are expressing concern over the manifold and destructive ways in which modernity is affecting their traditions, societies and peoples. In past generations, religious communities have for the most part embraced modernity and tried to deal with the problems it has wrought in ways that many now see as compromising their basic beliefs and values. Recently, more radical voices have spoken up against the ills of modernity. The particular voice in this chorus that has gained the most attention is from the Muslim communities around the world, but we hear the same types of concerns voiced by other religious communities, and these concerns frequently become the topic of discussion in interfaith encounters.

Through my own participation in Buddhist-Christian encounters, I have seen the emergence of at least two ways of dealing with these concerns. First is the way of fundamentalism. This way uncritically embraces the past and rejects modernity for a traditional faith-life based on, one may argue, premodern religious beliefs and practices. The problems with this approach are becoming more and more evident in light of the various violent forms that fundamentalism is taking to achieve its goals. Fundamentalism, be it Muslim, Buddhist, Christian, etc., attacks the modern worldview that has denied the validity of its own particular religious viewpoint. In this affirmation of its own religious claims against modernity, each also holds that it alone possesses the only proper way to believe and live. Therefore, fundamentalism creates its identity not only over and against modernity, but also over and against other religions in a manner that fosters division from, and, in some cases, violence against, peoples of these other religions.

The second way of dealing with the negative influences of modernity that I have found in interfaith encounters may be termed postmodern in the broad meaning of that word. That is, unlike the way of fundamentalism that seeks to return to the premodern, this postmodern way leads to a new future beyond modernism. It is this second alternative that I want to address in this article. I want to make it clear, however, that I am not in agreement with the postmodernist views of many contemporary writers. In fact, I see in the writings of certain French postmodernists a very negative relativism that can and may be used to reinforce the destructive and sometimes violent nationalistic tendencies we are facing in our world today. Indeed, a deconstructive postmodernism that totalizes the claims of cultural, ethnic, economic and sexual difference through the exercise of "identity politics" could rival fundamentalism in its divisive effects.

On the other hand, I do not want to get caught-up in what is becoming more and more popular today, namely, claiming that one's own view is truly postmodern and alternative views are not. So I will first explore the philosophical underpinnings of modernism that are being challenged in most postmodern thought today. Then I will look at a particular kind of postmodern vision that has been recently advanced and with which I agree. Finally, instead of just speculating on what kind of postmodern spirituality would best contribute to the realization of this vision, I will examine two particular spiritualities that I believe are already working to create such a postmodern world. Since, as we shall see, postmodernism seeks to embrace both East and West, I will discuss both the Buddhist F.A.S. Society and the Christian Focolare Movement.

1. Modernity

At the very core of modernity is the value given to individualism. David Griffin defines modern individualism to mean "the denial that the human self is internally related to other things, that is that the individual person is significantly constituted by his or her relations to other people, to institutions, to nature, to the past, even perhaps to a divine creator."[2] In this modern view, relations to others are regarded as external and not constitutive of the self. The person is believed to exist as a self-contained entity which then has external relations to others. Elsewhere, I have discussed at length the ways in which Buddhists and Christians like Keiji Nishitani and Thomas Merton have shown how this kind of understanding of the person is detrimental to the spiritual life.[3] It engenders a type of self-centeredness that isolates modern persons from a larger matrix of interrelatedness in which one can find one's true "home-ground," to use Nishitani's term. That is, if one tries to live either a Buddhist or a Christian spiritual life with this kind of individualistic self-understanding, one will not find a mode of being at home together with other persons, nature and ultimate reality in a way that is both true and fulfilling.

Postmodern writers have related this individualism and self-centeredness to the economic realm. Modern individualism in liberal capitalism accepts self-interest as a basis for the economic dimension of life, allowing thereby the desire for wealth and power to run uncontrolled in the marketplace. This has produced massive disparities between rich and poor throughout the world. Because modern capitalist society judges the worth of persons by the amount of their material possessions, poor people and poor countries are devalued and marginalized from the core of capitalist life, namely, from the gaining of more wealth and material property. Similarly, the value of things, including nature itself, is measured in terms of usability. Nishitani calls this dual effect of materialistic and self-centered individualism the "dehumanization of humankind" and the "denaturalization of nature."[4] The treatment of persons and nature as means for one's own material enhancement leads to the kind of economic and political imperialism, and the kind of environmental destruction, we see almost everywhere in the modern world.

Related to this kind of individualism is another aspect of modernity which Griffin calls "dualism."[5] This refers to such dualisms as that between the human person and nature. The human person is understood to be quite different from and of greater value than the rest of creation. Therefore, nature is something to be studied by science and controlled by technology for purely human benefit. This dualistic understanding of our relation to nature, coupled with self-centered individualism, has combined to reinforce the unlimited domination and exploitation of nature mentioned above.

Dualism is also related to the third characteristic of modernity, namely, secularization. Given that the person is understood to be independent and substantially different from nature, and given the Christian notion that God is a person who creates the world out of nothingness, then God is often seen as existing quite apart from this world. In the Middle Ages, divinity was seen as both transcendent and immanent, whereas to the modern mind, God is not to be found either within the human person or within nature. And as modern materialism has grown over the centuries, persons have become more and more interested in money and the material things money can buy. This attainment and enjoyment of material possessions, or consumerism, has become the focus of people's attention. And since these goals are achievable within a totally secular economic and social structure, God and religion have become more and more irrelevant. This process of secularization has ended in modern atheism.

Related to this secularism is the fourth characteristic of modernity, namely, scientism. Science rather than God is the object of modern faith. It is science, not God, that will meet our secular materialistic and consumeristic needs in this world. Science, not revelation, will give modern people what they need to know to have a materially better life. The natural sciences as well as the psychological, social, political and economic sciences are "believed" to be able eventually to solve all of our problems. This is the modern "myth of progress." Modernity has cut itself off from the past because it sees the past as being of no real value in the achievement of its goals. These goals are achievable as we progress into the future. Historically, this move marks the modern period from the previous Renaissance that looked backward to the earlier classical period of Western history for its inspiration. Modernity, on the other hand, always has a fascination with the new, always believing that it will be better than the past. And this better future is not being built by God, but by the advances of our own modern sciences.

Finally, scientism also gives modernity a widely accepted reason for rejecting religion. Science has been very successful through the practical application of an empiricist epistemology. Scientism, however, claims that this method of the modern natural sciences is the only method for ascertaining the truth. Theology cannot produce cognitive assertions that can be verified empirically. Therefore, religion cannot offer us any real truths about life. Only science can do that. The practice of religious spirituality or piety can give one a personal and subjective sense of comfort. It cannot give one any objective knowledge about the world. It seems to me that with all the problems facing modernity mentioned above, it is a pity that scientism places such narrow limits on our experience and knowledge. I share this concern with many postmodernists who believe that we must go beyond these and all the other limits of modernity in order to solve today's problems. In fact, many feel that the modern limits of scientism, as well as individualism, dualism, materialism and secularism, are at the foundation of many of these problems. Once they have been lifted, we may be able to discover new and better postmodern answers to the many difficult and even tragic issues facing humankind today.

2. Postmodernity

Griffin points out that postmodern thinkers have focused much of their attention on the first characteristic of modernity mentioned above, namely, individualism (p. 14). They have argued that relations are not accidental to human nature but essential to it. It is not that we are first self-contained entities that then engage in relationships that are external to who we are. Rather, our relations to others, society, family, nature and God are constitutive of our very identity, of our personhood. This more organic understanding of human existence also helps to overcome the second characteristic of modernity, namely, dualism. The postmodern vision does not see the person as fully distinct from others or from nature. The person is seen instead as interrelated with others and with nature. A truly postmodern person should not feel like an alien in a faceless society or in a hostile and indifferent nature. The postmodern ideal here is a real sense of at-homeness and kinship with other persons and with other species. It is this vision that is at the basis of the postmodern concern for social and economic justice, as well as ecological issues.

From the above, one can see that the individualism of modernity has led to a devaluation of the community and the natural environment as defining factors of personhood. Individual persons are seen as just individuals living in aggregate societies built on exploited landscapes. This implies a modern transition from being part of, and therefore at home in, a community and a natural setting to being alone and homeless in an impersonal society and natural environment. Peter Berger has said that "Modernity . . . is marked by homelessness."[6] Postmodernism, in contrast, has emphasized the communal nature of human existence and its connection to nature. It seeks, on the one hand, to re-create various forms of community on the local level and a greater sense of positive connectedness between communities, on the global level. On the other hand, it seeks to integrate the local and global communities of humankind into a more ecologically viable interconnectedness with the natural environment.

Besides breaking down the dualism between self and other and self and nature, the postmodern vision also overcomes the dualism between self and God. Postmodern theologians argue that since relations are internal rather than external, we are constituted not only by our relation to our social and natural environment, but also by our relationship with God. Our relationship with God is essential, not accidental, to who we are. Postmodern theology rejects modernity's pushing God to a transcendent position outside of our world in a manner that has led to the ultimate atheistic denial of God's very existence. That is, it rejects modern secularism for a type of postmodern panentheism. As Griffin puts it, it presents a vision "according to which the world is present in deity and deity is present in the world" (p. 17). This overcoming of secularization through the discovery of the immanence of the divine can also counteract the materialistic self-centeredness of modernity. The discovery of a spiritual dimension to life in which we share as brothers and sisters with one another and nature can engender a new sense of responsible kinship in this interrelated life. With this postmodern vision, one can see the value of living for others and of helping those most in need. A deeper happiness and fulfillment can be found in communion and sharing rather than in competitive and isolated self-affirmation and possessing.

Another aspect of modernism that is overcome in this postmodern vision is "the myth of the future" that rejects the contemporary relevance of the past. Since we are constituted by our relations, our life is seen as taking form in relation to our past. This leads to a new respect for tradition. Postmodernism, however, is not calling for a premodern traditionalism like that proposed by fundamentalism. The latter rejects change and the absorption into one's tradition of new elements from other traditions. Postmodernism is open to change and to more positive intercultural and interfaith exchanges in a manner rejected by fundamentalists. Postmodernists see the value of traditions sharing and working together to form a better future for all humankind in a way that respects cultural and religious pluralism.

Finally, the re-acceptance of God as a reality that affects our existence challenges modern scientism. This is not to reject scientific research or to deny the wonderful advances that science has made and its contributions to the betterment of life. Rather, it is just to say that science cannot tell us everything about life. Nor can it guide us in how to live our life. The empirical knowledge of science can tell us some important things about life and can change some things for the better, but it cannot tell us about the ultimate meaning of life, and it cannot tell us how best to live a meaningful life. The postmodern re-discovery of the sacred in life can provide us with meaningful narratives with which to live. It will be the project of spiritualities in a postmodern age to help persons make this discovery and live these narratives in more satisfying lives as human beings. Such postmodern spiritualities would foster spiritual lives in a more communally-centered matrix that is related to nature in a positive and integrated way. They would foster spiritual values in local community life as well as foster a greater sense of the global community of humankind.

Postmodern spiritualities would achieve these goals by drawing on past traditions while being open to new ways of expressing those traditions in building the future. This is especially the case in terms of going beyond the patriarchal past that has been so much a part of the spiritual traditions of the world. The goal of such postmodern spiritualities would not be just personal transformation, but social transformation toward the ideal of a more equal, united, peaceful and ecologically sound world community. In the achievement of this ideal, postmodern spiritualities would also seek greater interfaith collaboration. Their members would see themselves as persons in different traditions who are ultimately fellow pilgrims traveling together on a path that leads to a common ideal of a more just, equitable, united and peaceful world. And as some postmodern philosophers have pointed out, there is no single metanarrative to include the various stories lived by these fellow travelers on the way. Each has his or her story to be lived by those who share it and to be appreciated by those who hear it. Interfaith dialogue is a sharing of stories that fosters mutual understanding and appreciation among fellow pilgrims. In this way of dialogue, the foundation is laid for possible collaboration to realize common local goals as well as common international goals that foster the ideals of world peace and justice.

In what follows, I will present two stories of what I perceive to be postmodern movements in Buddhism and Christianity. In telling their stories, I will present the ways in which they come to terms with the problems of modernity discussed above. And, I will point out how they are working to build a postmodern world along the lines of the vision also mentioned above. The Buddhist postmodern movement that I will discuss is the F.A.S. Society in Japan. The Christian postmodern movement is the Focolare Movement that began in Italy but is now worldwide.[7]

3. The F.A.S. Society

The story of the F.A.S. Society begins with its founder, Shin'ichi Hisamatsu. Hisamatsu was born in 1889 to very devout Buddhist parents. He planned to attend a religious university, but before doing so, Hisamatsu lost what he later called his "medieval faith" in the Buddha and a world after death. He embraced instead a "modern faith" in the self-conscious individual person as a rational and moral agent building a better world here and now.[8] He went to Kyoto University to study philosophy in order to better understand this "modern standpoint."

While at Kyoto University studying with the great founder of the Kyoto School of Japanese philosophy, Kitaro Nishida, Hisamatsu had a religious and philosophical crisis. He felt that his self was "shackled" and "choked by the clinging web of the spider of sin" (p. 20). It is not clear what exactly Hisamatsu meant by sin, but he seemed to be overcome by his inability to live the kind of modern rational and moral life he had thought possible. The study and application of purely rational and moral philosophy was of no help to him. His attempt to live in this modern way was always compromised by a deeper self-centeredness. So, not choosing to return to his earlier Buddhist faith, he chose to practice Zen meditation. Through this practice in 1915, he awakened to his True Self, to what Hisamatsu called his "Formless Self." In this Awakening, he solved his problems at their root so that they "melted away like ice from within" (p. 26).

In this Awakening, Hisamatsu transcended the secularism and scientism of the "modern standpoint" that join in denying the validity of any kind of "religious" knowledge and insist that human problems must be defined and addressed in purely rational and empirical terms. This modern approach could not reach deep enough to solve Hisamatsu's problems that were caused by a fundamental self-centeredness at the core of his being. What did reach into this depth and bring him the freedom he was seeking was the "religious" knowledge of Zen Awakening. Hisamatsu would later refer to this experience as opening up for him a "post-modern" vision that was beyond both the medieval and the modern visions of life. Zen Awakening has given him the means of overcoming the limits of modern autonomous reason without returning to a medieval faith. And this Awakening became a new standpoint from which he criticized the secular standpoint of modernity and went on to propose the creation of a spiritually-based "post-modern" world.

Almost thirty years after Hisamatsu's original Zen experience, the members of the Young Men's Buddhist Association of Kyoto University found themselves in the midst of World War II. They soon became dissatisfied with the lack of spiritual guidance given by the organization in the face of the war situation. Two students were asked to explore how to reform the organization. One of these students was Masao Abe. Their exploration led them to Hisamatsu, who then greatly impressed the group. Hisamatsu helped the students examine how to attain Awakening and to confront the issues of the day from the standpoint of this Awakening. Awakening provided them with a spiritual foundation that went beyond the narrow secularism of modernity. It also led them to a deeper religious self-understanding from which to address the social problems of the day, such as war and peace and the economy and poverty. As I have observed elsewhere, "Hisamatsu and his followers felt that [a] world of peace can become a historical reality through the efforts

of persons who are awakening to their True Self and compassion-
ately choose to work on the basis of that Awakening for the liberation of all humankind."[9]

In 1958, Hisamatsu gave a new name to his group that had
grown out of the Kyoto University branch of the Y.M.B.A. He called
the group the F.A.S. Society. "F" for "Formless Self" means that the
Society seeks spiritual Awakening to the True Self so hidden by our
modern secular society. "A" for "all humankind" means that this
Formless Self encompasses all humanity. This discovery of a deep
spiritual interrelatedness of all humankind overcomes the individualism of modern society. "S" for the "supra-historical creation of
history" means that this Awakening to the Formless Self that embraces all humankind can become a transhistorical basis for the
Society to use in creating a new postmodern age.

Hisamatsu saw history as coming to the end of the modern age
with its basis on purely secular and individualistic rationality. He
felt that humankind is now realizing the limits of modern life built
on this basis. And he believed that a postmodern age is about to
emerge that will have a new spiritual and communal basis which
will overcome the egoism, materialism, nationalism, racism, etc.,
that so divide and oppress modern humankind. He believed that
the F.A.S. way of living was a "post-modern way of being."[10] It is a
way of living united with all humankind on a spiritual standpoint
that can serve as a basis for building a truly peaceful and just
world. Hisamatsu worked through the F.A.S. Society for this ideal
until he died in 1980.

Masao Abe, who is now one of the leaders of the F.A.S. Society,
gives a two-fold rationale for Hisamatsu's postmodernism.[11] First,
Abe points out that from Hisamatsu's Buddhist point of view, the
modern standpoint of autonomous reason must be replaced with
the postmodern standpoint of the True Self because autonomous
reason cannot in itself solve the problems of humankind. F.A.S. is
not anti-reason, but it feels that while reason may present positive
moral ideals, these ideals are compromised in practice by the deep
selfishness of the human psyche. In Buddhist Awakening, one finds
a deeper Center—the True Self—that can liberate one from the
fundamental selfishness that inhibits one from achieving one's ideals. Based on this standpoint of the Awakening of the True Self
("F"), the liberated person can live a universal love of all humankind ("A") forming history ("S") with a truly compassionate motivation. In this way, one can overcome the materialistic self-interest
that plagues modernity. If this deep self-centeredness is not rooted

out of humankind, reason may come up with solutions to various particular problems, but these solutions will always be compromised by self-centeredness and new problems will constantly arise from the same source. Awakening provides the necessary depth standpoint from which to exercise reason successfully.

The second rationale for Hisamatsu's postmodernism is that modernism's understanding of the self is not adequate to solve the particular problems faced by humankind today. The value given to autonomous reason by modernity is based on a Cartesian notion of the self as an independent and rational being. The radical individualism of this notion cannot provide an adequate standpoint to enable humankind to enter a new age that demands the building of a united global community. To build this kind of united humankind, we need to see humanity as "a community with a single destiny— one living self-aware entity."[12] It is this communal understanding of the self that one discovers in Zen Awakening. The True Self embraces all humankind as one reality and can thereby provide an adequate understanding of the self to overcome modern individualism and build a postmodern unity of humankind: "It is precisely humankind [understood] as a self-aware entity which can develop a unified, cooperative human community in the complete sense of the term" (p. 253).

The F.A.S. Society is devoted to the task of living this postmodern mode of communal life now as a contribution to the building of this more united postmodern humankind. For them, any postmodern spirituality must contribute to this project by overcoming the limits of modernity in the context of the spiritual life of its community. For the members of the F.A.S. Society, this means the reappropriation of traditional Rinzai Zen practice in a fashion that adds a new communal element to the practice. In this way, they draw on tradition, as opposed to the futurism of modernity, and yet do not fall into the kind of pure traditionalism found in fundamentalism's rejection of modernity. For example, instead of each individual member having his or her own *koan*, the Society uses one "fundamental" *koan* for all its members. This "fundamental" *koan* was chosen because it brings one to the deepest Awakening from which one can answer all other *koans*. However, one effect of having all the members use one *koan* is the fostering of a sense of equality and solidarity among its members. And when the members work on the *koans*, they do so together in pairs. This fosters a sense of "mutual inquiry" that strengthens the "dynamic unity" of the community.

Hisamatsu says that "the present world can be called a world without love."[13] Modern society sees itself as "a mere aggregate of individuals."[14] What is needed is a spiritual vision of humankind as a unity to be realized through the mutual love between its parts. Spirituality can help this realization of a more united humankind through this vision of unity and its actualization through mutual love. To make his point, Hisamatsu uses the metaphor of a fire: "If we spread this warmth externally, in the same way a charcoal fire lights in one spot and spreads, everyone in this room will become warm."[15] A postmodern spirituality will provide a fire of love and unity that will warm and bring together all humankind in a fashion that overcomes the "cold and self-centered" individualism of modernity.

Finally, we can see that the F.A.S. postmodern spirituality seeks to awaken all humankind to a spiritual standpoint that sets aside the secular standpoint of modernity. This deeper spiritual Awakening can free humanity from its modern enslavement to material things and self-centered purposes. This new freedom can in turn lead to people overcoming the divisions they have created among themselves. For Hisamatsu, this "communalism" is the active functioning of the essential unity of humankind that is now being blocked by self-centeredness. If this unifying energy of humanity's fundamental unity can be realized in society, there will be a breaking down of the various "isms" that separate us into groupings that seek only their own self-interest. This in turn will be expressed in a new international community transcending modern nationalistic structures in a "sharing of all wealth . . . all material and spiritual wealth" for the good of all humankind.[16] It is for such communal and social transformation of humankind that the F.A.S. spirituality was established. In this way, it transcends the kinds of modern spiritualities that seek only personal and individual transformation, and shows itself to be a truly postmodern Buddhist spirituality.

4. The Focolare Movement

The story of the Focolare spirituality begins at the very same time as the story of the F.A.S. Society. While Hisamatsu was meeting with young Buddhists during World War II in Japan, a woman named Chiara Lubich was meeting with young Christians in war-torn Italy.[17] Before the war, Lubich was a teacher and a student of philosophy at the University of Venice, but she was forced by the war to return to her family in Trent. Lubich and her friends began to share together a new spiritual experience in the city of Trent that was bombed heavily by the Allied forces.

One of her companions was Dori Zamboni whom Lubich tutored in philosophy. One day in 1943 when they were studying Kant, Lubich had a very deep realization that the rational approach of modern philosophy could not give her the understanding of truth for which she was looking. In that moment, when she set aside the light of reason, she felt herself illumined by what she calls "a light which comes from above, an understanding which is not a fruit of our intelligence, but which comes from God."[18] Lubich called this light the "Ideal" which for her is ultimately God. One interesting thing about this experience of the light of God is that Zamboni also shared in this experience of Lubich's. And when Lubich shared her discovery with her other companions, they too received this light as a kind of charism. Until then, each had his/her own individual and secular ideals. But in this communal mystical experience of God, each discovered a common Ideal as the standpoint of his/her collective spiritual life. So, I see this collective mystical illumination as moving Lubich and her companions from a modern rationalistic and individualistic "standpoint," to use Hisamatsu's term, to a postmodern spiritual and communal standpoint.

During the following years, Lubich and her companions continued to meet in the bomb shelters. They would take only the gospels and read them in the light of the Ideal in order to illumine the meaning of the scripture for their lives. In this radical way, they began to develop a new and collective form of spirituality that draws on tradition but also develops it in what I hope to show is in a postmodern direction.

The traditional basis of Lubich's spirituality is the experience of God as Love.[19] However, this experience of God-Love was not only a personal one for each member of the community. It was also a communally lived experience. This communal experience of God-Love was profoundly trinitarian. The essence of God was experienced as a communion of love that determines the nature of the three persons of the Trinity. As in postmodern thought, relations are not external to persons, but constitute their nature. The Father just is the giving nature of God-Love that can be so in relation to the Son who receives that love. And the Son just is Son in the dynamic of God-Love with the Father—a dynamic Love in which the Son returns all to the Father. The mutuality of this dynamic relatedness of God-Love is the person of the Holy Spirit in which all persons are united.

Lubich and her companions found that through their communal spirituality, with the grace of God, they could actually participate in this mutual indwelling (*perichoresis*) of the persons of the Trinity (p. 50). This is not to say that they can dwell within one another as do the divine persons; rather, they found that God could dwell within and among them in a way that united them in a mutual in-existence through the intersubjectivity of the love they have for each other. Lubich and her companions experienced God-Love present in the midst of their community as a trinitarian mutuality that penetrated them in a manner that enwrapped them together in that mutuality. In so doing, the unity achieved transfigured their relations, and thereby their persons, in the image of the Trinity (p. 52). They were made one as God is one.

From this communal transformation, these young women concluded that their new spirituality would make a contribution to the realization of Jesus' last prayer: "That all may be one as you, Father, are in me, and I in you; I pray that they may be [one] in us" (Jn 17:21). They also found that by living this trinitarian relationship among themselves, their lives were transformed. Again, in postmodern thought, relationships are constitutive of who we are as persons because "traces" of the other are within the self. In Lubich's trinitarian experience, others could be "lived" by the self in a dynamic mutuality of love and unity that reflected the dynamic love and unity of the Trinity. Living together in this communal, trinitarian way became the basis for personal transformation as well as for social transformation.

As for personal transformation, I have argued elsewhere that the new communal spiritual life of Lubich's community involves both *kenosis* and *ek-stasis*. Unity demands a kind of kenotic love that empties the self of any independent self-enclosure. Lubich says of God:

> God is one and triune. Because of their very same nature, which is love, the three live in unifying themselves (by emptying themselves) and in doing so they each re-find themselves. . . . The three make themselves one out of love, and in the One Love, they rediscover themselves. (p. 47)

So, Lubich and her companions would "empty themselves" before each other in order to take the other into her heart. Each would also share themselves with the other, allowing themselves to be taken into the other's heart. When this *kenosis* became mutual, there would be a kind of mutuality, a unity in which the persons would refind themselves made one with the other. And since the persons were outside themselves, as it were, there was a kind of *ek-stasis*, an ecstasy of mutual love. *Ek-stasis* is a category discussed by a number of postmodern thinkers. Here, it indicates a communal reality. It is not that one is in an ecstatic individualistic union with God. Rather, it is a collective ecstatic unity with others outside of themselves in the mystical, communal presence of God among them in a manner that "lives" the trinitarian unity of God. Lubich observes, "We had the impression that the Lord was opening our eyes and hearts to the kingdom of God in our midst, to the Trinity dwelling in this small cell of the mystical body."[20]

It was in this spiritual atmosphere of joy that Lubich and her companions lived during the war. Hence, when persons went to be with them, they said that it was like being near a "focolare," or a fireplace. This word indicates the light, warmth, and joy of gathering around a "family fireside." This later became the name of the movement to which Lubich and her companions gave birth. One is here reminded of Hisamatsu's metaphor of the charcoal fire.

Since this ecstatic or joyful unity was not a purely individual matter but was ultimately communal, it also became the basis of the Focolare's work for social transformation. The members of the community emptied themselves before every person they met in a selfless imaging of God-Love. In the war situation, to be one with others meant to share their sometimes desperate situation. Lubich and her companions shared an apartment and began to live the "communion of goods." They put all in common and used everything for those most in need. Soon over five hundred people joined them and through this communion of goods all of the wounded, poor, and hungry of the city of Trent were taken care of so that no one went without. Again, one is reminded of Hisamatsu's statements on the importance of the communion of goods.

Because of the success of this work, Lubich and the new Focolare community saw themselves as not only founding a religious community, as would be the case in the older paradigm of individualistic spirituality, but as also laying the basis for social transformation. Unlike Hisamatsu, Lubich does not use the term "postmodern," but she does refer to creating a "New Humanity." Just as the persons of the Trinity are distinct persons in their own right and yet interdependent in their unity, so humanity can achieve a similar unity that still maintains the diversity of human-kind. In Lubich's thinking, this unity is not just a possibility, but reflects the true nature of humankind. Given her trinitarian per-spective, she feels that God did not just create each person in his image. He created humankind as a whole in the image of the Trin-ity. Humankind is created to be united in love as the persons of the Trinity are united, but to achieve this unity there must be a spiri-tual change in how people see themselves and the world they share with others. Creating a new society means to create new people freed from the restricting limits of modernity.

Lubich's Focolare spirituality has various practices that help their members overcome their modern limitations and develop a personal sensitivity to unity in order to better work for a more united world. For example, the practice of "making oneself one" with others mentioned above overcomes the perceived duality be-tween self and other. Also, in a way similar to Hisamatsu's collec-tive, single *koan* practice, the whole Focolare tries to put the same verse from scripture into practice each month. The verse is chosen from the monthly scripture readings shared by most Christian de-nominations. Persons of other religions choose a similar verse from their own scripture. The Focolare members come together at least once a month to share their efforts, successes and failures. These and other practices of living their faith in daily life in a collective manner provide a counter to modern individualism. Also, the prac-tice of the communion of goods counters modern materialism and consumerism. However, as is true of all authentic Christian spiri-tualities, real spiritual growth does not just depend on techniques. The Focolare's communal and spiritual environment provides a mutuality wherein God can be present transforming their lives by his grace. And the experience of this mystical, communal presence counters the secularism of modernity. In light of these practical examples, one can see why I refer to the Focolare as a spirituality for the postmodern age.

One final element of the Focolare spirituality that reminds me of certain strands of postmodern thought is what Lubich calls the "key" to their life of unity. This is the experience of Jesus forsaken.[21] Jesus experienced the absence of God when he cried out from the cross, "My God, my God, why have you forsaken me?" At that point, he so totally identified himself with humankind's sinful and suffering condition that he experienced the absence of God. But as Godself, in that moment he also identified himself with all human pain and suffering. Therefore, we can find Jesus forsaken as the presence of God in the seeming absence of God in the suffering of humankind today. In terms of one's own sufferings, Lubich says "We too . . . have experienced that in embracing the cross one does not find only suffering. On the contrary, one finds love, the Love that is the life of God himself within us."[22]

Unlike in some premodern spiritualities, Lubich does not recommend that one just passively accept and embrace the cross as penance leading to union with God. Rather, she sees in Jesus forsaken the "key" to unity. One finds in the sufferings of life an experienced absence of God that is paradoxically a presence of God. This God-absent-yet-present in Jesus forsaken transforms the suffering into a love that when mutual generates unity. In the experienced absence of God in suffering, there is an actual presence of God-Love penetrating the person with a trinitarian life that more deeply unites that person with God and others. Jesus forsaken is God-Love penetrating and transforming humankind into a more united image of the Trinity. So one does not just passively accept the cross; rather, one uses it as a "springboard" to a more loving way of living with God and others. Also, in Lubich's spirituality, one finds the face of Jesus forsaken in the sufferings of others and is moved thereby to compassionate action. One feels moved to respond to the cry of Jesus forsaken in the poor and oppressed. One is moved to try to liberate all the crucified parts of humanity so that all can share fully in a more just society. It is precisely these very active communal and community building dimensions to Lubich's experience of the cross that make it so postmodern.

One can appreciate Lubich's contribution to postmodern thinking on the experience of God if we consider what some postmodernists call the "non-absent absence" of God, or God's "presence of non-presence."[23] Here they are speaking of the presence of what is absent to one's experience. God is not just absent as in modernity, nor is God just present as in the medieval world. Rather, he is present to us in certain "traces" of his absence. Given the relationality of postmodern thought, these traces are understood to enter our consciousness, making God present even in his absence in a manner that marks our identity. I see this kind of phenomenon in Lubich's experience of Jesus forsaken. The experience of Jesus forsaken is an experience of the absence of God, the absence of love, light, goodness, beauty, etc. Yet that absence, that forsakenness of God, is itself a presence of God. It is in that void and darkness that God penetrates the person and opens the mind and heart of the person to a new life of unity.

To conclude our story of the Focolare, after World War II Lubich was joined by more and more persons who wanted to live this spirituality of unity. Focolare centers, which are at the heart of larger Focolare communities, opened around the world. In 1962, Pope John XXIII approved the Focolare as a spirituality in the Catholic Church. It seems to me that he understood the Focolare Movement to be in line with his vision of the new church to be born from Vatican II. The Focolare has become ecumenical with a large percentage of its members in Europe belonging to Protestant denominations and its members in the Near East belonging to the Orthodox churches. Lubich herself has been given awards for her work in the Lutheran, Anglican and Orthodox communities. The Focolare is also an interfaith spirituality with participants from the Muslim, Jewish, Hindu and Buddhist communities. For this broad work in the religious world, Lubich was awarded the Templeton Prize in 1977. She and most of her first companions live in Rome at the international center of the Focolare Movement.

5. Conclusion

I hope this short article on F.A.S and Focolare as examples of postmodern spiritualities has shown how two well-established communities are trying to move humanity beyond the limits of modernity. There are certainly many other spiritual movements that are going in this same direction. Indeed, it is very common for persons of various faith communities to discover, in the context of interfaith dialogue, that they are really fellow pilgrims on this same path. They realize that they are facing the same untruths in the modern world and are working to liberate a suffering humanity and build a more peaceful, united and just postmodern world. In this regard, interfaith collaboration seems to be the order of the day.

Finally, it is interesting to note in this regard that one of the leaders of the F.A.S. Society, Masao Abe (mentioned above as one of the founding students of the Society and now a leading figure of the Kyoto School of philosophy) traveled to Rome in March 1993 to be hosted by the Focolare Movement's Center for Interreligious Dialogue. It was arranged for him to meet with the Vatican's Pontifical Council for Interreligious Dialogue, Joseph Cardinal Ratzinger, a number of Catholic theologians and Pope John Paul II. Abe was struck by the similarities between his and Lubich's spiritualities and visions of the future of humankind. The encounter was of such depth that Abe now considers himself an "informal" Buddhist member of the Focolare Movement. This informal relation has been affirmed by Lubich herself. It is this kind of interfaith encounter that is a "sign of hope" for the realization of the postmodern vision of a new civilization of peace in the future.

Notes

1. Diogenes Allen, *Christian Belief in a Postmodern World: The Full Wealth of Conviction* (Louisville: John Knox Press, 1989), p. 3.

2. David Ray Griffin, ed., *Spirituality and Society: Postmodern Visions* (Albany: State University of New York Press, 1988), p. 3.

3. See my *Spirituality and Emptiness: The Dynamics of Spiritual Life in Buddhism and Christianity* (New York: Paulist, 1991), Chapter 2.

4. Ibid., p. 32.

5. Griffin, *Postmodern Vision*, p. 3.

6. Peter Berger, *Facing Up to Modernity* (New York: Basic Books, 1977), p. 61.

7. See Mitchell, *Spirituality and Emptiness*, Chapters 6 and 7, for a more in-depth comparison of the F.A.S. and Focolare Spiritualities.

8. Shin'ichi Hisamatsu, "Memories of My Academic Life," *The Eastern Buddhist* 18.1 (1985): 10. Subsequent citations are parenthetical.

9. Mitchell, *Spirituality and Emptiness*, p. 148.

10. Shin'ichi Hisamatsu, "After My Student Years," *F.A.S. Society Journal* (Winter, 1985–86), p. 2.

11. Masao Abe, "Hisamatsu's Philosophy of Awakening," *The Eastern Buddhist* 14.1: 31–33.

12.   Masao Abe, *Zen and Western Thought* (Honolulu: University of Hawaii Press, 1989), p. 249.

13.   "The Vow of Humankind: Talks by Shin'ichi Hisamatsu: Part IV," *F.A.S. Society Journal* (Winter, 1988), p. 12.

14.   "An Interview with Shin'ichi Hisamatsu," *F.A.S. Society Journal* (Winter, 1986), pp. 3–4.

15.   "The Vow of Humankind," p. 13.

16.   "An Interview with Shin'ichi Hisamatsu," p. 7.

17.   For a detailed account of Lubich's life during World War II, see Edwin Robertson, *Chiara* (Ireland: Christian Journals, 1978).

18.   William Proctor, *An Interview with Chiara Lubich* (New York: New City Press, 1983), pp. 27–28.

19.   For an in-depth theological analysis of Lubich's experiences of and reflections on God-Love, see Marisa Cerini, *God Who is Love in the Experience and Thought of Chiara Lubich* (New York: New City Press, 1992). I give subsequent citations parenthetically.

20.   Chiara Lubich, *May They All Be One* (New York: New City Press, 1984), p. 52.

21.   For Lubich's discussion of the relation of Jesus Forsaken to unity in her spirituality, see Chiara Lubich, *Unity and Jesus Forsaken* (New York: New City Press, 1985).

22.   Lubich, *May They All Be One*, p. 68.

23.   Mark C. Taylor, "Reframing Postmodernisms," in *Shadow of Spirit: Postmodernism and Religion*, ed. Philippa Berry and Andrew Wernick (London and New York: Routledge, 1992), p. 26.

GÜNTHER M. BOLL

Answering to Pluralism:
Fr. Kentenich's Concept of a
Secular, Marian Spirituality

This paper takes a look at the concept and life-work of a man whose most central concern was the creation of a "lay spirituality," and who is certainly one of the pioneers of a secular spirituality for the future—Fr. Joseph Kentenich (1885–1968), the founder of the Schoenstatt Movement.[1] It is obviously not possible in the scope of this paper to give a complete survey of his spirituality. However, every concept, if it is holistic, if it has grown organically, has a nucleus which contains everything in essence ("Das Ganze im Fragment"). With this as my starting point, I shall circumscribe Kentenich's lay spirituality for the future in two steps, considering first his basic premise, then, secondly, the Marian modality of his work.

1. The Basic Premise of His Secular Spirituality

In order to understand Kentenich and his spirituality, it is essential to grasp the basic insight which motivated him to develop a new and timely expression of Christian spirituality. This was his view of Christianity in a pluralistic society. His entire pedagogical and pastoral practice is an attempt to offer an answer to the totally changed situation of the Church in the world by drawing from the heart of Christian spirituality. We often do not recognize clearly in what a radically changed situation the Church finds herself today, because she is inevitably drawn into the changes and developments going on in human society. In all the many and var-

149

ied features of this change in our century we can discover a common core: a pluralism that is spreading inexorably over the whole world. Every country and culture, which for centuries has been uniformly marked by a common scale of values, experiences today that this consistent and relatively unchanging social climate is being destroyed. As Kentenich put it, this process continues "like a consuming fever."[2] This applies to all religions and cultures. Fundamentalism is an attempt to stop this process, to preserve a common milieu. It still has to be seen in how far it can succeed. Yet almost everywhere on our globe, the various religions and *Weltanschauungen* exist side-by-side and intermingle. Even the traditionally Catholic countries and regions are drawn into the pluralistic whirlpool. It is in this context that for some decades people have been speaking about a worldwide diaspora situation of Christianity, and of Catholicism in particular.

This is of importance in the context of our discussion, because this situation presents a tremendous challenge to the Church and its pastoral efforts. In the past centuries one could trust in a Catholic milieu to act as a "hidden co-educator," because the individual Christian was born into it, supported and upheld by it. Today, however, education has to enable the individual to live in a pluralistic surrounding.

With a view to this situation, Kentenich wrote in 1961 in Milwaukee:

> Everywhere Christians and non-Christians come face-to-face. Everywhere they confront each other in an existential way. There is no longer a 'Great Wall of China' to separate the different *Weltanschauungen* physically and intellectually. A common world culture increasingly and almost irresistibly encompasses peoples and nations like a gigantic net. Willingly or unwillingly it brings people closer, making all without exception dependent on one another. Distances disappear. . . . We are well advised to gear ourselves mentally to a sufficiently long domination by such a diaspora situation of Christianity and make our preparations accordingly. A diaspora situation requires of necessity a comprehensive education towards life in the diaspora.[3]

Here we find the most typical, and for the Church most helpful, element of Kentenich's life-work: his charism for education.

When he analyzed the situation of the Church in our pluralistic society, he immediately drew the conclusion: education and the pastoral practice have to adapt themselves in order to do justice to this challenge. He therefore came to the clear insight that the traditional spirituality of the Church, in particular in the way it is passed on to the vast majority of the laity, is not in step with the new situation of the Church in the postmodern world. It is necessary, if the Church is to survive, and above all if the Church is to carry out her mission, to develop a new, secular form of Christian spirituality in the foreseeable future.

Perhaps it is a good idea, particularly with a view to the laity in the Church and their circumstances, to take a look at the developments within the Church in our century. The legacy of the past centuries was the clearly visible division of the sociological body of the Church into two parts; there were clear differences between the clergy and the laity. It was said that the ordination of the one led to the subordination of the other group. As far as the religious life was concerned, people were more or less aware that genuine Christian striving for holiness was only possible for the clergy or religious.

As long as there was a united Catholic milieu, such a state of affairs could exist. However, with the continuous development of an emancipated and secularized world, a new situation has arisen. In many ways it is similar to the situation of the early Church. The dividing line, as at the beginning of the Church, no longer runs between the clergy and the laity, but between Christians and non-Christians, between believers and non-believers. This has resulted in a change of emphasis within the Church.

Already toward the end of the nineteenth and at the start of the twentieth century, there were developments aimed at giving the laity a different status and a different self-appreciation. After all the centuries governed by a different mentality, in particular as a result of the opposition to the Reformed Churches that had abolished the ministerial priesthood, such attempts naturally gave rise to many tensions and could proceed only by small steps. Even "Catholic Action," which was founded by the official Church, understood the apostolate of the laity in the world as sharing in the hierarchical apostolate of the Church. The laity were and remained an extension of the hierarchy. In view of the challenge of the pluralistic world all around, these were half-hearted steps that could not offer a solution for the future.

The Second Vatican Council brought about a decisive divide in this development by stating: "The lay apostolate . . . is a participation in the saving mission of the Church itself. Through their baptism and confirmation, all are commissioned to that apostolate by the Lord himself" (LG 4.33, p. 59).[4] By reflecting on her essential nature, the Church discovered her real form: as the chosen and graced People of God, all the members of the Church are fundamentally equal. The necessary and enduring difference between the clergy and the laity recedes behind the common grace of redemption by Christ and the common mission to heal and sanctify the world.

As a result, the actual and fundamental differentiation again comes clearly into the foreground: between the redeemed and the unredeemed, between believers and nonbelievers, between Christians and non-Christians. All the baptized, those with an official status as well as all the other members of God's People, are called to live up to the grace of their baptism. Inwardly this means allowing this new, divine life to come to maturity in a holy life; outwardly it means bearing witness to Christ, to the reality of the arrival of God's kingdom.

This confronts us with the challenge and task that result from the all-comprising change in our understanding of the Church and the situation of the Church in a pluralistic society. It is necessary to develop a spirituality that does justice to the lay state and is rooted in the world, so that individual Christians, in particular those living in the world, are enabled to live their Christianity convincingly.

Let us now take a brief look, an all too brief look, at Schoenstatt's spirituality, which Kentenich developed out of such insights and attempted to realize in the communities that make up his work.

He called the Christian world of the future, in distinction to the Church of past centuries, a markedly elective Christianity: "We are obviously dealing here with a Christianity that places the main emphasis on the personal choice of its members, on their enlightened, personal decision, on their vigorous will to carry through that decision and to conquer."[5] Kentenich distinguishes this "elective" Christianity from what he calls "inherited" Christianity:

> It is not satisfied, as was the case with inherited Christianity ("Nachwuchschristentum"), with creatively attracting others mainly by its influence and by carefully passing on common customs and morality, so that its children and members spontaneously and without reflection more or less effortlessly grew into the life, work, and being of the

Christian community. . . . An inherited Christianity is fine when Christianity governs and permeates a more or less united and insular cultural sphere. This was the case in the past, when the West was a united, Christian world. Today this is no longer true. . . . Today one has to speak of the transformation of an inherited Christianity into an elective Christianity on every continent. (p. 50)

Having sketched this picture of the Church in a pluralistic setting, Kentenich proceeds to draw the pastoral consequence for the spiritual formation of the faithful:

Therefore, present-day diaspora Catholicism has to confront its children and members all the time with making new, personal decisions. . . . It is far more important than before to train the conscience, so that it can become the immediately obligatory norm for our life and actions. It is far more necessary than before to educate ourselves and others to exercise the true freedom of God's children. . . . An elective Christianity clearly lives from this form of education for genuine and generous freedom. (p. 51)[6]

From the above it will be clear that a spirituality which attaches such a high value to the freedom and dignity of the individual Christian no longer places the Church's laws and commandments in the foreground, but rather the attractive force of the ideal of Christian holiness. Once such an attitude and form of the spiritual life has successfully made itself felt, the inner life and climate of the Church will definitely have been transformed.

This shows in particular in a second fundamental tendency of Schoenstatt's spirituality: its great emphasis on the secular reality. In an almost programmatic statement, Kentenich called this dimension "Workday Sanctity" (*Werktagsheiligkeit*). Our Christian lives must be lived in our normal working day, in the midst of the world, not in special areas and detached from the world in which we live and work. That is why Kentenich placed great emphasis, along with the great spiritual traditions, on "seeking God in all things." In the process he very consciously placed the stress on "*all* things." In explanation he added: "in all things, in all events, in all people."[7] From this one can understand why he conceived of "Workday Sanctity" as an harmonious interplay of attachment to God, our working world, and other people. Our religious life and striving to set up bonds with God can and should take place in harmony with our bonding to things and people, and should prove itself precisely there.

The theological background to this is a theology of creation that takes God's presence in the world very seriously in practice, and with great realism counts upon our bonding to created things, and very particularly to people. These bonds will mature organically under the influence of grace to bring about an ever deeper bonding with God, in accord with the laws of transference and transmission. That is to say, the creatures that reflect to us the beauty and goodness of God effectively draw us closer to God. But things have not merely the "function to attract," as Kentenich described their pedagogical purpose, but also the equally important "function to disappoint." Our hearts always want more than they can actually find in creation. According to God's plan, each such disappointment should be an invitation to make use of created things' "function to lead us further"—even though painfully—so that we may enter more deeply into God's heart.[8] In the end, every spirituality that is close to life, if it is Christian, will lead us into a personal covenant of love with God, who is our final goal.

With this vision of the future, and with his interpretation of the *vox temporis* as the *vox Dei*, Kentenich is situated right in the mainstream of the further development of the Church. The disastrous polarization between "progressive" and "conservative" tendencies, and the disproportionate concentration on problems within the Church, may blur our vision at the moment, but the Council has set the direction, and the development continues inexorably. It requires re-thinking in the Church and a liberating answer. In this sense Kentenich was a pioneer of a new, secular spirituality.

2. The Marian Modality of His Spirituality

With the second focal point of his spirituality, Kentenich finds himself completely at odds with the main trends and tendencies in the Church today. He was convinced that Mary will play a very significant role in the future development of Christianity and the life of Christians. He was not just a great devotee of Mary himself; he did not just give his spiritual family a Marian direction from the very first; he also saw Mary as the great educator of the new Christian. In his opinion, we find ourselves in that Kairos in salvation history in which the position of God's Mother in the New Testament salvation event should be fully recognized both in theology and in our actual spiritual lives.

His Marian concept has two focal points. The one is the theological clarification of Mary's objective position in God's plan of salvation; the second, which is of particular importance in our context, is the answer we give in our spiritual lives to this God-willed position.

Kentenich tried to explain Mary's position in the salvation event in his definition of her "personal character." He was well-aware that he was only taking up and giving expression to what was already there in the actual faith of the Church. He formulated his insight concisely as follows: Mary is the associate and helpmate of Christ in his entire work of redemption. Toward the end of his life, he experienced a monumental confirmation of his Mariological position. In its final chapter to the Constitution on the Church, the Second Vatican Council, in a way no previous Council had done, enlarged in detail on "the role of the Blessed Virgin in the economy of salvation" (LG 8.2.55, p. 87):

> The Blessed Virgin was eternally predestined, in conjunction with the incarnation of the divine Word, to be the Mother of God. By decree of divine Providence, she served on earth as the loving mother of the divine Redeemer, an associate of unique nobility, and the Lord's humble handmaid. She conceived, brought forth, and nourished Christ. She presented Him to the Father in the temple, and was united with Him in suffering as He died on the cross. In an utterly singular way she cooperated . . . in the Savior's work of restoring supernatural life to souls. (LG 8.3.61, p. 91)

In the understanding of the Council, Mary was the "associate" of Christ not merely because she was his physical mother, but because she accompanied him throughout his life. Outwardly accompanying him, inwardly cooperating with him, and "embracing God's saving will with a full heart," Mary "devoted herself totally, as a handmaid of the Lord, to the person and work of her Son. In subordination to Him and along with Him, by the grace of almighty God she served the mystery of redemption. Rightly therefore the holy Fathers see her as used by God not merely in a passive way, but as cooperating in the work of human salvation through free faith and obedience" (LG 8.2.56, p. 88).

Kentenich's understanding of Mary's "personal character" as "associate and helpmate of Christ" thus anticipates the very language used in the Constitution, conforms to its dogma, and actually applies it. He believed that if Mary freely cooperated in the work of human salvation during the earthly lifetime of Jesus, she surely continues to fulfill her God-given calling and mission now. She is, as Kentenich said in summary, "the associate and helpmate of Christ in his *entire* work of redemption." In other words, now that she is at the side of Jesus in heaven, she performs an on-going task in the Church and for the Church. As the Council declares, Mary's

> maternity will last without interruption until the last fulfillment of all the elect. For, taken up to heaven, she did not lay aside this saving role, but by her manifold acts of intercession continues to win for us gifts of eternal salvation. By her maternal charity, Mary cares for the brethren of her Son who still journey on earth. . . . Therefore the Blessed Virgin is invoked by the Church under the titles of Advocate, Auxiliatrix, Adjutrix, and Mediatrix. (LG 8.3.62, p. 91)

The Council finally summarized Mary's activity in the Church by stating that she "cooperates with a maternal love" in the "birth and development" of the faithful (LG 8.3.63, p. 92).

This provides us with the starting point for the pastoral and pedagogical consequences Kentenich drew from this Catholic understanding of Mary's position and activity in the salvation event. According to him, what is actually meant by the traditional invocation of Mary as "our Mother," "our Advocate," "our Mediatrix" is her task to be our motherly educator. In 1954, during the Church's first Marian Year, Kentenich enlarged upon his picture of Mary as the Educator of Christians in a series of Lenten sermons held in the Holy Cross parish in Milwaukee, Wisconsin. He started with the words Jesus spoke as he was dying, and which the Church regards as his last testament: "Ecce Mater tua," "Behold your Mother" (John 19:27). In the history of spiritualities in the Church down through the centuries these words are understood as not having been addressed to the beloved disciple alone, but in him to all Jesus' disciples throughout the ages. Mary's "spiritual motherhood" in the Church and for the Church is the real focus of her mission and activity from heaven.

This belief and vision has a very practical application with regard to our question about a lay spirituality for the postmodern era. If Mary's spiritual motherhood includes God's commission to be the "motherly educator of Christians," it must be met with a corresponding answer on our part, that is, the willingness to be educated by her. This willingness has found practical expression in the "consecration to Mary," which has been alive in the Church for centuries.[9] According to Kentenich, this is not a single, isolated, pious act, but requires us to set up inner, vital bonds with Mary in our lives, as a way to live our bonding with God. This total self-giving to Mary is an important help in our postmodern era for becoming fully human (*Mensch-werdung*) and becoming fully Christian (*Christ-werdung*).

According to Kentenich, what is of particular importance for pastoral pedagogy is that here the psychology of love has a great role to play. As person-related thinkers like Martin Buber have pointed out clearly, it is only when we give ourselves to another person that we can wholly discover and find ourselves. In the process it is important *who* the person is to whom I give myself. The deeper someone is bonded to another person, the stronger is the influence of that person on the educand's attitude. Marian movements have experienced that if people live according to their consecration, this total self-giving to Mary, they are helped to become fully human, sound personalities. Kentenich formulated this process as follows: Through bonding with Mary to a Marian attitude.

Mary stands before us as the great "believer," the "exemplary disciple" of Jesus, as the New Testament depicts her. She is the "model" for Christians, because she united her whole life with Christ and committed herself totally to his work. Mary's educational influence therefore has only one goal: that Christ may be born in us. Experience over the centuries bears witness to the truth of the motto "Per Mariam ad Jesum," "Through Mary to Jesus."

In our postmodern situation as Christians, in the midst of a pluralistic society, we have the tremendous difficulty of faith, of learning to believe. All too often the supernatural world and reality, the Persons of Christ and God the Father, seem pale and distant. Faith has often remained too intellectual; it has too seldom penetrated to the deeper levels of the soul and has not been able to send down sufficiently strong roots into our hearts. For us to survive as Christians in the icy air of the spiritual-intellectual world around us, this is not sufficient.

It seems to be sort of a Marian charism that Mary is able to connect early experiences (e.g., childhood experiences with our mothers) with central religious experiences. What results is a certain warmth and joy in the faith. This is what is meant by a saying of Pope Pius X, which Kentenich repeatedly quoted, apparently as a result of his own experiences, that devotion to Mary "is the easiest, surest, and shortest way to arrive at a 'vitalis Christi cognitio'."[10] A vital, not just an intellectual knowledge of Christ, but a self-giving to Christ that comes from the heart and is the expression of its power to love—that is what Mary wants to give us through our bonding with her.

As historical witnesses that also exercised an influence on the formation of Schoenstatt's spirituality, Kentenich had recourse to the Marian Sodalities and Grignion de Montfort. With the latter he shares a vision of the future of the Church that will be essentially influenced by Mary through the dedication of Christians to her. Already in 1954, in Milwaukee, he wrote: "It is to be expected that the consecration to Mary will prove to be a dominant and permanent gift that is intended to imprint Mary's features on the Church in a very special way. This will transfigure the Church and hence influence her future image essentially."[11]

Of course, he was aware that we are passing through an era of all-comprising chaos in which, along with many other truths of our faith, also those concerning Mary are under attack. He also saw that it is precisely the Marian dogmas and forms of spirituality that hamper ecumenical dialogue. Nevertheless, his words of farewell to his spiritual family were: "Together with Mary we go, with hope and joy, confident in the victory, into the postmodern age."[12]

When we try to summarize what has been said, I should like to take up a well-known statement of Karl Rahner and connect it with Kentenich's concept. In the last years of Rahner's life, when he saw the worsening situation of the Church in a pluralistic society, he made an almost prophetic pronouncement that was taken up everywhere by people on the alert. He said, "The faithful of the future will be mystics, or they will cease to exist."[13] What he meant was that when all outward support from a Catholic or Christian milieu falls away, when believers have to decide time and again for Christ and to live out the grace of their baptism in surroundings that follow a completely different outlook on life and way of life, they will only be able to be Christians because they are borne by the experience of a deep encounter with God. "Mysticism" is here meant in the wider sense of an experienced union with God.

I personally believe that in this point Fr. Kentenich is in complete agreement with Karl Rahner—the inmost, the deepest and most personal core of a lay spirituality is this experienced encounter with God. However, the original element that Kentenich offers the Church on the way to this goal can be added to Rahner's statement: "The faithful of the future will be *Marian* mystics, or they will cease to exist."

Notes

1.   For biographical information, see Engelbert Monnerjahn, *Father Joseph Kentenich: A Life For the Church* (Cape Town: Schoenstatt Publications, 1985).

2.   Joseph Kentenich, "Oktoberbrief, 1948," p. 18. I cite from a nonedited, private copy.

3.   Joseph Kentenich, "Wahlchristentum," *Regnum: Internationale Vierteljahresschrift der Schönstattbewegung*, Heft 2, 1990, pp. 49–50. The translation is mine.

4.   Cf. *Lumen Gentium* 33, in *The Documents of Vatican II*, gen. ed. Walter M. Abbott, S.J., trans. ed. Joseph Gallagher (The America Press, 1966), p. 59, n. 167. Hereafter I use this translation, citing passages from LG parenthetically.

5.   Kentenich, "Wahlchristentum," p. 50. Cf. Ignatius of Loyola, *Spiritual Exercises*, Twelfth Day. The quotations from "Wahlchristentum" that follow are cited parenthetically.

6.   The emphasis on freedom is characteristic of Fr. Kentenich's spirituality from its earliest expressions. In the so-called Pre-Founding Document of the Schoenstatt Work, dated 27 October 1912, he offered an acute symptomology of modernity, firmly rejected a fundamentalist course "backwards . . . to the Middle Ages," and embraced instead a communal program of concentrated self-education: "Under the protection of Mary we wish to learn to educate ourselves to become firm, free, priestly personalities" (*Schoenstatt: The Founding Documents*, privately translated and published by the Schoenstatt Sisters of Mary [Waukesha, WI, 1993], p. 15). Later, when Fr. Kentenich was arrested by the Gestapo and eventually imprisoned, along with other Schoenstatt members, in the con-

centration camp at Dachau, the gift, proper exercise and sacrifice of freedom became a dominant theme of his writings, as he directed the striving of the persecuted Schoenstatt Family toward "the glorious freedom of the children of God" (Romans 8:21).

7.   The theological context is the spirituality of faith in Divine Providence. See Joseph Kentenich, *Texte zum Vorsehungsglauben* (Vallendar: Schoenstatt, 1970).

8.   Cf. Hans-Werner Unkel, *Theorie und Praxis des Vorsehungsglaubens nach Pater Joseph Kentenich* (Vallendar: Schoenstatt, 1980), p. 129.

9.   For two recent studies of the subject, see René Laurentin, *The Meaning of Consecration Today: A Marian Model for a Secularized Age* (San Francisco: Ignatius Press, 1992); Arthur Burton Calkins, *Totus Tuus: John Paul II's Program of Marian Consecration and Entrustment* (Libertyville, IL: Academy of the Immaculate, 1992).

10.   Joseph Kentenich, *Maria, Mutter und Erzieherin: Eine angewandle Mariologie* (1954; Vallendar: Schönstatt, 1973), p. 72. The translation is mine.

11.   Ibid., p. 327.

12.   Joseph Kentenich, "Grußwort, 7 September 1968," p. 7.

13.   Karl Rahner, *Shriften zur Theologie*, Bd. 7, p. 22.

PART III

Social Representations

ANN W. ASTELL

Feminism, Deconstructing Hierarchies, and Marian Coronation

As E. R. Carroll observes, "Christian piety knows few titles for the Virgin Mary older than queen."[1] The belief in Mary's queenship—attested to in Scripture itself and clearly evident in Christian writings and art from the sixth century on[2]—has traditionally gained expression in cultic coronations, which honor Mary under various royal titles, implore her intercession, and pledge her the love and service of her subjects. Coincident with the triumphal mariology of the 1950s and renewed papal and popular declarations of Mary's sovereignty,[3] the rise of feminism as a postmodern movement has placed Mary's status as queen and the cultural symbolism of her queenship at the center of a heated debate about women's nature, mission, and subjectivity—a debate focused on issues of hierarchy.

Feminism, as an ideology and form of cultural critique, shares with postmodernism in general a radical urge toward the deconstruction of hierarchies, both conceptual and sociological. Beginning with a denial of man's ontological superiority over woman, feminism as a movement has traditionally expressed itself in demands for equal rights for women—political, educational, economic, and sexual—and extended itself into the whole-scale dismantling of patriarchal institutions, all of them based on hierarchies affirming inherent masculine superiority and preserving male control.

The fundamental terms with which feminism defines itself derive from both Hegelian and Marxist models of historical class conflict and the psychoanalysis of Freud. Conceiving of the world as composed of male "haves" and female "have nots," feminists simultaneously appropriate and reject the subject position, negating patriarchal negation as a means to obtain a new, positive self-identity. As an adversarial movement, feminism thus tends to internalize essential features of the patriarchalism it mirrors, contradicts and opposes. The woman who regards herself as not inferior to man continues, in short, to take her bearings from him and measure herself according to his standard, not her own. In the words of Luce Irigaray, "Demanding to be equal presupposes a term of comparison. Equal to what? What do women want to be equal to? Men? . . . Why not to themselves?"[4]

Perhaps the most original among French feminist philosophers, Irigaray warns that unless "women's liberation has a dimension other than the search for equality between the sexes . . . , feminism may work towards the destruction of women and, more generally, of all values" (pp. 31–32). Opposing the demands of "certain tendencies of the day" and "certain contemporary feminists" for the "neutralization of sex," Irigaray insists that "trying to suppress sexual difference is to invite a genocide more radical than any destruction that has ever existed in history" (p. 32). The historical exploitation of women, which has been "based upon sexual difference," cannot, in Irigaray's view, be resolved through the erasure of woman as a distinct *genre* of humankind; it "can only be resolved through sexual difference," through "defining the values of belonging to a sex-specific *genre*" as men and women.

The much deplored lack of an independent female standard, of a realized womanly ideal and positive role model, has prompted considerable new interest in the person of Mary. The guiding motif of "not inferior," of negated negation, however, continues to frustrate the feminist approach to Mary in two opposed, hierarchically defined directions: from below and from above. From a feminist perspective, Mary's greatness as queen, seen from below, accentuates the inferiority of ordinary fallen women. Seen from above, Mary's queenship, conferred on her by a masculine Godhead, affirms the subordination of even the greatest of women.

Marina Warner best articulates the feminist critique of Mary's dogmatic and devotional queenship. Considering the four key Marian dogmas—Mary's Immaculate Conception, her perpetual virginity, her divine motherhood, and her Assumption—Warner observes that "the Virgin Mary . . . is theologically and doctrinally defined as wholly unique and yet set up as the model of Christian virtue"[5]—the greatness of Mary's being inevitably driving her adherents into a proletarian "position of acknowledged and hopeless yearning and inferiority" (p. 337) and thus securing the Church's authority and power. As "an icon of the ideal, the Virgin affirms the inferiority of the human lot" (p. 254), her unspotted goodness preventing "the sinner from identifying with her" (p. 235) and accentuating the painful "feeling of sinfulness" (p. 254).

In Warner's analysis, Mary's hierarchical greatness, seen from below, undercuts her exemplarity for contemporary women because the ideal she represents is, by definition and in practice, "unobtainable" (p. 337). Similarly, Mary Daly observes that whereas Catholicism, unlike Protestantism, "has offered women compensatory and reflected glory through identification with Mary,"[6] its Mariology nonetheless excludes women from a full share in Mary's status on two grounds. Both "the inimitability of 'Mary conceived without sin' " and "the inimitability of the Virgin-Mother model (literally understood)" have left all women as women "in the caste with Eve" (pp. 81–82).

Mary's coronation is particularly vexing because it symbolizes Mary's elevation over other women and over humanity in general, and thus strengthens the hierarchical structuring of society as a whole. The symbolism of the crown, Warner writes, is "not innocent" (p. 104); it projects "the hierarchy of the world onto heaven," gives it divine ratification, and thus upholds "the status quo to the advantage of the highest echelons of power," honoring earthly queens "to the exclusion of other women" and the poor. Anticipating others, like Nicholas Perry and Loreto Echeverría, whose analysis of Marian dogma and devotion links it inextricably to conservative, Right Wing politics,[7] Warner finds in Mary's coronation as Queen of heaven and earth "an assertion of the Church's power" (p. 116), a support for papal authority, and a bulwark for temporal monarchies and dictatorships. Indeed, Warner insists, "It would be difficult to concoct a greater perversion of the Sermon on the Mount than the sovereignty of Mary and its cult" (p. 117).

Seen from above, Mary's queenship is equally abhorrent to Warner. Noting that artistic representations of Mary's coronation typically show her kneeling and being crowned by Christ, God the Father, or the Trinity,[8] Warner emphasizes that Mary survives as "a goddess in a patriarchal society" (p. 191) only because she herself, elevated far above other women, bows before a masculine Godhead and thus emulates the "sweetness, submissiveness, and passivity" that the Christian West expects of women in relation to men.

The feminist attempt to deconstruct these Marian hierarchies, which assign Mary a medial position above the rest of humankind and below the Father-God, has typically gone in one of two directions, both of them heterodox. The first denies Mary's supernatural greatness—her sinlessness, her virginity, her bodily assumption—in order to bring Mary closer to ordinary women and accommodate her image to what Warner calls "the new circumstances of sexual equality" (p. 339). The second emphasizes Mary's greatness to such an extent that she stands as a powerful queen and goddess ruling independently at the side of the Father-God, equal to him and in actual opposition to him.[9] Either move—to lower Mary's status or to raise her—deconstructs a hierarchy, but only at the cost of emptying Mary's historical life of its moral significance. Conceived of as either a goddess or an unexceptional woman, Mary ceases to be an inspiring ideal and example for women. In Warner's words, "Mary cannot be a model for the New Woman" (p. 238).

Warner's conclusions about the inimitability of Mary have been contested from two, very different directions: from the secular perspective of postmodern semiology, as articulated by Julia Kristeva, and that of contemporary women's religious experience, as manifested in popular piety and widespread postmodern movements of renewal within Christianity. Kristeva's critique of Warner appears in a uniquely personal 1977 essay entitled "Stabat Mater,"[10] which reflects in its form and content Kristeva's own experience of maternity.

Calling Christianity "doubtless the most refined symbolic construct in which femininity . . . is focused on Maternality," Kristeva perceives in the paradox of the Virgin-Mother "one of the most powerful imaginary constructs known in the history of civilizations."[11] Following Warner, whose influence she acknowledges, Kristeva surveys the history of Marian dogma in three main streams of development: the dogmas which assimilate Mary's life to the pattern of Christ's; the dogmas of "power," which name Mary as Lady, Protectress, and Queen; the titles and devotional images by which Mary becomes the human focus of both courtly and filial love. Unlike Warner, however, Kristeva finds in the image of Mary a remarkable portrait that satisfies all the "discontents" of the human species—a portrayal that not only "gratifies a male being" and "reduces [his] social anguish," but also "satisfies a woman so that a commonality of the sexes is set up beyond and in spite of their glaring incompatibility and permanent warfare" (p. 163).

Kristeva's recognition that the image of Mary provides in the Catholic world a crucial means of mediation between the sexes recalls Luce Irigaray's insistence that defining the difference between man and woman must be coupled with the discovery of a "third term" to intervene in the male/female binary, occupy the "gap" between the sexes, and thus unite them. Irigaray herself characterizes this third thing which inhabits "the realm of sexual difference" as a mutually experienced "feeling of wonder, surprise, and astonishment in the face of the unknowable."[12] While, she says, "this communion is often left to the child, who is a symbol of an alliance" (p. 176) between the sexes, the bond "uniting or reuniting masculine and feminine must be both horizontal and vertical, terrestrial and celestial" (p. 174). "For this," she says, "we need 'God,' or a love so scrupulous that it is divine" (p. 176). While Irigaray suggests that angels, as divine mediators who "circulate" among God and men and women, best represent this divine/secular presence, Kristeva points instead to the image of Mary the Mediatrix.

Kristeva's analysis focuses on the paradoxes characteristic of Marian dogma—Mary's sinless humanity, virginal motherhood, imitable singularity, deathless death, humble queenship. Taking a psychoanalytic approach, Kristeva argues that the virginal-maternal image of Mary answers to deep-set human fears and longings and represents "a way (not among the less effective ones) of dealing with feminine paranoia" (p. 180) through a "skillful balance of concessions and constraints" (p. 181). In the present-day secular world where "that clever balanced architecture . . . appears to be crumbling"—a "motherless" world deprived of the cultural influence Marian dogma once exerted—women are newly vulnerable to the various forms of feminine paranoia, some of which are manifested in Kristeva's own fragmented, nightmarish musings about pregnancy, labor and birth, which intrude in a contrastive typeface upon the main body of her text.

In giving birth to a son, in becoming a mother herself, however, Kristeva identifies in a new way with not only her natural mother but also Mary, the Sorrowful Mother, whose mother-love for the Crucified sets the standard for an unconditional love that is stronger than death and which exceeds in its demands the claims that mere morality derives from the Law. Unlike Warner, therefore, Kristeva turns and returns to Mary as an unsurpassed model of, and the indispensable cultural symbol for, the selfless, death-defying mother-love that Kristeva calls "herethics." Even today, perhaps especially today, as Kristeva says, "the music of the *Stabat Mater* . . . swallows up the goddesses and removes their necessity" (p. 185).

The purely secular, "religionless Christianity" of Kristeva's semiological and psychological refutation of Warner complements the refutation that comes from the side of popular piety and contemporary Marian spirituality within the Church. In opposition to Warner's prediction of an inevitable decline in Mary's cult and a rejection of her regal image, the last two decades have witnessed a charismatic awakening of popular devotion to Mary the Queen, especially through the publicized reports of visionaries and international pilgrimages made to the sites of various apparitions.[13]

The frequency and urgency of modern Marian apparitions, beginning with those at LaSalette (1846) and Lourdes (1858), have helped to inspire widespread movements of renewal within the Church and new lay spiritualities with a definitive Marian character. What unites them all is the insistence that genuine devotion to Mary requires not only veneration and invocation, but also imitation—so much so that Mary can actually appear again on earth in every person consecrated to her. Both the Focolare and the Schoenstatt Movements, for instance, emphasize the Christian calling to be an *altera Maria*, a living apparition of Mary, an *apparitio Matris*. In the words of Fr. Joseph Kentenich, Founder of Schoenstatt, "May everyone who sees us, wherever we may be, be increasingly directed by our appearance, by our whole being, to the appearance, the being, the life-work of the Blessed among women."[14]

The compelling idea that the Mother of God wants to appear again on earth—not only in multiple visionary sites and shrines, but also in every child of God and in the Church as a whole—combines Marian coronation and imitation in a way that feminist thinking has generally termed impossible. As we have seen, Warner and Daly regard Mary's cultic coronation as separating her from other women; Mary's dogmatic perfection as precluding identification with her.[15] Warner, moreover, acknowledges in the prologue to her book that her theoretical understanding is the "outcome of a private journey" and rests on the assumption that "millions of Catholics," especially women, have had the "same [exclusionary] experience" of Mary.[16] In direct contradiction of Warner's view, however, a strong coronation trend in Schoenstatt has intensified the striving in the Apostolic Movement as a whole, and especially in the women's branches, to be and become "Mary for our times." Not all women, in short, share in the experience that Warner de-

scribes. The question therefore arises: What does Marian coronation signify within Schoenstatt spirituality, and how does it reconcile Mary's exceptional greatness and giftedness, on the one hand,
with her universal imitability, on the other?

Schoenstatt's founder, Fr. Joseph Kentenich, prepared the
Schoenstatt Family to crown the picture of our Lady of Schoenstatt for the first time in 1939, when the rise of National Socialism
in Germany and the beginning of World War II signalled a time of
persecution for the Apostolic Movement and its leaders. Later, on
October 18, 1944, Kentenich and a small group of fellow prisoners
in the concentration camp at Dachau offered a crown to the Mother
Thrice Admirable as Queen of the World. At the end of the war
Kentenich returned alive to Schoenstatt, and on October 18, 1946
he solemnly renewed the two previous coronations in an assembly
of the Schoenstatt Family. Since then the coronation trend has
spread through the ranks of the Movement, and the picture of the
Mother Thrice Admirable and Queen of Schoenstatt has been
crowned on public and private occasions, by priests and lay people
alike, in Schoenstatt Shrines and churches, in schools, hospitals,
homes and offices all around the world.

When Kentenich articulates the reasons for the act of coronation, he typically begins by reviewing Mary's titles to queenship—
in particular, her Divine Motherhood, which makes her "Queen
Mother" in relation to Christ the King, and the "right of conquest"
by which Mary, as Christ's Bride and Co-Redemptrix, has merited
queenship through her unique cooperation in the completed and
on-going, objective and subjective, work of redemption. Kentenich
then emphasizes yet a third reason for crowning Mary as Queen:
the right of election. To crown Mary is to choose her voluntarily as
Queen, "to elevate her again and again, freely and willingly, to the
throne of our family and of our hearts."[17] Thus the act of coronation
in Schoenstatt always implies a personal consecration and instrumental self-surrender to Mary, and the willingness to be used by
her as her child and instrument in the spirit of the inscription:
servus Mariae.[18]

When Kentenich articulates these three Marian titles of
queenship—inheritance, conquest, and election—he recalls traditional Catholic teaching. Schoenstatt is original, however, in its
treatment of the act of election as mutual and in its emphasis on
the reciprocity of consecration and coronation. This mutuality and
reciprocity, which essentially characterizes Schoenstatt's Covenant spirituality, answers to the problem highlighted by the femi-

nist critique—namely, the apparent gap between Mary's unique supernatural greatness and her universal model character.

The so-called "little consecration" that Schoenstatters use daily to renew their Covenant of Love with our Lady of Schoenstatt is a traditional prayer commonly used in Marian Sodalities. It begins with the words: "My Queen, my Mother, I give myself entirely to you." As Kentenich understood and explained it, however, "The covenant character presupposes that when we address our Lady, when we offer ourselves to her, when we give ourselves to her, she does the same to us."[19] He insists that the consecration prayer is actually a dialogue, not a monologue; that the donation of self is not one-sided, but rather a mutual exchange between the Covenant partners; and that "when we say: I give you my eyes, I give you my hands, I give you my heart, we should hear in faith: But I also give you my eyes, my hands, my heart."[20]

This emphasis on a mutual consecration and bilateral Covenant relationship between the Blessed Mother and her devotees affected Kentenich's interpretation of both Marian instrumentality and the cultic act of coronation. To be "an instrument in Mary's hand" is not, in his understanding, so much to be used by her as her slave and servant, but to be her child, a living image of Mary, vitally united with her in attitude and action, and therefore an extension of Mary's own self.[21] The so-called "Instruments' Hymn," composed by Kentenich in Dachau, implores the Blessed Mother: "Keep us as your instruments, now and always, Queen and Mother. . . . Let us walk like you through life. Let us mirror you forever. / Strong and noble, meek and mild, peace and love be our endeavor. / Walk in us through our world. Make it ready for the Lord."

The coronation that symbolizes such an instrumental surrender is similarly understood to be mutual. As Kentenich explained in 1967,

> It works like this (as we have always seen it in our family): to the extent and at the moment that we place the crown on the head of our Lady in acknowledgement of her sovereignty, she gives us the crown in return. At the very same moment as we crown her, she makes us little kings and queens. . . . [She makes us] aware of our rank as a child of God and member of Christ.[22]

Unlike Warner, who finds "both humanity and women . . . subtly denigrated" (p. xxi) in the coronation of Mary, Kentenich sees the acknowledgement of Mary's queenship in symbol and practice as a way to counteract human degradation in all its contemporary forms, from the overt attack on life itself, to sexual harassment and promiscuity, to the crippling loss of self-esteem, motivation, idealism and hope that is so evident today, especially among women, racial and ethnic minorities, the young, and the poor.[23]

Honoring Mary is, he insists, the way to gain possession of our own royal selves and discover the human dignity in others. Crowning Mary allows us to discern "a mysterious marian crown on the head of every woman and girl"; in her "woman has again become a queen."[24] In the image of *Maria Regina* we do not only find "a clear concept of the fully redeemed person," but also "a climax and direction for human striving."[25] In Mary we not only see "the idealization of our own nature,"[26] but through her motherly mediation we also receive the means, the grace, and the guidance to realize it, as far as that is possible on earth. Mary offers us, as Kentenich often said, love for love, faithfulness for faithfulness, a crown for a crown.

Kentenich's emphasis on a mutual coronation clearly affirms the hierarchical relationships feminism attempts to deconstruct. Seen from below, "Mary outshines all created things here on this earth. . . . She is the Queen of Apostles, the Queen of Martyrs, the Queen of Virgins, the Queen of All Saints. . . . She is simply the crown of the whole human race."[27] Seen from above, "Mary is and remains a created being. Even though she is the masterpiece of God's omnipotence, wisdom, and kindness, there is an infinite distance between her and the infinite God."[28]

At the same time, however, Schoenstatt's spirituality puts these hierarchies into a creative, dialogic interaction that avoids the psychological, theological, and social dangers attendant upon a one-sided, monologic experience of them. Unlike Warner, for whom Mary's divine greatness either precludes her human smallness, or vice versa, Kentenich sees the Marian mystery as encompassing both smallness and greatness, humanity and divinity: "Lowliness and exaltation—these are two abysses which condition each other and attract each other. How vitally all this was actualized in the life of the Mother of God,"[29] who is both the humble Handmaid of the Lord and the sovereign Queen of Heaven. In Schoenstatt the act of crowning Mary as Queen allows that same Marian mystery to become experiential in the lives of Mary's children who are great not in spite of, but precisely because they are small, crowned because they crown.

In the image of the one paying homage to the Other—the child kneeling before Mary's picture, or Mary herself kneeling before the Divine Child in the crib—feminists like Marina Warner, Mary Daly, and Simone de Beauvoir tend to see only a humiliating female defeat. Julia Kristeva reminds us, however, that Mary's humility has "its counterpart in gratification and *jouissance*," that "the low-ered head of the mother before her son is accompanied by the immeasurable pride of the one who knows she is also his wife and daughter" (p. 172). The paradox to which Kristeva points, which discovers in the distance between us and Mary, between Mary and God, a "third term" of ecstatic wonderment, is the same paradox to which the act of coronation gives expression in a reciprocal ex-change of visible and invisible crowns. As an outward sign of a mutual covenant of love, the exchange of crowns—from below and from above—reverses all hierarchies, even as it upholds them, and allows the humility of God and Mary to exceed our own. Human and divine, "all love crowns."[30]

Notes

1. E. R. Carroll, "Mary, Queenship of," in *The New Catholic Ency-clopedia*, Vol. 9 (New York: McGraw-Hill, 1967), p. 386.

2. Elizabeth hails Mary as "the Mother of my Lord" (Luke 1:43), using the Old Testament phrase for a Queen-Mother to honor the royal Mother of the Messiah, and the Johannine description of the woman adorned with the sun and crowned with stars (Apoc. 12:1) soon gained a Marian interpretation. A fresco on a wall of the Church of S. Maria Antiqua (early sixth century) in Rome shows a crowned image of Maria Regina. Among the traditional hymns honoring Mary as Queen, "Regina Caeli" and "Ave Regina Caelo-rum" date from the tenth century, "Salve Regina" from the twelfth. Among the early Western theologians who honored Mary as Queen are Idelfonsus of Toledo (d. 667), Ambrose Autpert (d. 784) and Paschasius Radbert (d. 860). For a survey of historical references to Mary as Queen, see Hilda C. Graef, *Mary: A History of Doctrine and Devotion*, 2 vols. (London and New York: Sheed and Ward, 1963). See also S. G. Matthews, ed., *Queen of the Universe* (St. Meinrad, IN: St. Meinrad Seminary, 1957).

3. Pope Pius XII consecrated the world to the Immaculate Heart of Mary, Mother and Queen on October 31, 1942; dogmatized her

Assumption in 1950; and declared her Queen of Heaven in 1954. See *Munificentissimus Deus*, ActApS 42 (1950): 768–69; *Ad Caeli Reginam*, ActApS 46 (1954): 625–40.

4. Luce Irigaray, "Equal or Different?" trans. David Macey, in *The Irigaray Reader*, ed. Margaret Whitford (Oxford: Basil Blackwell, 1991), p. 32. The passages that follow immediately, cited parenthetically, are from the same essay.

5. Marina Warner, *Alone of All Her Sex: The Myth and Cult of the Virgin Mary* (New York: Macmillan, 1976; Vintage Books, 1983), p. 334. Subsequent citations are parenthetical.

6. Mary Daly, *Beyond God the Father: Toward a Philosophy of Women's Liberation* (Boston: Beacon Press, 1973), p. 81. Subsequent citations are parenthetical.

7. See Nicholas Perry and Loreto Echeverría, *Under the Heel of Mary* (London and New York: Routledge, 1988).

8. See also Penny Schine Gold, *The Lady and the Virgin: Image, Attitude, and Experience in Twelfth-century France* (Chicago: The University of Chicago Press, 1985). Art historians indicate that the earliest representations of Mary as Queen (as, for example, in the twelfth-century apse of S. Maria Trastevere) show her already crowned and enthroned next to Christ, whereas later representations depict her kneeling and being crowned.

9. See, for example, Daly, p. 87; James M. Somerville, "Maria Avatara," in *The Goddess Re-Awakening: The Feminine Principle Today*, ed. Shirley Nicholson (Wheaton: The Theosophical Publishing House, 1989), pp. 179–86. The treatment of Mary as a goddess owes much to Jungian archetypal theory. It extends the theological view of Mary as co-regent, which in the late Middle Ages sometimes opposed Mary's mercy to Christ's justice, depicted her as the powerful equal of Christ, and emphasized her intercessory powers on behalf of humankind to the exclusion of her personal adoration of God and obedience to his will. See Graef, p. 297. The extent of Mary's power as Queen has not gained a definitive dogmatic statement.

10. The title of the essay alludes to Jacopone da Todi's famous medieval sequence about the sufferings of the Sorrowful Mother at

the time of the Crucifixion. Many composers, among them, Palestrina, Pergolesi, Haydn, and Rossini, have set it to music.

11.   Julia Kristeva, "Stabat Mater," in *The Kristeva Reader* (New York: Columbia University Press, 1986), pp. 161, 163. Subsequent citations are parenthetical.

12.   Irigaray, "Sexual Difference," trans. Seán Hand, in *The Irigaray Reader*, pp. 171–72. Subsequent citations are parenthetical.

13.   See Joan Ashton, *Mother of All Nations: Visions of Mary* (Harper San Francisco, 1989) for an account of recent apparitions in Yugoslavia, Africa, Italy, Australia, Nicaragua, Portugal, Ireland, Egypt, France, Japan, and Spain. As Ashton notes, "In most of her manifestations [Mary's] aspect has corresponded partly if not entirely with the great sign in Heaven of the Book of Revelation, Chapter 12" (pp. 11–12). These regal apparitions of Mary—among which the appearances in Fatima (1917) and Medjugorie are probably the best known—combine motherly tenderness and queenly power in the person of Mary with apocalyptic warnings and calls to conversion, prayer, and penance.

14.   Fr. Joseph Kentenich, *Sign of Light for the World*, translated and privately published by the Schoenstatt Sisters of Mary (Constantia, South Africa, 1980), pp. 12–13.

15.   As Lawrence Cunningham observes, "For feminist critics like Warner, the Virgin reflects a kind of profound schizophrenia in Christianity. Mary is honored as the ideal feminine but, in that very act of honor, other women are degraded" ("Mary and Contemporary Experience," in *Mother of God* [San Francisco: Harper and Row, 1982], p. 96).

16.   Warner talks about herself as a "devout Mariolater" (p. xxi) in a Catholic school where "holiness [was] a shallow affair" (p. xx) consisting of beautiful ceremonies, and where she experienced "absolute misery . . . when confronted, in puberty, by the Church's moral teaching." Her book, she says, has resulted from an attempt to understand her childhood and adolescent experience of Mary's holiness.

17.   Joseph Kentenich, "Second Founding Document, October 18, 1939," in *Schoenstatt: The Founding Documents*, rev. ed., privately

translated and published by the Schoenstatt Sisters of Mary (Waukesha, WI, 1993), p. 45.

18.   Leaden seals with the inscription "servus Mariae" date from the fifth or sixth century and attest to an early Christian trend of consecration to her. In the Middle Ages Mary often received chivalric honors as a lady served by her knights and courtly lovers. In the seventeenth and eighteenth centuries Saints Alphonsus Ligouri, John Eudes, and Louis de Montfort promoted practices of "the slavery of Mary." The lightframe in the Schoenstatt Shrine spells out the words: "Servus Mariae numquam peribit."

19.   Joseph Kentenich, "My Queen, My Mother: Extracts From a Talk Given to the Schoenstatt Family, 22 January 1967, at Dietershausen," privately translated and published by the Schoenstatt Sisters of Mary, n.d.

20.   Ibid.

21.   The traditional motto, "Servus Mariae numquam peribit," which appears above the altar in the Schoenstatt Shrine is regularly translated, not according to its literal Latin meaning ("A *slave* or *servant* of Mary will never perish"), but in the context of Schoenstatt's Covenant spirituality: "A *child* of Mary will never perish" (stress added). In Schoenstatt the emphasis on the gender-neutral "child" (in German, *das Kind*), which is often used to characterize both Mary's and Christ's relationship to God, enhances Mary's ability to mediate in what Irigaray calls the "divine space" between the sexes, unite them in a common spirituality, and serve as a model for men and women alike.

22.   Kentenich, "My Queen, My Mother."

23.   The Schoenstatt Movement has proven its effectiveness not only in the inner cities of the United States and Europe, but also in third world and developing countries, such as Burundi, South Africa, India, the Philippines, Mexico, the Dominican Republic, and many South American countries. For a recent study that combines Mariology with Liberation Theology, see Leonardo Boff, O.F.M., *The Maternal Face of God: The Feminine and Its Religious Expressions*, trans. Robert R. Barr and John W. Diercksmeier (San Francisco: Harper and Row, 1987).

24.   Joseph Kentenich, *The Jewel of Purity*, 2nd ed., privately translated and published by the Schoenstatt Sisters of Mary (Waukesha, WI, 1973), p. 7.

25.   Kentenich, *Sign of Light*, p. 18.

26.   Ibid., p. 10.

27.   Ibid., pp. 45, 51.

28.   Joseph Kentenich, *God My Father*, privately translated and published by the Schoenstatt Sisters of Mary (Waukesha, WI, 1977, repr. 1992), p. 66.

29.   Joseph Kentenich, *He Exalts the Lowly*, trans. M. J. Hoehne, privately published by the Schoenstatt Sisters of Mary (Waukesha, WI, 1982), p. 35.

30.   The last phrase is an oft-repeated motto in Schoenstatt.

THOMAS RYBA

Postmodernism and the Spirituality of the Liberal Arts: A Neo-Hegelian *Diagnôsis* and an Augustinian *Pharmakon*

The love of money is the root of all evil.

1 Timothy 6:10

Some years ago when I was Director of Planning, Research and Evaluation at Harry S. Truman College in Chicago, I sat on a committee constituted to increase the enrollments. Within committee, there were some fundamental disagreements about which strata of the population of Chicago were to be our target groups. Some of the committee members were in favor of the "sow's ear" approach—as I like to call it. They wanted to improve the image of the college to make it more appealing to those Yuppies who had begun to gentrify the area in their never ending quest for cheap properties to rehabilitate and resell. Since our college was located in the Uptown area of Chicago, this posed a difficult problem.

Uptown, a fashionable neighborhood in the 30's—and favorite crib for mobsters—had become by the early 80's a neighborhood of crack and flop houses, drug and psychiatric halfway houses, and wino bars, as well as a roosting place for immigrant minorities, recently arrived in this country but in flight to other more hospitable environs. On Friday and Saturday nights, Wilson Avenue—the avenue that runs directly in front of the college—turned into a sexual smorgasbord; anything wanted sexually could be had, and in any permutation and combination. On weekend nights, a steady procession of cars driven by "coke heads," "chicken hawks" (pedophiles) and other heterosexual and homosexual buyers cruised the neighborhood hoping for a drug score, a sexual score, or both.

Half of our committee members believed that we should concentrate our energies on improving the image of our college; that we should de-emphasize its real nature, location and student body and develop a *positive* image which would attract a "better" clientele. The other half thought we should concentrate on the college's strengths within the reality it inhabited and thus attract students from the surrounding neighborhoods, students who otherwise had no hope of a college education. Ultimately, the disagreement came down to one about the mission of Truman College. I counted myself among the group that saw the college's mission as one to the community. We argued that the college should serve as a point of political crystallization and action. The other group thought in terms of what the college ought to be, assuming that the gentrification would eventually be complete so that the college ought to begin to court the Yuppie vanguard. The President, who was both more opportunistic and politically expedient than any member of either group, had his own *agendum* (for which the notion of the college's mission was just so much window dressing). After one heated discussion, I tried to lay out the arguments in support of an enrollment campaign which would treat the college as it actually existed and according to its mission to the community in which it found itself. To underscore my points I remember saying, "In short we simply ought to tell the *truth* about Truman College, we simply ought to tell the *truth*." I remember the response of the President because of the chilling chord it struck in me and some of the others. He thought a moment and then grinning his best used-car salesman smile he said, "The truth. Now, *there's* an idea. It just might *sell*." The response of Truman College's president in his equation of the truth with an idea and an idea with a commodity form, the social dynamic of the environment in which Truman College was nested, the attempt of a faction of the enrollment committee to substitute a nonexistent image for the reality which truly grounded the college, these are all aspects of education in a postmodern world.

It is the thesis of this paper that what was especially intensified at Truman College in the early 80's has become more generally symptomatic of the character of education—and more specifically liberal education—under the conditions of postmodernism. But it is also my thesis that postmodernism is merely the complex of symptoms of a deeper malady. Given this thesis, it is my purpose in this paper to diagnose the phenomenon known as postmodernism. This means that I shall give a neo-Hegelian reading of postmodernism to show it to be a deceptive set of symptoms representing a deeper, underlying malaise. After explaining the grounding of the phenomenon of postmodernism in the deeper (but hidden) essential condition of our time, I hope to show how the Augustinian spirituality can provide a medicine for the amelioration of this contemporary *Zeitgeist*. The equation of the *Zeitgeist* and the essential condition of the time is possible along both Marxist and Thomistic lines, the soul—according to St. Thomas—being the form of the body, and the essence of social relations—according to Marx—being rooted in the relations of production.

1. A Neo-Hegelian Diagnosis of the Postmodern Symptomology

There is a tendency among those thinkers who have resignedly accepted the postmodern condition to portray postmodernism as the inevitable result of intellectual production. Although postmodernists generally construe the history of philosophy and the history of hermeneutics in a fashion which is not developmental, they nevertheless imagine that postmodernism—as a movement which puts an end to the hope for finality or totality—is at least a positive development in this sense. One of the difficulties with the case they make for the paradoxical finality or totality of postmodernism is that this case is generally driven exclusively by concerns which come from within philosophy or hermeneutic theory. They often portray much of the debate over postmodernism as a theoretical enterprise in such a way that theory is pictured as calling social realities into existence. In their fear of totalizing explanatory theories, they ignore the material and practical grounding of theoretical discourse. Moreover, with rare exception, they foreclose the hope that something beyond the postmodern is even conceivable. Though they may make reference to external social conditions to prove that this new *epistêmê* accurately describes the contemporary reality, they almost never pose the question as to whether the notion of postmodernism, perhaps, stands to social realities as an ideological superstructure.

In fact, it is my thesis that this is precisely the relationship between postmodern intellectual production and the real world. To put it simply, I will argue in this section that postmodernism, as a philosophy of contemporary existence, stands to the economic base of late capitalism as a reflex of that base, and that cultural existence and societal relations in the late twentieth century are the phenomenal surface of a deeper economic essence. This thesis has uncomfortable implications for the elite involved in cultural productions, perhaps the most annoying of which is that in attempting to be radically *avant garde* in their fragmentation of reality, they are actually cooperating with the cunning of capitalism in its most recently developed form. In short, it is an implication of my thesis that some of the most anti-bourgeois of twentieth century thinkers are in reality the most bourgeois. Though this thesis has a Marxist flair about it, my argument should not be interpreted as indicating complicity with the Marxist project. Though I accept the Marxist analysis of societal relations in part, I reject Marxism's totalizing eschatology. (I also reject as incomplete and distorted his notions of human nature and class conflict.) In the same way, though I shall employ the Hegelian interpretation of appearance to characterize the postmodern form of life, I reject the claim of the Hegelian philosophy to have provided—before the fact—a road map of Spirit's course and its ultimate destination. If there is any sense in which my own thesis is postmodern, it is in the rejection of any philosophical claims to a realized totalization or of any society's legitimate claims to totalitarian control. The eclecticism with which I freely borrow from Hegel, Marx and Augustine to demonstrate my thesis might also—wrongly—be construed as postmodern, as well. This is a charge I deny. In this respect, I simply claim to be a part of a Christian philosophical and theological tradition going back to Pantaenus Sicilianus.

The touchstone for a diagnosis of postmodernism is contained in those passages in Hegel's works where he presents his descriptions of appearance. The most vivid of these occurs in the *Phenomenology of Spirit* where he describes appearance as follows:

> Appearance is the process of arising into being and passing away again, a process that itself does not arise and pass away, but is *per se*, and constitutes reality and the life-movement of truth. The truth is thus the bacchanalian revel, where not a member is sober; and because every member no sooner becomes detached than it *eo ipso* collapses straight-away, the revel is just as much a state of transparent unbroken calm. Judged by that movement, the particular shapes which the mind assumes do not indeed subsist any more than do determinate thoughts or ideas;

but they are, all the same, as much positive and necessary moments, as negative and transitory. In the entirety of the movement, taken as an unbroken quiescent whole, that which obtains distinctness in the course of its process and secures specific existence, is preserved in the form of self-recollection, in which existence is self-knowledge, and self-knowledge, again, is immediate existence.[1]

Later, Hegel tells us that appearance never exists immediately for consciousness but must always be mediated by consciousness. To attempt to understand the fragmentation and pure difference which characterizes the realm of appearance, a realm which is as much a realm of melded homogeneity, consciousness returns to itself for the criterion of appearance's truth. In so doing, however, it distinguishes the realm of appearance as a realm of external, objective processes over and against its own subjectivity which is not similarly protean. It thus looks to itself for the truth about the contradictions in the realm of appearance. "Away remote from the changing vanishing present (*Diesseits*) lies the permanent beyond (*Jenseits*): an immanent inherent reality (*ein Ansich*), which is the first and therefore imperfect manifestation of reason . . . " (p. 191). The result, according to Hegel, is that our consciousness' attempt to read this appearance is analogous to a syllogistic inference where the major proposition = the inner being of things, the minor proposition = the appearance of things, and the conclusion = our understanding (ibid). But it is a syllogism in which the middle term possesses an over-determination of meaning. It means so many things that it means nothing. In other words, we are in the position of the thinker who has the conclusion and the apparently meaningless middle term of the proposition but who must find the major premise, a major premise about the inner being of things, this inner being having been concretely and contradictorily instantiated in the realm of appearances. The difficulty is that the contradictory nature of the realm of appearance makes such an abduction impossible. The nothingness of the realm of appearance is such that it suggests nothing about its relevance for understanding or about its relation to the general nature of reality.

Now Hegel was aware that understanding might stop precisely at this point. For example, Kant's attachment of a subjective meaning to appearance "put the abstract essence immovably outside . . . [of appearance] as the thing-in-itself beyond the reach of our cognition."[2] But neither subjective idealism—with its exclusive knowability of phenomena—nor any approach which attempts to return to objectivity and totality through abstract immediacy will be sufficient. Rather, Hegel's insight is that the turning point for the understanding of appearance is reached when we realize that "it is the very nature of the world of immediate objects to be appearance only. Knowing it to be so, we know at the same time the essence, which, far from staying behind or beyond the appearance, rather manifests its own essentiality by deposing the world to a mere appearance" (*Logic*, p. 188). The way this deposition is accomplished is through reflection upon how we can make sense of appearance. Appearance is understood as manifesting the truth of reality only when one has understood how and why the instrumentalities of consciousness function to bring reality out of appearances. But this is an understanding which cannot confuse reality with either appearance, *per se*, or the instrumentalities which are useful in its interpretation. Appearance, for Hegel, thus functions like a partially silvered pane of glass. In mediating the outside view it also reflexively makes us aware that it is only a view *for someone*. Without the instrumentality of that pane (that is, appearance) we would have no awareness that the experience of the scene was positional, that is to say that it had a subjective center. But in coming to this awareness we also look beyond the pane which—dissolving in its instrumentality—becomes transparent to us, the viewers.

There are, in these meditations of Hegel, some affinities with Walter Truett Anderson's description of the postmodern worldview as *practical* self-consciousness of "the belief-about-belief."[3] But there is a major difference. Anderson, like many postmodern thinkers, forever throws away the hope that any *epistêmê* can have complete explanatory sufficiency, whereas Hegel believes that in reflecting upon the purpose and use of various epistemological paradigms it is possible to understand the reality they mediate. In short, Hegel does not make the typical postmodernist inferential leap: that from the obsolescence of all previous epistemological paradigms, one can jump to the conclusion that there will never be a final paradigm or that there is no such thing as truth. Rightly or wrongly, Hegel claimed to have discovered a method by which the progression of successive epistemologies could be read as disclosing the possible relations between consciousness and supersensible reality. His only error was in imagining that he could see the final end of the path.

Marx adopted the Hegelian notion of appearance as a point of departure useful for diagnosing the dissonances between the appearance of a societal form and its underlying material essence. Unlike Hegel's understanding of epistemological development, the Marxist analysis presupposed the importance of material conditions, particularly the organization of the means of production, as the driving force not only behind societal relations but also as that which was ultimately responsible for the various epistemological paradigms which surfaced throughout history. Inasmuch as these paradigms have most often reflected the reality of the organization of the means of production, they have generally reflected the interests of those who control these means. In short, the dominant ideologies of any period are conscious or unconscious reflections of the values of the economic elite. It is to the advantage of the ruling elite to keep this economic structure and the values which drive it hidden. As John McMurtry put it: "[I]t is always the case with the mature Marx that he sees in the ruling-class economic structure and its laws the 'inner-most secret' of this or any other historical society; the 'secret' that is systematically 'hidden' by the legal and political superstructure, the ideology, and the forms of social consciousness of the society in question. . . ."[4]

When the contradictions between forms of social practice are profound, Marxists read this as indicating a basic instability in the society, an instability attributable to class conflict rooted in a fundamentally unjust economic system. The more just the economic system, the fewer the contradictions between theory and practice. For Marx, the ideal society would arrive when social appearance no longer masked economic reality but when the social and economic were in concord and clear for all to see without illusions. But this presupposes the arrival of a society in which class conflict had ceased and the dissonance between theory and practice was resolved. Thus, just as the actual or the substantial stands behind appearances for Hegel, so too a notion of a hidden essence (of society's economic base) stands behind the deceptive appearances by which a society tries to cover its conflicts and its underlying reality.

What I should like to suggest is that Marx's appreciation of the diagnostic value of the Hegelian notion of appearance shows us the way to find what grounds the appearances of postmodernism. It helps us to understand that postmodernism as a condition (and as a worldview) is nothing more than the ideological reflection of late-twentieth-century capitalism. In other words, for all their talk about the anti-totalitarian dimensions of a worldview which sees difference as primary, in which the possibility of any totalizing epistemologies, ethics, politics or histories has been negated, and in which individual freedom is unbridled, the postmodernists have become marionettes who—for the most part—are unaware of the ideological relations binding them to an economic form. Because they share a form of life in which human social reality is fragmented, and because they assign the status of ultimacy to their worldview, they find it impossible to think about reality in any way which makes it other than fragmented. The result is an orientation to existence in which the exhaustion of thought and moral values is thematic.

The difficulty, as Jean Baudrillard has observed, is that the protean nature of capitalism has allowed it to undergo a number of mutations never anticipated by Marx.[5] (So much for Marxist science's ability to predict specific historical outcomes.) According to Baudrillard, capitalism has entered a triumphant phase characterized by a new set of economic conversion laws. These laws are the abstract representations of those concrete historical relations which are the hidden form beneath the contemporary raiment of culture, a raiment mirrored in the Hegelian notion of appearance. In this new historical phase, economic exchange value has been superseded by sign exchange value, and the economic infrastructure determinative of exchange value has been supplanted by the various coda which determine the value of semiotic exchange. The new tableau of relations consists of those fundamental laws representing the transmutability of use value, economic exchange value, sign exchange value and symbolic exchange.

The notions of use value and economic exchange value are a part of the standard Marxist technical vocabulary. According to Marx, the use value of things or commodities is the utility of a thing. It is (a) "limited by the physical properties of the commodity," (b) "has no existence apart from that commodity," (c) is "independent of the amount of labor required to appropriate its useful qualities," (d) becomes "a reality only by use or consumption," (e) "serve[s] directly as the means of existence" and (f) "do[es] not express the social relations of production."[6] The wealth of a society is based upon use value, in the final instance.

On the other hand, the exchange value—as expressive of "the proportion in which values of one sort are exchanged for those of another sort"—seems to be accidentally related to the time, place and circumstances of the exchange (*Capital* 1:43). This accidental appearance of exchange value is deceptive because, according to Marx, the abstract labor invested in the production of a commod-

ity (which is measured temporally, qualitatively and quantita-
tively) provides the universal feature upon which exchange may be
objectively based. The ease or difficulty with which a commodity is
produced is proportional to its exchange value, and both the conditions of production and exchange value are, in turn, a reflection of
the development of the means of production in that society. The
exchange value of a commodity is thus the measure of the labor
value attached to it under particular conditions of production.
What this means is that the exchange value stands to the relations
of production as its shroud of appearances, a sort of Hegelian phenomenal shroud which simultaneously covers and discloses the
underlying form of social relations of production. Commodities are
exchanged either for commodities or for capital (which is the ab-
straction of the exchange value of commodities). Things with use
values need not embody labor value, as is the case with pristine
nature. Also, things may embody labor value without being commodities, if there is no desire on the part of their owner to trade
them (*Capital* 1:47–48).

Baudrillard takes the Marxist understanding a step yet further
to accommodate the radical changes symptomatic of postmodern
capitalism. In late capitalism, the notion of utility is no longer the
reality principle of the object, but is augmented (or replaced) by
the notion of its signification. He argues that a further variety of
exchange must be introduced to make the behavior of individuals
under the condition of postmodernism intelligible. This is sign exchange value. Postmodern society is distinguished from classical
capitalist society in that economic circulation is not limited to
commodities and capital but extends to a new realm, that of signs.
In addition to commodity production, the postindustrial society is
also driven by productive semiosis which consists of the creation of
values and coda which dictate the legibility of objects. However,
signs or coda cannot be properly equated with the use value or
exchange value of other commodities because they do not admit of
crystallizing labor in quite the same way as other capitalist commodities. Their value lies in the aura of signification they confer
upon their objects, possessors or manipulators in terms of prestige,
power, smartness, etc., a kind of value which is not necessarily
related to the sedimentation of labor power. If use may be spoken
of at all, the usefulness of these signs is found in their power to
generate capital or confer power, a utility which—because of the
nature of these signs—comes *ex nihilo* from the desires elicited
from semiotic consumers by the emblematic attractiveness of

these signs under the conditions of their manipulation by the media wizards. Thus, though demarcating a distinct realm of value, signs can be *exchanged* for capital or commodities. Semiotic production, therefore, takes its place in postmodern, postindustrial society alongside commodity production, and issues from semiotics mills (such as advertising agencies and political consultancy firms) where account executives, spin doctors and image makers loom appearances in which commodities and personalities can be cloaked and invested with magical virtue. An empty fame conferred upon a particularly unproductive member of society would be an example of one such semiotic investment.

The symbolic is important to Baudrillard because it stands in opposition to the values embodied in post-industrial capitalism. Only it can break that complex circuit of the postmodern economy defined as a system of exchanges between use value, exchange value and sign value. As a value—if a value it may be called—the symbolic is axiologically *sui generis* and thus completely irreducible to transmutation into other exchange values so long as it still retains its unique meaning. It stands as fundamentally opposed *to* and transgressive *of* the economic order because its meaning deconstructs that order. However, the symbolic may be appropriated within the economic system (as are myths often appropriated to bolster a sagging ideology), but once appropriated, it never functions as it did before it was thus violated. The reason for this irreducibility, though Baudrillard does not quite say it, is that in the symbol sign and coda are fused. To remove either the sign value or the coda from their relation of interpenetration in the symbol is to destroy integral meaning and impact of the symbol. To paraphrase George MacDonald: in the symbol, the meaning comes with the thing itself.[7] Untampered with, the symbolic is transcendent, though it is transcendent in a peculiar sense. Because Baudrillard has, *a priori*, ruled out either an egological or theological transcendental referent, he cannot explain whence the symbolic emerges to stand against the economy of the sign. The symbolic's transcendence is thus radical and apophatic. The best he is able to do is to express the obscure hope that the backbone of the postmodern economy may be broken by "a pure event, an event that can no longer be manipulated, interpreted, or deciphered by any historical subjectivity."[8] If the symbolic transcends the notion of a utilitarian economy, it is because its way of exchange is one which radically transgresses the assumptions behind the rationality of utilitarian economic action. More precisely, the symbolic is operative in all of those things, actions or processes when the use value, the exchange value and the semiotic exchange value are annihilated. Examples of such transgression are religious sacrifice (the annihilation of use value), the defacement of currency (the annihilation of exchange value) or the desecration of a secular icon (the annihilation of sign exchange value).[9]

What all of this means is that today capitalism hides behind the cloak of what has been called virtual reality or hyperreality. It is the realm in which everything can be semiotically transformed into anything else so that all things are convertible into commodity forms or capital. The fragmentation of the self, of the family, of traditional values, of communities, of educational curricula, of epistemological paradigms, and so on, occurs because of the advantage such atomization holds for profit. If it can be demonstrated that there are no abiding essences, no abiding natures, no abiding identities, no abiding qualities then, *ipso facto*, all of these things become volatilized as semiotic consumables so long as there are means for producing more of them. And of the readiness of the producers, let there be no question. The dissolution of reality's constancy drives people to desire constancy of some sort and to purchase it at a price, if necessary. Late capitalism is driven by that lucrative realization— a realization which is one of the contradictions in the heart of Marxism itself—that needs and desires can be produced without limit. Contained in this recognition is the faintest suggestion that even the Marxist eschaton may not be able to contain the force of desire.

But there is another side to postmodernism's proclivity to denature reality; it is related to late capitalism's need for a protean work force conformable to its own mutations. If one's identity is decentered or dispersed, then it becomes much easier for that identity to be retooled for a new occupation. The (apparently) arbitrary logic of fashion—driven as it is by the cycling of capital and signs—thus becomes the dominant logic of social reality. Today we put on new selves, new bodies, new values, new sexualities, new religions, new philosophies with the same ease and boredom that the bourgeois French woman of the nineteenth century put on the latest Parisian fashions. Capitalism no longer makes any pretense to support the supposedly stalwart values of the middle class; a managed relativity now reigns and capitalism thrives on the profits it produces.

Here, the academic establishment—particularly in this country—is no exception. Since the early to mid sixties it has been driven by a production model immortalized in the imperative: "Publish or perish!" It is little wonder that in those disci-

plines centered on texts, disciplines such as literature, philosophy
and religion, we find the academic productivity model most powerfully driving research. These are, after all, disciplines whose
pragmatic value is most questionable and hardest to measure.
The number of articles produced thus becomes a convenient
gauge. But if productivity is to be the measure of value, then these
disciplines require an *epistêmê* which validates them. It is little
wonder then that the hermeneutics of the relativity and over-
determination of meaning are embraced even to the point of ex-
cluding other hermeneutics which are not so relativistic. It is a
question of embracing that which will make one prosper. The
postmodern paradigm is favored in these disciplines precisely because demands have been made upon their practitioners which
reward originality and volume as ends in themselves. The written
piece thus becomes a means to an end and not a proximate end at
all. The philosophy of relativity is embraced because it means
freedom to write and propose anything, and such undisciplined
and untruthful freedom makes production easy. The textualists in
the liberal arts are the slaves of the postmodern form of life. And
the postmodern form of life is driven by the late capitalist mode
of production.

2. The Postmodern Condition and the Augustinian Medicine

In bringing these ruminations to an Augustinian conclusion, I
am in the position of preaching to the already converted. I am not
so sanguine to think that the medicine I prescribe for the postmodern condition will be convincing to anyone who is not already a
Christian. Indeed, it may not even be convincing to Christians.
Nevertheless, I cannot resist making a few observations in regard
to what we can learn from Augustine about how to answer the
challenges of postmodernism. In taking the thought of Augustine
as a draught for ameliorating the postmodern condition, I am
aware that a medicine—when it does not lead to a cure—is only a
temporary measure. But there is, at least, a medicine. And where
there is a medicine there is hope. A second point. Nothing I am
about to say about Augustine's spirituality is particularly *new*, but,
then, progress in Christian theology should not be measured by the
very criterion which makes postmodern thought a slave to market
forces, anyway. There is great depth to that observation of C.S.
Lewis that the best theologians do not attempt to be original, but

they merely give original expression to the old. In this sense, Augustine's own thought was—in its time—a new expression of an original *Lebensphilosophie* which was, at the time he was writing, nearly four hundred years old.

Augustine's spirituality is a medicine against postmodernism precisely because it goes to the root causes of the postmodern condition, and it does so in a way which has profound implications for the way Christians ought to practice the liberal arts. What I should like to distinguish, here, are those assumptions which are a part of his fundamental theology *vis-à-vis* those assumptions which are a part of his understanding of the role of the liberal arts in shaping Christian character.

First, Augustine offers a rival theory of desire and utility which, though it does not explain why postmodernism possesses the features it does, suggests an alternative to either capitulation to the late capitalist form of life or acceptance of the Marxist eschatology.[10] In brief, Augustine recognizes that all humans are driven by desire but this desire is the result of the separation of humankind from their appropriate object. In the unseparated state, humans would have not experienced desire because the perfect fulfillment to which human nature is proportioned would have been realized. In post-lapserian existence, however, human beings are separated from their final fulfillment and thus live in a constant state of incompletion and need, a need which is potentially infinite. Augustinian thought lends itself to an orthodox Marxist (and contra-Baudrillardian) interpretation in this sense: both maintain a hierarchy of fundamental human needs which cannot all be arbitrarily engineered. Just as Marx postulated a set of fundamental needs that are rooted in the species being of humankind—needs such as food, clothing, fresh air, sunlight, adequate living and working space, cleanliness of person and environment, rest, variety in activities, play and aesthetic stimulation, a set of fundamental needs which form a hierarchy with respect to subsistence—Augustine, too, would presumably recognize the importance of these needs. However, he would add to the list (as a need of finality) the need for union with God. In other words, Augustine posited outright what Marx denounced as a ruling class ideology imposed upon the proletariat and deducible from a society's economic structure and what the neo-Kantians developed as an extension of the aesthetic sense. Augustine posited the need for God as an irreducible drive in human behavior.

Now, though God is the only need that can bring ultimate

fulfillment, he is still a need among others. Augustine recognized human existence as driven by exchanges and utility directed to the achievement of union with God. The utility of an exchange is measured by the fulfillment we associate with the acquisition of the needed object. Although needs may be met through the acquisition of specific objects, all *natural* human needs are renewable because all natural objects are consumable. ("If you thirst, though you drink, you will thirst again.") Therefore, the objects of human needs fall into a hierarchy of consumability with God being the only durable object of need who, when once acquired, brings final human fulfillment. The economy of nature is such that all objects can be used as means for the acquisition of fulfillment.

Where the Augustinian theory of utility differs from capitalism is in its axiology. On the surface, the rational calculation involved in acquiring the valued objects would not seem to be so different in the capitalist system of exchange and the Augustinian economy of salvation. But things are not always what they seem. True, Augustine would have little sympathy with the desires of consumers for commodities or status outside of whatever is necessary for subsistence. He was, after all, a monk. The production and semiosis typical of postmodern society would have struck him as catering to the superficialities of human existence and not to its proper end, union with God. No doubt, he would pose asceticism as an answer to our amazing cultural prodigality. That is to say, he would be signaling his transcendence of the capitalist theory of utility. In this, he would be prescribing a symbolic act in the Baudrillardian sense for he would be answering abundance and pleasure with a refusal, that is with an act that makes no sense according to the capitalist logic which always searches for an eventual reward in terms of use value, exchange value or sign value.

But aside from this refusal and deferral, Augustine would also introduce a positive social stipulation that directly addresses the dehumanization rampant under postmodernism. Though recognizing that God is the ultimate object of humankind's desire and that humans indeed employ a variety of artifices to storm the gates of the kingdom of God, Augustine would stipulate that union with God can be achieved only through the instrumentality of the love of neighbor, an instrumentality of a very anti-capitalist kind.

In stipulating—as Jesus had done (and as had Hillel done before Jesus)—that the whole of the law is subsumed under the two commandments to love God above all things and to love your neighbor as yourself, Augustine set the conditions on the usufruct nature of one's neighbor and one's self. The conditions are deceptively simple. Since in loving oneself one expects for oneself all the good things which satisfy natural needs and supernatural needs, the use of your neighbor for the attainment of union with God implies (a) that you will really *love* your neighbor, (b) that in loving your neighbor you must never allow him or her to stand as a final end which supplants God; (relative to God) he or she must remain only a means (or proximate end), and (c) that to achieve union with God you will do all in your power to provide for your neighbor every natural and supernatural good that you provide for yourself. Condition 'a' is perhaps the most important because it precludes an economic interpretation based upon the capitalist understanding of utility. It must not be construed as an exchange of the love of neighbor as the purchasing price for salvation—though it has been thus construed at different periods as such. Rather, it is a gracious and holy affection in which no *practical* distinction is made between self and other. When directed toward non-Christians, its gratuitousness is especially symbolic in the Baudrillardian sense because this extraordinary charity stands as absurd to the rationality of capitalist exchange.

To describe the Christian economy of salvation as a community bound together by mutual love and instrumentality directed toward union with God might seem sufficient. But Augustine's analysis does not stop here, because a further clarification is required: the death to self (*psuchê*) prescribed by Christianity must be complete. Just as the individual must not rest in the other as a proximate end (or as a substitute final end), so too the individual cannot rest in himself/herself as a proximate (or final) end. Thus, the fulfillment of the individual is achieved only when the complacent culturally-defined self has been obliterated and obliterated along with it all distinctions between the self's welfare and the welfare of the other. In loving the self, you love your ultimate end through yourself and the other. But in loving the self and the other, one is engaged in the process of making one's own egotistically constructed self *nothing* at the same time one is aiding one's neighbor in the annihilation of his or her egotistically constructed self. In this process, too, one engages in the Baudrillardian symbolic act. For in the *kenosis* of self toward union with God, one negates the chief identity produced by *classical* capitalist society, that of the egotistic rational actor. But, unlike the deconstruction of self which becomes a possibility in postmodern capitalism, the Augustinian deconstruction is not a deconstruction designed to expand the field of desires, nor is it a deconstruction designed to fragment the self and then to commoditize the pieces. In this, the Christian deconstructive message of death to self is a profoundly symbolic refusal, because, if pure, it cannot be transmuted into any economic value.

How does this Augustinian interpretation of utility in the pursuit of ultimate value provide a program for thought and action in the postmodern world? The answer to this question possesses complications which differ according to whether we pose this question about our day-to-day existence outside of the classroom or whether we pose it to ourselves with respect to the roles we play as teachers of the liberal arts.

Taking the last interrogation first, I think that it would be absurd to suggest that the curriculum of the liberal arts as Augustine experienced it has much substantively to do with university education today. We are not seeking thoughtlessly to revive outdated pedagogic methods or to urge a return to obsolete subject matters or conceptions of the sciences. As creatures of our time, we are responsible for addressing the conditions of our time, but we must do this without capitulating to our age's indefensible and anti-Christian assumptions. It is with respect to this last imperative that Augustine still has much to remind us.

The liberal arts may be considered in two different ways: according to their respective objects and according to the way in which they affect the subjects studying them. Thus the worth of the liberal arts may be construed according to the kinds or extent of knowledge which they provide or it may be construed according to the manner in which they shape the character of the people studying them. Corresponding to the subject-object distinction which characterizes the liberal arts are two symbolic dimensions: one from the side of the object, one from the side of the subject. The objective symbolic dimension represents the inventory of symbolic acts, events or artifices as these are remembered and transmitted as a part of what constitutes cultural history. To be sure, this inventory never constitutes the whole of any liberal art, and it may not even be present in a given liberal art (mathematics, for example) but its presence is a (too often silent) testimony to the higher aspirations of a particular culture. In effect, the symbolic inventory of a culture includes all accounts of paradigmatic behavior (philosophical, fictional or historical) which bear testimony to transcendent values, accounts not reducible to matters of pure egoistic self-interest and, thus, not susceptible to the hermeneutics of suspicion.

Corresponding to these inventories would be the expectation that the student engaged in the study of the liberal arts or the professor teaching them would also take them up and emulate them.

Now in describing these accounts as symbolic, I am not maintaining that they are solely religious, even though the religious are my sole concern in this piece. Secular symbolic acts are certainly possible in the Baudrillardian sense: we are all aware of transcendental values of a non-religious nature which have been pursued with great human energy but also with a complete disinterest in their use, economic exchange and semiotic exchange values. In its pure form, this is simply a restatement of the notion of art (or science) for art's (or science's) sake. But this cannot be the Christian's route. Here, Augustine's own example is instructive.

In rethinking the utility of rhetoric for the Christian, Augustine transformed the Ciceronian/Quintilian ideal. Instead of accepting *docere* [to instruct], *delectare* [to delight] and *movere* [to move] as equivalent ends for the Christian rhetorician, Augustine made instruction most important, made the moving of an audience/reader of secondary importance and almost entirely discounted the importance of delight.[11] In his spiritual utilitarianism, Augustine saw little benefit for rhetoric outside of the end of teaching, because it was instruction which led most directly to God.[12]

For the Christian, the end of human existence is not of the natural order and—until union with God is achieved—remains unattained. The liberal arts may be useful for developing latent human capacities, but if these are taken as ends in themselves, instead of as proximate ends on the way to salvation, they—in a real sense—eclipse God. This means that, according to Augustinian principles, the Christian's involvement in the liberal arts must always be directed—because of the responsibilities to neighbor and self—toward prosecution of the ultimate end of Christian existence. Those Christians who study the liberal arts and those who teach them can live in only one possible relation toward them, the relation of pilgrim and vehicle for pilgrimage. Thus the Christian professor must be engaged in two tasks: that of ceaselessly finding new forms by which the message of salvation can be re-*incarnated* in culture and that of doing the intellectual work necessary to ensure that the truth of that message will not be undermined, a task which necessarily subserves the former. This conception of the professor's role bears affinities with H. Richard Niebuhr's notion of *Christ the transformer of culture*, that stance of Christians taken toward the secular which is thematically embodied in the works of John the Divine, Clement

of Alexandria, Kierkegaard, Tolstoy, Ritschl and—most important
for our purposes—Augustine of Hippo.[13]

The role of the professor in culturally reincarnating the kerygma will of necessity focus on grace. Gratuitous acts, because
they have no part in the process of economic calculation, are
transgressive of postmodern culture. In fact, the more gratuitous
the act, the more transgressive the act. God's incarnation in Jesus
Christ and Jesus Christ's death on the cross are a greater scandal
to the postmodern world than to any previous period not only
because of their ultimacy but, also, because of the strength of
what they oppose. They are poised over and against capitalism in
its most powerful and dehumanizing stage. If some of that scandal seems to have been lost on the postmodern world, it is not
because the symbol has died but because its meaning has been
semiotically adulterated or co-opted. Nevertheless, in the incarnation and the crucifixion one finds the realization of exactly what
Baudrillard has been seeking: a pure symbolic act. Its transgres-
sions against both the economy of exchange and the postmodern
order are legion. God (the supreme value) in a supremely gratuitous act empties himself of his power, becoming weak and pitiful
like those he will die for. Incarnate, he prefers to live, anonymously, in the company of the poor, the impotent, the sinful, the
marginalized. In his critique of wealth, Jesus Christ does not set
himself against its utility in procuring the necessities of life; he
sets himself against a style of existence which continually seeks
money as an equivalent to excessive material comforts, prestige
and power. His own simple existence represents a lived refusal in
the face of everything that the world of power and wealth might
offer. Indeed, in living to embody the kerygma of God's gracious-
ness while subjecting himself to suffering, a criminal's death and
annihilation, Jesus Christ simultaneously transgresses the Jewish
understanding of righteousness and the Greco-Roman conception
of practical rationality. Triumphing over death—the very symbol
of the economy of exchange—Jesus Christ offers a similar conquest to anyone who will believe in him and sincerely imitate—
however imperfectly—his own gracious existence.

The weight of the responsibility for reincarnating this Christian proclamation means that Christian educators must use all of
the symbols at their disposal to draw their students out of fragmentation and dispersal within the economy of the sign. Program-
matically, this entails a number of things. First, by personal example, Christian professors will teach the value of heroic anonymity,

because at present only anonymity insures against absorption in the sea of semiotic commoditization. Second, by personal example, Christian professors will demonstrate heroic dedication both to the ultimate end of proclaiming the foundational symbols of Christianity (as well as the transcendent symbols of all peoples) and to the proximate ends of instruction and research in their chosen fields. Third, Christian professors will take responsibility for realizing the symbolic in life, first, through their actions and, then, through the actions of their students.

In an academic setting, our options for free action in the deconstruction of postmodern capitalism are more limited than those in the non-academic world. Still, our ultimate impact will, conceivably, be much greater. Joachim Wach in his essay, "The Christian Professor," made the observation that two avenues of witnessing to the truths of Christ are available for the Christian professor.[14] One is the esoteric way of the closed hand: without an overt profession but through one's demeanor, actions and intellectual pursuit of truth and goodness one suggests the Christian ideal, until the student broaches the question of belief. This is the way of the greatest anonymity; it is the way of Christian professors acting *incognito* as *agentes in rebus* or even as *agents provocateurs*. Its great advantage is the advantage of all secret movements: by deferring recognition they cannot be infiltrated or appropriated.

The other is the way of the open hand. One simply professes (and most certainly acts out) Christian truth at every appropriate opportunity in the course of one's academic life. Of the two methods, the latter is certainly the most difficult because it entails that the professor act as a believer without compromising the academic integrity of his discipline but all the while bringing that Christianity into a dialogue with its subject matter. In the case of the postmodern epistemological paradigm, it means that the professor will provide *alternatives* to ways of thinking which compromise the dignity of the individual or which deny the possibility of truth or salvation. And it means that he/she will do this without being coopted by the very form of life that he/she opposes. But, finally, it means that the professor will issue a call to action, first, a call for the local action necessary to build academic communities of Augustinian solidarity and secondly a call for the replication of Augustinian communities in the society as a whole.

Applied to the mundane world, I suppose this must ultimately mean the transformation of the economy of late capitalism into an economy of God's love. As *theoretically* attractive as I find Augustine's observations—as I said much earlier—I am less sanguine about the possibility of this hope ever being universalized. The postmodernists are right at least in this sense: we seem, again, to have entered a period in which the culture of Christendom is no longer dominant. In many respects, the strength of Christianity as a historical force and worldview is on the wane; the great tape of history is being played backwards. To my mind, the bricolage which goes by the oxymoron "postmodern culture" most closely resembles the syncretism of late antiquity. And it is, perhaps, for this reason that some renovation of Augustine's theology—a theology of the Patristic period—may put us in possession of a shelter by which to weather the coming age.

Practically, the best we can hope for is to build small communities in which these exchanges of love are possible. Practically, we can avoid participating in any societal exchanges where symbols, transcendent values, and humans are turned into commodities purchasable for a capitalist profit or for advantages which are not tantamount to the values of the Christian tradition. Practically, in the day-to-day world, we can also make others aware when they, their symbols or their values are being thus traded and when they have sold these as cheap commodities.

Notes

1.   G. W. Hegel, *The Phenomenology of Mind*, trans. J. B. Ballie (New York: Harper and Row, 1967), pp. 105–06. Subsequent citations are parenthetical.

2.   G. W. Hegel, *Hegel's Logic: Part I of the Encyclopedia of the Philosophical Sciences* (1830), trans. William Wallace (Oxford: Oxford University Press, 1975), pp. 187–88.

3.   Walter Truett Anderson, *Reality Isn't What It Used To Be* (San Francisco: Harper Collins, 1990), p. 253. Anderson predicts that this self-consciousness will result in five megatrends: "(1) changes about thinking; (2) changes in identity and boundaries; (3) changes in learning; (4) changes in morals, ethics and values; and (5) changes in relationships to traditions, customs and institutions" (p. 254).

4.   John McMurtry, *The Structure of Marx's World-View* (Princeton: Princeton University Press, 1978), p. 94.

5.   Jean Baudrillard, *For a Critique of the Political Economy of the Sign*, trans. Charles Levin (St. Louis: Telos Press, 1981), pp. 143–63.

6.   Karl Marx, *Capital*, trans. Ernest Untermann (New York: Modern Library, 1906), 1:42; Karl Marx, *A Contribution to the Critique of Political Economy*, ed. Maurice Dobb (New York: International Publishers, 1970), p. 28. Subsequent citations are parenthetical.

7.   George MacDonald, *Little Daylight*, adapted and illustrated by Erick Ingraham (New York: William Morrow, 1988), p. 26. I thank my daughter Elizabeth for this reference and the opportunity to read this fairy tale to her at least three times a week.

8.   Jean Baudrillard, *Forget Foucault* (New York: Semiotext[e], 1987), p. 70.

9.   See Baudrillard, *For a Critique*, pp. 123–42. What Baudrillard has in mind may best be expressed by reproducing his tableau of the transformations possible under the political economy of the sign. The possible varieties of the transmutation of value can, *mutatis mutandis*, be represented as follows:

Use Value (UV):
    1. UV=EcEV   2. UV=SgEV   3. UV=SmE

Economic Exchange Value (EcEV):
    4. EcEV=UV   5. EcEV=SgEV   6. EcEV=SmE

Sign Exchange Value (SgEV):
    7. SgEV=UV   8. SgEV=EcEV   9. SgEV=SmE

Symbolic Exchange (SmE):
    10. SmE=UV   11. SmE=EcEV   12. SmE=SgEV

Although Baudrillard does not offer an example for each of these transmutations, thinking through the various relations in order to come up with a concrete interpretation is fruitful. Transmutation 1 represents the exchange of an object's use value for its exchange value. A farmer bringing a crop to market and accepting money dictated by the market value of the produce would represent such an exchange. Transmutation 2 represents the transmutation of an object's use value into its sign exchange value. The SAAB, a rather ugly Swedish automobile (by virtue of its being advertised as the thinking man's car) suddenly becomes the icon of the academic elite, thus driving profitability for the motor company up in the process of enhancing the wealth and intellectual class status of the professors who own them. Transmutation 4 represents the reverse of relation 1 and may be termed consumptive transformation of exchange value: something we all accomplish when we buy and consume the farmer's produce. Transmutation 5 represents the exchange of something's economic value for its sign value. An example would be spending twice as much money on a jacket simply because that jacket sported the Chicago Bulls team emblem. The iconic legibility (and totemic identification involved) would make the item more semiotically valuable, despite the fact that the labor process was not significantly different for jackets made out of identical materials. Transmutation 7 is the reverse of transmutation 2. It might consist of taking the legible object, say the "thinking man's car," and employing it to do what any auto can do, namely to pull things. However, if one were really under the thralldom of the coda of the car, then perhaps certain objects would be seen as *infra dignitatus*. One who bought into the legibility of the SAAB might, therefore, never be caught dead pulling a bull out of a ditch or pulling a U-Haul trailor. Relation 8 is the reverse of 5 and is well represented by those who sell the memorabilia of Hollywood stars (or the relics of saints) for money.

The last three relations (10, 11, 12) represent the transmutation of the symbolic into exchange value, processes which never take place without violating the nature of the symbol they transmute. Traditionally, these have been associated with desecration of holy objects, though not exclusively so. Picking one's teeth with the small end of a crucifix might be an example of transmutation 10. Transfer of honorific titles from Jesus Christ ("King of Kings," "the eternal king") to Elvis Presley in order to sell records would be an example of transmutation 11, or the selling of "Pope-sicles" during a papal visit. An example of transmutation 12 might be wearing a gold crucifix because on the Euro-trash scene a gold crucifix and decolletage provide a deliciously provocative (and thus, status-conferring) juxtaposition of the sacred and the profane. In this case, the de-contextualization of the symbol co-opts its normal effect and inverts it—a process of semiosis common to Western black magic. More interesting, however, is symbolic exchange's transgression of the economic order represented by relations 3, 6 and 9, relations which make no sense in terms of a utilitarian axiology. A non-theurgic thanksgiving sacrifice of a large beast of burden would be an example of transmutation 3 (use value to symbolic exchange). Such a gratuitous act of worship cannot be understood within the capitalist calculus of utility. Winning ten million dollars in a lottery and giving all the money to the poor, or burning hundreds of dollars of paper currency to protest a military action, might be examples of transmutation 6. Finally, the early Christian refusal to sacrifice to the sterile cult of the Roman gods would represent a transgression of the signs in relation 9.

In light of this tableau of relations and its interpretation, Baudrillard constructs a number of proportions, all of which are important to an understanding of what is at stake in postmodern culture. Most important is the following:

$$\frac{EcEV}{UV} = \frac{Sr}{Sd} \text{ vs. Symbolic exchange}$$

Baudrillard's point is that the relationship between the economic exchange value (EcEV) and use value (UV) is as accidental as the relationship between signifier (Sr) and signified (Sd) according to Saussurean semiotics. There is no fundamental necessity at all to either relation. In its most radical form, the condition of postmodernity means that the signifie and the economic exchange value so dominate postmodern society that the reality of things signified and the real utility of things are swallowed up in a nest of never-ending irreal exchanges. Thus the economic exchange value is cut free from its moorings in use and has reality only in terms of previous economic exchanges as dependent upon semiosis and its various coda. Likewise, any given signifier simply refers back to a chain of previous signifiers, none ever finally touching the signified. No wonder then that, epistemologically, the postmodern period is characterized by the hegemony of anti-foundationalism. The interesting question, a question Baudrillard never quite answers, is how the symbol is able to transgress the established order of exchange. To put it in the form of Baudrillard's equations:

$$\frac{EcEV}{UV} = \frac{Sr}{Sd} \text{ vs. } \frac{SmE}{?}$$

If, as Baudrillard suggests, the symbolic has the power to speak in spite of the attempt of other systems of exchange to co-opt it; and if it is possible for it to radically transgress the economic order, then perhaps what distinguishes symbolic exchange from the other exchanges is that it does not stand in opposition and in accidental relationship to the transcendent, but—perhaps as scholars of religion have long maintained—it mediates the transcendent. A symbol would thus be a *presentational* sign which—in proper context—presents the very reality it signifies. As such, it would really be joined to the referent or signified. In a materialist sense, that is precisely what the symbolic does. When enacted it demonstrates the folly of the economic: it shows it to be an arbitrary system of exchanges. It tears aside its veil so that the great wizard Oz (the system of postmodernity) is seen for exactly what he is: a dumpy little man pulling levers and strings (capitalist axiology). In Hegelian terms, the postmodern condition is the phenomenal shroud of a hyper-realized profit motive. Symbols thus become the means for coming to this realization.

10.   The following are some of the places where Augustine discusses his notions of enjoyment and use in relation to the two greatest commands: *On Christian Doctrine* 1.4.4, 1.22.21; *Commentary on John's Gospel* 40.10, 123.5; *City of God* 14.13. Anders Nygren provides an extensive listing of all passages having to do with Augustine's interpretation of the two commandments in relation to love, enjoyment and use in *Agape and Eros*, trans. Philip S. Watson (New York: Harper and Row, 1969), pp. 476–558. Nygren's interpretation, though a standard for the subject and very rigorous, is dictated by his program of demonstrating the dilution of the *agapê* in the thought of Augustine, a program which—at points—forcibly compromises the consistency of Augustine's theological project.

11.   Aurelius Augustine, *Concerning the Teacher and On the Immortality of the Soul*, trans. George G. Leckie (New York: D. Appleton-Century, 1938), pp. xii–xiii.

12.   One might think that Augustine would have no use for the liberal arts as a whole, given his severe reordering of rhetoric. But, contrary to this expectation, he had high regard for their value in perfecting the interior virtues and powers. See Leckie's introduction to *Concerning the Teacher*, p. xxvii.

13.   H. Richard Niebuhr, *Christ and Culture* (New York: Harper and Row, 1951), pp. 190–229.

14.   J. Wach, *Understanding and Believing*, ed. Joseph Kitagawa (New York: Harper and Row, 1968), p. 160.

PHILIBERT HOEBING, O.F.M.

St. Francis and the Environment

When problems of the environment are addressed, one finds some writers arguing for the rights of animals and endangered species; others defending the rights of humans and their technological achievements; others taking the position that humans are just another species on the planet, and that the evolutionary process would continue even if humans destroyed their environment and themselves. The debate about contemporary environmental issues thus raises basic questions: "What is a human being?" and "What should the relationship between the human species and the nonhuman world be?"

In the field of environmental ethics, two fundamental sets of questions recur. The first asks: "What sorts of things have moral standing?" In other words, do things that are nonhuman have moral standing? Apart from human beings, do endangered species have moral standing? Do only the higher animals have moral standing? The second set of questions is related to the first: "When moral standing of nonhuman beings is determined, then how does one evaluate a situation that involves a conflict of moral interests?" How does one determine which endangered species is more deserving of protection than another? Some moral norms or principles must be established to respond to the above questions.[1]

Environmentalists, scientists, philosophers and theologians have proposed various avenues of approach to these questions. One approach that includes the spiritual and suggests an ecological spirituality is called "deep ecology." In 1973 Arne Naess, a Norwegian philosopher, distinguished between deep ecology and shallow ecology.[2] According to Naess, the proponents of shallow ecology are opposed to pollution and the loss of resources because of their

201

negative effect on the health and affluence of people in developed countries. The advocates of deep ecology, on the other hand, go beyond the scientific level to the level of self and world wisdom. Opposing the shallow ecological view that there is no value except that which is valuable for humans, deep ecology argues that seeing value in this way reveals a kind of racial prejudice. In attempting to bring an appreciation of the spiritual into ecology, Naess emphasized the importance of the insights that the world religions and philosophies can offer in regard to the relationship of humans to nonhumans.

This essay presents a theological approach to the relationship between humans and nonhumans based on the life and ideals of St. Francis, as developed by Blessed John Duns Scotus, a thirteenth-century professor at the University of Paris. This Franciscan approach revolves around the Primacy of Christ and the value of every single creature, human and nonhuman. In both Francis and Scotus these two theological positions are intimately connected. St. Francis (d.1226) in his unique way was able to appreciate that each and every individual in nature is part of God's creative goodness, and Scotus (d.1308), a philosopher's philosopher, gave Francis' ideals a theological explanation. One might argue that St. Francis was a proponent of a kind of deep ecology long before the postmodern age.

A timely theological and spiritual approach to environmental issues recognizes that how a person views the nonhuman world affects the way one looks at God and other human beings. In the postmodern world, nature cannot be regarded simply as an "it" to be exploited. J. Baird Callicott, for one, is convinced that the old mechanistic idea of nature is dying and that a new holistic, organic worldview is emerging. An advocate of Aldo Leopold's "land community," in which human beings are members of the world of nature and not the supreme rulers, Callicott believes that we are beginning to see nature as an organic system in which human beings are one of the components.

This postmodern systems-model must be considered when one is addressing issues of the environment and spirituality, because it reflects contemporary dissatisfaction with the modern anthropocentric approach to the world. Selfish exploitation and abuse of our natural resources, especially during the modern period of colonization and the industrial revolution, have put us in a position where we are more and more aware that our very existence depends on (and is perhaps coterminous with) nature. We have invaded nature so that its boundaries and the boundaries of culture (as defined by technology) are less and less distinguishable. As Callicott explains, "Nature as Other is over. Everywhere man's works insidiously pervade, if they do not palpably dominate, the landscape . . . . A new dynamic and systemic postmodern concept of nature, which includes rather than excludes human beings, is taking shape."[3]

In a world where the God-made and the man-made overlap, nature tends no longer to be "Other" in either the premodern sense, which associated nature with God and the sacred, or the modern sense, which perceived nature as a lifeless "matter" to be mastered, used and exploited. In the premodern view of nature there was a hierarchically and teleologically structured universe. Every species and every individual had a place in this structured universe. The saints of that period would read both the Book of Nature and the Bible to understand God's plan for themselves and the nonhuman world. The modern period, in contrast, viewed the world of nature as a great machine, emphasized the role of reason, and eliminated hierarchical and teleological structure. The language of nature was mathematics, and the human individual became the center of knowledge and decision. God who had been the Ruler of the world of nature was displaced by autonomous individuals who were creators of themselves and who harnessed nature to their own purposes.

Today the human race is at a crossroads because today as never before the human race can see the results of carelessness, greed, selfishness and war on our fragile planet. The anthropocentric model, which recognizes the human as having intrinsic value and all nonhuman nature as existing only to serve the needs and interests of the human, clearly needs to be reevaluated.

The postmodernist movement presents a radical challenge to the myth of inevitable progress through technology or reason, and what is called "constructive postmodernism" opens the way for a new ecological spirituality. Unlike "deconstructive postmodernism," which tries to go beyond the scientific certainty of the Enlightenment by denying any reality outside the norms imposed by culture and language, "constructive postmodernism" does not necessarily exclude all of the views of the premodern and modern age in building a new worldview.[4]

As David Griffin expresses it: "[constructive postmodernism] involves a unity of scientific, ethical, aesthetic, and religious intuitions. It rejects not science itself but only that scientism in which the data of the natural sciences are alone allowed to contribute to

the construction of our worldview."[5] A constructive postmodernism, in short, embraces more values than those that are established
by the scientific method. It does not simply return to the premodern views of nature and God, but combines elements of both premodern and modern attitudes and puts them in creative tension.

What is needed is an approach that allows humans to consider
themselves to be different from nature without dominating over
her, so that they can be co-creators of the future with God and
nature and at the same time responsible stewards of nature. This
implies a complex relationship between the human and the nonhuman. Exercising responsible stewardship places humans in a hierarchical relationship "above" nature, while the attitude of reverence and service places us "below" nature and "with" nature in
relation to God. Such a view recognizes God as the loving Creator
of all; it values the "difference" between and among creatures; it
fosters a loving, redemptive attitude toward the beautiful, albeit
wounded and endangered nature that is not absolutely "Other," but
rather "brother" and "sister" to us. Such a Christian postmodern
spirituality sees the individual as belonging to Christ, who is the
beginning and end of all.

This attitude is best represented in the life of St. Francis of
Assisi, whose example offers a timeless imperative to us. In the
eyes of St. Francis, all of creation is an act of God's love, and each
and every individual has value because it comes from God's loving,
creative act. This recognition of uniqueness and individual difference (so unlike the "individualism" fostered during the modern
period) gains its classic theological expression in the "haecceity"
("thisness") of the saint's Franciscan heir, John Duns Scotus—the
"haecceity" that later inspired the "in-scape" of the poet Gerard
Manley Hopkins. While the theology and spirituality of Scotus
share some elements with contemporary Creation Spirituality,
they preserve a Christology and a soteriology that powerfully resist
the temptation to a New Age-like escapism.

Others have recognized the relevance of Franciscan spirituality to contemporary ecology. Lynn White, Jr., for instance, in his
much publicized and critiqued presentation, "The Historical
Roots of Our Ecological Crisis," delivered to the AAAS on December 26, 1966, made a special reference to Francis of Assisi.[6] He
called the present ecological crisis a religious crisis resulting from
the application of religious principles to the world of nature, and
he blamed the Judaeo-Christian tradition in particular. White nevertheless praised Francis for his love of nature, indicating that

Francis had attempted to set up a democracy of all God's creatures, but was so heretical in his view of nature that St. Bonaventure attempted to suppress the early accounts of Franciscanism.
White concluded that St. Francis, whose ideas were not developed
by his followers after his death in 1226, ought to be proclaimed
the patron of ecology.

Pope John Paul II actually did proclaim St. Francis to be the
patron of those who promote ecology in 1979. More recently, in his
New Year's letter, "Peace with All Creation," dated January 1, 1990,
the pope showed concern for the environment and the need for an
ethics to protect the earth from destruction, and he gave various
reasons why all nations should assume responsibility to work for a
restoration of a healthy environment. He asked those people who
have no particular religious convictions to be moved by concern
for the common good. He asked those who believe in God to appreciate the unity and order that has come from God. In a special way
he called those who believe in Christ to assume their responsibility
for the environment because of this belief. The Holy Father concluded his New Year's letter by reminding his audience that he had
in 1979 proclaimed St. Francis as the patron of those who promote
ecology, and that "the poor man of Assisi gives us striking witness
that when we are at peace with God we are better able to devote
ourselves to building up that peace with all creation which is inseparable from peace among all peoples."[7]

The papal letter may be considered a two-edged reply to people like White. In praising Francis as a model and patron of ecological concern, the pope in effect refutes the charge of Franciscan
heresy. Against White's charge that Franciscans subsequently suppressed the views of St. Francis, I am arguing in turn that the
intuitions and nature mysticism that are found in St. Francis were
the source and basis of the theology and philosophy of both St.
Bonaventure and Bl. John Duns Scotus, and that Scotus' teachings
on the value of the individual and the absolute Primacy of Christ
are particularly important for the ecological spirituality of the postmodern age.

St. Francis was neither a pantheist nor a romanticist in his
appreciation of the world of nature. A true mystic who appreciated
the goodness and love of God in his creation, Francis was a nature
mystic and may have been the first nature mystic. In his study of
Francis and nature mysticism, Roger Sorrell holds that there is no
strong evidence for nature mysticism in the Hebrew, classical or
Christian worlds until the thirteenth century.[8]

St. Francis is unique in his approach to nature, because he did
not draw away from the world in order to go to God but believed
that the goodness and love of God were evident in his works. Francis was not trained as an intellectual; he neither studied nor
adopted the Christian Neoplatonic attitude toward creation, which
advocated withdrawal from nature and the world in order to
achieve union with God. In his original and radical way Francis
perceived the connectedness of the world and, since everything
came from a loving Father, he regarded everything as part of the
family of God.

In affirming the goodness and beauty of creation, Francis not
only departed from Neoplatonism; he also took a stand in opposition to Catharism. The Cathars, a non-Christian religious group
strongly influenced by Manichean dualism, were active in Italy at
the time of Francis. They taught that the spiritual world came from
an all-beneficent divine power, while the material world came
from an evil power. They also had various dietary rules and would
not eat certain foods. In striking contrast to the Cathars, when
Francis wrote his rule for his Brothers, he allowed them to eat of
any food put before them. Francis in his own unique and radical
way thus affirmed the goodness of material things and made a very
liberal statement by the standards of the thirteenth century, when
members of religious groups were expected to be more ascetical
than lay people and refrain from eating various foods, especially
meat. St. Francis was not a vegetarian and, as much as he loved the
nonhuman world, did permit his brothers to eat meat.

Francis intuitively recognized the value of each individual,
realizing that each creature came from the creative hand of God
who was infinitely Good, and he was able to appreciate the hand of
God in all of creation. In his famous "Canticle of Creatures" Francis
invites everyone to be at one with the universe and to experience
"brotherhood" and "sisterhood" with all of creation. According to
Eric Doyle, Francis was inspired to write the Canticle in part because of the way people misused the world around them.[9] Already
at his time Francis was aware that humans were abusing the gifts
of God. In his "cosmic humility," Francis recognized that he shared
in the drama, rhythm and worship of the whole universe and that
all was dependent on God.

It is, however, too simplistic to think that Francis believed in a
democracy for all of creation and that all of the members of nature,
human and nonhuman, were equal. Many admirers of Francis are
continually amazed by Francis' ability to communicate with the

world of nature and are delighted by the many stories of his love for animals. There are more of these happenings in Franciscan *legenda* than in the lives of other ascetics; they display certain common elements that show the distinctive quality of Francis' love for animals and instruct us about his view of human beings and their relationship to nature.

To take one incident out of the many in the life of St. Francis, his famous Sermon to the Birds illustrates the complexity of his perception of humanity's place in the world of nature. This incident occurred on his first trip between Cannara and Bevagna when Francis saw a very great crowd of birds and said to his companions: "Wait for me here on the road. I am going to preach to our sisters, the birds." The account continues as follows:

> And he went into the field toward the birds that were on the ground. And as soon as he began to preach, all the birds that were on the trees came down toward him. And all of them stayed motionless with the others in the field, even though he went among them, touching them with his habit. But not a single one of them made the slightest move, and later they did not leave until he had given them his blessing.[10]

Sorrell, in his analysis of this important incident, shows how Francis exercised his role as a representative of God in his preaching to the birds. Before Francis spoke to the birds, he asked help from God; then he addressed the birds in his usual manner, which was to say: "May the Lord give you peace." In his message to the birds Francis told them that they should thank and love God for the goods that he had given them. By preaching to the birds, Francis thus showed himself to be both in control over nature and in its service; the birds, for their part, responded by listening and only left when he had given them his permission. Sorrell sees the incident as indicating that Francis considered himself an agent of God in this situation. For Francis there is a hierarchy in nature; man is the highest of God's creations, and all of creation is related to the All-Good God. Francis, however, differs from other ascetics in that he sees the goodness and the interdependence of all of nature.

Francis loved God in nature; he also loved God in humanity— the humanity of Christ and the humanity of the poor. One cannot separate Francis' love of nature from his love of Christ and his love of the leper. He was intimately aware of human suffering in the marginalized and the poor; he devoted himself to their service and shared in their lot; he insisted that they share in the worship of the universe. One of Francis' early biographers relates how his life was changed when he embraced a leper whom he met one day while he was riding his horse. Before this incident Francis had avoided lepers, and if he ever did come close to one, he would look away and hold his nose. After his encounter with the leper his love of Christ and nature flowered.[11]

A true nature mystic, Francis was also a mystic of the "historical event" who especially cherished the celebrations of the Birth of Christ and his Passion and Death. The devotion to the humanity of Christ did not originate with Francis, but was strongly supported and encouraged by him and his Franciscan followers, so that the Christian spirituality of the Western World was different after the time of Francis than it had been prior to the thirteenth century.

Inspired by the Christ-centered and nature-centered mysticism of St. Francis, John Duns Scotus, a thirteenth-century Franciscan philospher and theologian, developed a view of the universe and world which concerned the value of the individual and the role of the humanity of Christ in the creative act of God. On the occasion of the Second Scholastic Congress that was held at Oxford and Edinburgh on the seventh centenary of the birth of Scotus, Pope Paul VI rightly described him as a "true follower of St. Francis."[12] An examination of Scotus' teachings on the individual and the Primacy of Christ suggests their relevance to contemporary ecological issues.

1. The Philosophy of the Individual

As we have seen, the life and actions of St. Francis readily illustrate his awareness of the value of individuals. He saw every individual as a gift from God and each creature mirroring the perfections of God. Francis was able to perceive "the goodness of God within his own soul and in all created things, which produced an especially profound love for those which he thought of as representing some truth about God or religion."[13]

Inspired by Francis' intuitive appreciation of the individual, Scotus developed his philosophical "haecceity" to solve the philosophical problem of individuation which was much debated at that time at the University of Paris. The newly recovered works of Aristotle—in particular, those which presented his teachings on the nature of the intellect and its knowledge of universals—were provoking much dialogue and many disputes and arguments in academic circles there.

The questions centered on the nature of knowledge: How do people know? What can they know? How are general concepts formed? Medieval philosophy developed three basic positions on the subject: extreme realism, moderate realism and nominalism. Scotus was a moderate realist in that he accepted the view of a common nature that was individualized in nature.

Scotus argued that the intellect in this life could have direct knowledge of the singular thing—a view he held in opposition to that of many of his contemporaries, who taught that the intellect knows universals immediately but singulars only indirectly. Some Islamic philosophers, in applying this principle to the Divine Mind, argued that God had no knowledge of individuals and only knew universal Ideas. Scotus and other Christian philosophers did not appreciate such a view, because it denied divine providence and God's concern for his creation.

Scotus' more basic disagreement with his contemporaries, however, was not about the knowledge of individuals, but what caused or produced the individual. Scotus argued that God in the act of creating has given each individual its own "haecceity." The word derives from the Latin word "haec," meaning "this," and translates literally as "thisness." In their dictionary of terms, Felix Aliuntis and Allan Wolter explain that *haecceity* "designates the unique formal principle of individuation that makes nature, which all individuals of the same species have in common, to be just this or that individual and no other. Scotus regards it as a distinct positive formality over and above the common nature of the individual (*natura communis*)."[14]

In the Scotistic vision, God, in his infinite love and wisdom, creates each individual as distinct from another. It is this *haecceity* that gives each creature its special value and real worth in the eyes of God. According to Scotus, even God could not replicate the individual which He has created and to whom he has given *haecceity*. The common nature (universal) is made completely incommunicable to another individual creature after God's creative work. Commenting on the importance of the principle of individuation for Scotus, Allan B. Wolter and Blane O'Neill observe: "If we reflect on this Scotistic conception of individuality in the context of what he believes God to be, we discover that it means that God's creative love wanted just this person or this creature to exist, rather than its twin or perfect copy."[15]

Such a position has enormous ramifications for contemporary ecology and ethics in general. Scotus offers a theology and a cosmology according to which the very nature of beauty and order in the universe requires not only a multiplicity of species, but also a number of individuals within a species. Scotus expressed this view in a scholastic disputation about whether angels were only specifically different or whether or not there could be individual angels within a species. There Scotus argued that God could create an unlimited number of individual angels within a species, and that it was fitting for him to do so to show his beatitude and goodness. He extended the argument to comment on God's creation of the universe, observing that its beauty required many species and many individuals within those species.

The individual is of the utmost importance, then, not only in Scotus' theory of knowledge, but also in his theology and moral philosophy. As Archbishop Cardinale observed in his inaugural address at the Second International Congress on the Seventh Centenary of the Birth of John Duns Scotus:

> In the philosophical system of Scotus the individual reigns supreme, against the general trend of his age which gave pride to the universal and relegated the individual to the domain of the accidental and perishable. Medieval man thought and lived within the orbit of a deep collective consciousness; he was absorbed into a strong social structure where he easily lost awareness of his individuality and personal responsibility. Reacting to the common trend, St. Francis of Assisi emphasized the importance of the individual in his rule, leaving much to the inspiration and guidance of divine grace. Scotus who translated into metaphysical language "the most beautiful Franciscan ideal of perfection and the ardour of the Seraphic spirit" bases this integration on the principle of differentiation and individuation.[16]

2. The Primacy of Christ

Like his teaching on the individuality of creatures, Scotus' belief in the absolute Primacy of Christ supports a relationship between humans and nonhumans that is, first of all, reverent and loving, and, secondly, salvific. Although the doctrine of Christ's

Primacy is found in the writings of the early Greek Fathers who influenced medieval thought, especially through the School of St. Victor, Scotus is one of the most important defenders of this theological view, which has become part of the Franciscan tradition.

What do we mean by the Primacy of Christ? Basically this: that Christ is the first-willed among all creatures and, at the same time, the Exemplar and Final Cause of all the rest of creation. Every creature that comes from the creative act of God is marked by Christ and for Christ. Every individual is dignified by its relationship to Christ, who is the first of God's creations (cf. Colossians 1:15–20).

Scotus' theology of the predestined Christ led him to reject the arguments that tried to show that Christ became man because of man's sin. Scotus taught that the Word would have become man even if Adam had not sinned. As a matter of fact, Christ did redeem man, but it was an act of liberality and mercy, and not an act that was necessary. Scotus viewed the act of redemption as an act of love for the human race that allowed people to fulfill their role in loving God.

The basic argumentation of Scotus, based on theological truths, is that God is love and that God, being infinite love, loves himself necessarily because he possesses all goodness. This act of love takes place in one single act which can be directed to different objects. Because the love of God is diffusive, however, he also desires co-lovers. From this principle Scotus argues that God predestined Christ as the Alpha and Omega of all creation. Because God willed to be loved by another to the highest degree, the Father willed the existence of Christ who could love God infinitely. From these principles Scotus argued that the whole of creation is permeated with love. Human beings too, created in the image and likeness of Christ, are a part of creation because of God's desire to have co-lovers.

The sensible creation also fits into this plan of God, as it is made for man to love God. Scotus agrees with Aristotle's view that man is the "end" of sensible things, but he gives a different interpretation to the value of nonhuman creation, emphasizing that God does not simply intend the inanimate creation as something for humans to use for their own benefit; rather, God intends that humans should love him through the nonhuman world, which is "ordered to predestined man," that is, ultimately to Christ:

> [God] wills for [the] sake [of human beings] those things which are remote—for instance, this sensible world—in

order that it may serve them, so that what is stated in the
second book of [Aristotle's] *Physics* is true: 'Man is the end
of all sensible things,' for . . . that which is closer to the
ultimate end is customarily said to be the end of those
things which are more remote. Hence, man will be the end
of the sensible world; whether it be because God wills the
sensible world to be ordered to predestined man or whether
it be because His more immediate concern is not that the
sensible world exist, but rather that [through it] man love
Him. (*Opus Oxoniense* III, d.32, TTn.6)[17]

Scotistic commentators believe that the Subtle Doctor is giving the cosmos a Christic shape in this and other passages where he
refers to the soul of Christ as the exemplar cause of the angels, and
the body of Christ as the exemplar cause of all material creation.
The view of Scotus that all of creation comes from the the love of
God and that Christ is the Alpha and Omega of all gives Christ an
organic function in the cosmos.[18]

Père Teilhard de Chardin was especially interested in this aspect of Scotus' arguments for the primacy. Chardin is, of course,
often quoted by environmentalists and well known for his attempts
to develop an evolutionary understanding of human faith and development. He discerned God's creative energy in operation at all
times and in all places, as well as a cosmological pattern that
included the redemptive act of Jesus Christ and evolved toward a
total fulfillment of creation in and through the Cosmic Christ.

A fascinating, long-time dialogue took place between de Chardin and Fr. Allegra, a Franciscan scripture scholar, while they were
in China. For three years these two friends discussed the differences and similiarities between Teilhard's views on evolution and
the Cosmic Christ and Scotus' theology of the predestined Christ.
Fr. Allegra vividly recalls one day when he was reading to Teilhard
from a theological manual about Scotus' concept of Christ as predestined and his conviction that Christ would have come but not as
the suffering Redeemer if man had not sinned; Teilhard responded
emphatically: "There you have the cosmic theology, the theology of
the future."[19]

Chardin's remark, which identifies Scotus' predestined Christ
with the cosmic Christ and Scotistic theology with "the theology of
the future," confirms the general argument I have been advancing
in this essay. The Franciscan Christology of Scotus offers us a vision
of an evolving and developing cosmos destined for Christ in which

human beings have a primary role and responsibility as co-creators. His doctrine of *haecceity* underscores the importance of each individual species and creature in the eyes of God and the interdependence of all things. His Franciscan poverty and saintly life oppose the greed and selfish consumption of resources that has contributed to the present ecological crisis. Finally, the "cosmic humility" he inherited from the nature mysticism of his father Francis opposes the extreme anthropocentricism which has been prevalent in the Western world during the industrial revolution and the age of technology.

From spiritual leaders like Bl. John Duns Scotus, who was beatified by Pope John Paul II on March 20, 1993, we can learn how to overcome the individualism of our soteriology, together with its acosmic style. If the contemporary Creation Theology espoused by ecologists like Thomas Berry and Matthew Fox reminds us of the goodness of creation,[20] the ecological crisis in which we find ourselves also reminds us "that up to the present time all of creation groans with pain like the pain of childbirth" and "waits with eager longing for God to reveal" his glory and deliver "creation itself . . . from its slavery to decay" (Romans 8:19–22). Science alone cannot solve our problems, and ethics apart from religion has proven itself unable to offer much direction. We need a "deep ecology" and a spirituality like that of St. Francis if we are to value properly the creatures who are no longer simply "Other," but "brother" and "sister" to us.

Notes

1. To offer a case in point, most environmentalists would not find ethically acceptable the position taken by a recent writer who claimed that he would rather shoot a human being than a snake, because the human race is overpopulated and is ruining the environment for everything else.

2. See Arne Naess, "Identification as a Source of Deep Ecological Attitudes," in *Radical Environmentalism*, ed. Peter C. List (Belmont, CA: Wadsworth, 1993), pp. 24–38.

3. J. Baird Callicott, "La Nature est morte, vive la nature!" *Hastings Center Report* 22.5 (1992): 16–23.

4. For a discussion of the difference between deconstructive and constructive postmodernism, see Charlene Spretnak, *States of Grace: The Recovery of Meaning in the Postmodern Age* (Harper San Francisco, 1992).

5. David Ray Griffin, ed., *Spirituality and Society: Postmodern Visions* (Albany: State University of New York Press, 1992), p. x.

6. Lynn White, Jr., "The Historical Roots of Our Ecological Crisis," *Science* 155.37 (1967): 1203–07.

7. Pope John Paul II, "Peace with God the Creator, Peace with All of Creation," *Origins* 14 (December, 1989): 465–68.

8. See Roger D. Sorrell, *St. Francis of Assisi* (London: Oxford University Press, 1988). For a lengthy treatment of the significance and meaning of the Canticle of Creatures, see pp. 115–24.

9. Eric Doyle, O.F.M., "Ecology and the Canticle of the Brother Sun," *New Blackfriars* 55 (1974): 392–402. See especially p. 397.

10. Marion A. Habig, ed., *St. Francis of Assisi, Writings and Early Biographies: English Omnibus of the Sources for the Life of St. Francis* (Chicago: Franciscan Herald Press, 1972), p. 1337. See Roger D. Sorrell, *St. Francis of Assisi*, pp. 55–68, for an explanation of St. Francis' nature mysticism and a discussion of his sermon to the birds.

11. See "Legend of Three Companions," in Habig, ed., *Writings and Early Biographies*, pp. 900-901.

12. Pope Paul VI, "Alma Parens," *Franciscan Studies* 17 (1967): 5–10. The pope called particular attention to Scotus' beliefs in the preeminence of love over knowledge, the Primacy of Christ, and the Immaculate Conception of Mary.

13. "Mirror of Perfection," in Habig, ed., *Writings and Early Biographies*, p. 1252.

14. In John Duns Scotus, *God and Creatures: The Quodlibetal Questions*, trans. Felix Aliuntis, O.F.M. and Allan B, Wolter, O.F.M.

(Princeton: Princeton University Press, 1975), p. 511. The so-called formality of *haecceitas* is important in the metaphysics of Scotus.

15.   Allan B. Wolter, O.F.M. and Blane O'Neill, O.F.M., *John Duns Scotus: Mary's Architect* (Quincy, IL: Franciscan Press, 1993), p. 37.

16.   Archbishop H. E. Cardinale, "The Significance of the Apostolic Letter, 'Alma Parens,' of Pope Paul VI," *Franciscan Studies* 27 (1967): 11–20. Archbishop Cardinale was the Apostolic Delegate to Great Britain at the time.

17.   See Allan B. Wolter, O.F.M., "Duns Scotus on the Predestination of Christ," *The Cord* 5 (1955): 366–72. The passage from Scotus is quoted on p. 369.

18.   See Robert H. Hale, O.S.B. Cam., *Christ and the Universe, Teilhard and the Cosmos*, ed. Michael Meilach, O.F.M. (Chicago: Franciscan Herald Press, 1972), pp. 48–49.

19.   Gabriel M. Allegra, O.F.M., *My Conversations with Teilhard de Chardin on the Primacy of Christ*, trans. Bernardino M. Bonansea, O.F.M. (Chicago: Franciscan Herald Press, 1970), p. 92.

20.   See Thomas Berry, *The Dream of the Earth* (Sierra Club Books, 1988); Matthew Fox, *Original Blessing: A Primer in Creation Spirituality* (Santa Fe, NM: Bear and Company, 1983). Fox and Berry have encouraged the development of a Creation Theology in contrast to the Fall/Redemption Model that has prevailed in the Judaeo-Christian tradition especially during the past five hundred years.

ROBERTO COLELLA

Science and Faith: Is It Possible for a Scientist To Believe?

The relationship between science and religion can hardly be described as a good friendship. Indeed, as part of our modern inheritance, the unspoken notion that science and religion, like reason and faith, are antithetic and contradictory pervades our culture to an extent that we do not even realize that it is there. Postmodernism in its various forms typically challenges such simple oppositions, however, and there are clear signs that this binary distinction is being called into question, partly as a result of a revolution within science itself.

During the academic year 1991–92 I had the opportunity to spend a sabbatical year in Paris. During this period my wife Adele and I were happily surprised to notice an intense activity in the form of books, conferences, and symposia on the theme of "Science and Faith," with the purpose of bringing them together after a long time of separation and antagonism. Significantly, this attempt toward a reconciliation is happening now in France, the country that so much contributed to the dichotomy between the two in the first place.

Three books figure prominently in my present discussion about science and faith. The first, the best-selling *God and Science* (Paris: Grasset, 1991), consists in a dialogue between J. Guitton, a highly respected Catholic philosopher and a well-known member of the French National Academy, and Grichka and Igor Bogdanov, young scientists whose fields of research are in astrophysics. In the dialogue between Guitton and the Bogdanov brothers, the scientists answer the questions posed by the philosopher about the laws governing the natural world. Intriguing questions are addressed: "Where is the universe coming from? What is the real? What are the relationships between conscience and matter? Why is there anything rather than nothing?" In every instance the philosopher, who is also a believer in God and the Bible, finds that the answers he receives from science give him comfort and strength in his faith. He finds no contradiction between the two; on the contrary, everything he hears about science strengthens his faith.

A collection of essays edited by Jean Delumeau, *Le Savant et la Foi* ([*Scientists and Faith*], Paris: Champs-Flammarion, 1989), sounds a similar theme. It consists of nineteen contributions from scientists, some of them highly reputed, who explain in often touching terms why they are Christian (mostly Catholic, some Protestant, and one Orthodox) and how they reconcile their faith with their scientific research. One of the essays is the result of a collaboration among some twenty scientists affiliated with the University of Paris-Sud (Orsay, Gif, Saclay, etc.), who hold monthly meetings to discuss issues of science and faith in relationship to their research activity.

A third book that attests to this renewed interest in the relationship between science and faith is another collection of essays, *Can Scientists Believe?* (London: James and James, 1991), written by scientists from different religious traditions and edited by Sir Neville Mott, winner of the Nobel Prize for physics in 1977. In it Mott himself explains how he became a Christian at the age of fifty, when, as head of the Cavendish Laboratory at Cambridge, England, he was invited by the vicar of the university church to join other leading scientists in contributing to a lecture series there about science and religion. Being agnostic, he felt a need to do some reading before discussing something about which he knew very little, and this was the beginning of his conversion.

In January 1992, the Catholic newspaper *La Croix* organized its second conference on "Science and Faith," a day-long conference which took place in a theater in Paris and was widely attended. Among the participants were scientists, theologians, historians, and philosophers, representing all the major religious traditions and including atheists of good will and with an open mind. Some of the participants were people of high professional standing, members of the French Academy. The opening addresses were delivered by Cardinal Jean-Marie Lustiger, Archbishop of Paris, and Professor Hubert Curien, minister in the French government for scientific research.

The recurrent theme of all the contributions at the conference was "Scientism is dead." In order to understand the significance of that pronouncement in the context of our discussion of spirituality and postmodernism, we must consider the historical development of science.

1. Modern Science and Determinism

In the ancient and medieval world, science and religion were part of the same cultural heritage; one was unthinkable without the other. What happened later to cause the chasm between them?

The story is well-known. Modern science developed in the sixteenth and seventeenth centuries, with Francis Bacon (1561–1626) and Galileo Galilei (1564–1642), in the aftermath of a great period, the Italian Renaissance, during which attention shifted from God to humankind, from supernature to nature. Raphael gave dramatic expression to this shift in his famous frescoe, "The School of Athens," where we see Plato, pointing to the sky, at the side of Aristotle, who stretches his hand toward the ground.

The historical rift between science and religion started with Galileo's clash with church authorities over Copernican theory, which was believed to contradict a literal reading of the Bible. Unfortunately, Galileo was unable to persuade the church authorities that the Bible teaches us "how to go to Heaven, not how the heavens go."[1] Darwin's theory of evolution did not help to bridge the gap between science and religion, which became wider and wider up until the beginning of this century.

Indeed, the scientific theories in vogue at the end of the nineteenth century characterized science in general as *deterministic*. Mathematics was a fully developed discipline, and physics was (and still is) a reading of the great book of Nature in the language of mathematics. In this deterministic view, given the conditions of a physical system *at a given time*, we know how the system will evolve later and can predict with absolute certainty the configuration of the system in the future, one hundred, one thousand years from now. The great triumph of the age was Newtonian mechanics, which could describe with great accuracy the motion of celestial bodies. Edmond Halley (1656–1742) was able to predict in 1705 that a certain comet, whose passage had been recorded in several reports in the West and Far East, would appear in the European skies in 1758, which is in fact what happened. How unfortunate that Halley had been dead for sixteen years when "his" comet appeared in the sky!

This was a great triumph for Newtonian mechanics, the most developed science of the time, and induced the feeling that every natural phenomenon could be predicted by human reason with unlimited accuracy. Until then, all scientific endeavors describing the origins of the cosmos referred to God as Creator. It was a noticeable omission, therefore, when the French mathematician Pierre Simon Laplace (1749–1827), in his book, *Exposition du système du monde*, failed to make any mention of God. Questioned by Napoleon about God's role in his theory of the world's origins, Laplace reportedly replied, "Sir, I do not need this hypothesis in my theory."

Toward the end of the nineteenth century, which saw such technological advances as electricity and the steam engine, which made such a deep impact in the life of the western world, confidence in science was unlimited. There was a general feeling that science would ultimately solve all the problems of society and the human condition. Suffering, diseases, poverty—all these evils would sooner or later be eliminated by science and its products. There was no place for God. Human reason could reach the ultimate truth without the need of a supernatural power. This set of euphoric expectations inspired the famous ballet, *Excelsior*, that was such a big hit in the European theaters at the turn of the century.

In philosophy these ideas culminated in schools of thought such as logical positivism, in which there was no room for a transcendent superior being. All these schools of thought are usually referred to under the general name of "scientism." When, therefore, H. Curien and the other participants in the 1992 conference in Paris boldly declared the "death of scientism," they marked the end of a whole historical development and celebrated the present, postmodern period in science.

2. The New Science: Causality and Probability

At the end of the twentieth century we are more ready than eighteenth- and nineteenth-century scientists were to recognize humbly that science has its own limitations and cannot cure all the evils of our human condition. This altered perception of science has been fostered by the advent of the so-called new science, which developed during the third decade of this century. Quantum Mechanics has revolutionized the way people think about the natural world. In the atomic and nuclear realm the deterministic model advanced by Laplace in his *System of the World* was no longer valid. Certainty had to be replaced by the notion of probability; the whole principle of causality had to be questioned and revised. For example, the notion of "orbit," perfectly valid when describing the motion of the earth around the sun, became meaningless in the new theory, which was designed to describe the properties of a negative electron moving around a positive nucleus.

A well-defined trajectory was replaced by a "probability cloud." We do not know where the electron is located at any given time; we only know the regions in space in which it is more likely to be found. Radioactivity is a physical process that illustrates this point even more clearly. If we expose a piece of silver, for example, to a beam of neutrons—the easiest way to perform this experiment is to introduce the metal specimen in the core of a nuclear reactor—a large fraction of silver nuclei will each absorb one neutron. They are said to be "in an excited state." This means that these nuclei will be slightly more massive than those present in ordinary silver. Instead of containing 60 neutrons and 47 protons, which is the nuclear composition of a large fraction of the nuclei present in an ordinary specimen of silver metal, the same material used for bracelets and medals, for example, those excited nuclei will now contain 61 neutrons and 47 protons. They will not be stable, however. They are too big. After a certain time they will decay into cadmium nuclei by emitting one electron. Now, focus your attention on a given excited silver nucleus. We know all the properties of such an object. Quantum Mechanics can be applied to describe the physics of such a system in the least detail. However, we are not able to predict exactly when the excited nucleus will disintegrate. We can only define an average lifetime. In other words, we can say that, 2.4 minutes following the removal of the silver specimen from the reactor core, 50% of the excited nuclei will transmute to cadmium; but we cannot say when a single given excited nucleus will disintegrate. It may happen one second, two seconds, or several hours after extraction. What is physically significant is only the average value of the lifetime. This is a clear example of a situation in which causality no longer works in the usual sense. We are no longer able to predict how a system will evolve in the future, given all the conditions at any given time. A radioactive nucleus does not behave like the Halley comet.

Another important feature of Quantum Mechanics is the equivalence between waves and corpuscles. The great triumph of Augustin-Jean Fresnel (1788–1827) was to show that all optical phenomena known at that time could be explained by considering light as waves. If you sit in a dark room with all the windows closed and let sunlight enter the room through an adjustable slit, you will see projected on the wall behind the slit a bright line, corresponding to the image of the slit. If you reduce progressively the slit aperture, you will notice that at some point, when the distance between the edges is less than 0.2 mm or so, the projected image becomes fuzzy. The bright line projected on the wall does not decrease in size; on the contrary, it will increase, and some other bright lines will appear on the sides of the central image. This curious phenomenon was observed for the first time in the seventeenth century by Francesco Maria Grimaldi, an Italian Jesuit. It could be explained, along with many other more complex optical phenomena, by Fresnel and others by postulating that light propagates like water waves.

However, at the end of the nineteenth century another curious phenomenon was observed. The German scientist Heinrich Rudolph Hertz (1857–1894) discovered that light impinging on a metal surface could cause emission of electrons. This phenomenon was called the "Photoelectric Effect" and is at the base of many devices used today to open and close doors automatically in elevators, stores, etc. Hertz studied very carefully the dependence of electron emission on light color and intensity and concluded that the wave theory of light was in complete contradiction with the experimental observations. The dilemma was solved in 1905 by Albert Einstein (1875–1955), who, with a stroke of genius, assumed that light propagates in bundles, little particles of electromagnetic energy called "photons." So here we have the following situation. When light goes through a fine slit, it behaves like waves. When it stimulates electron emission from metal surfaces, it behaves like particles. What is light, then, waves or particles? The new science answers: neither and both at the same time. Certain phenomena can only be explained by the wave theory, other phenomena by the particle theory, and a third class of phenomena by both.

Louis de Broglie, through another stroke of genius, later proposed that all particles, electrons, protons, neutrons, etc., enjoy the same property. Sometimes they behave like particles, sometimes like waves. A neutron beam going through a fine slit will spread and produce a diffraction pattern similar to that produced by a light beam. The same neutron, going through a counter, will produce a well-defined "click," typical of a particle striking a target.

As these examples indicate, our ability to grasp reality is limited. Waves and particles are different descriptions of the same reality, which we are not able to define in absolute terms, as claimed by the deterministic science of the nineteenth century. At this point we realize that we must give up the idea of grasping "the thing in itself." All this does not mean that the old, deterministic science was wrong, but only that it was correct under certain approximations which are not valid in the micro-world of atoms and nuclei.

The healthy effect of this great revolution brought about by the advent of the new science and Quantum Mechanics has been to shake the arrogance of those who believed that everything could be predicted, once the initial conditions of the system were known, and to introduce an element of chance. We might say, in different words, that there is a place for God in the new scheme of ideas.

Einstein's unenthusiastic response to Quantum Mechanics shows that he clearly perceived the "place for God" at the very heart of things. In the early stage of development of the new physics, he wrote to Niels Bohr: "Quantum Mechanics is very impressive. But an inner voice tells me that it is not yet the real thing. The theory produces a good deal, but hardly brings us close to the secret of the Old One. I am at all events convinced that *He does not play dice.*"[2]

Einstein's letters and essays are famous for their many references to God. Although he never associated with a synagogue and shunned all forms of organized religion, Einstein the scientist had a firm belief in God. Forty years before the 1992 conference in Paris declared the "death of scientism," Einstein had come to this same conclusion, as shown by a letter to his dear friend Solovine:

> You find it strange that I consider the comprehensibility of the world (to the extent that we are authorized to speak of such a comprehensibility) as a miracle or as an eternal mystery. Well, *a priori* one should expect a chaotic world which cannot be grasped by the mind in any way.... There lies the weakness of positivists and professional atheists who are elated because they feel that they have not only successfully rid the world of gods, but also "bared the miracles." Oddly enough, we must be satisfied to acknowledge the "miracle" without there being any legitimate way for us to approach it.[3]

As an exemplar of the "new scientist," Einstein rejects a science without faith, without a belief in the "miracle" that remains "unapproachable" and "mysterious." Perhaps the best description of Einstein's attitude toward religion appears on the back of the dedication page in a recent biography: " 'Science without religion is lame, religion without science is blind'—So Einstein once wrote to explain his personal creed."[4]

3. The Development of Science and Christianity

Given the death of scientism, the discoveries of Quantum Mechanics, and the obvious connection between faith and science in the life and work of men like Einstein, it is now possible to write a revisionary history of western science based not on the split between religious belief and scientific research, but on their intimate connection. We can view science and religion as two approaches, different but complementary, to the same reality. In fact, there has never been a good reason for an opposition between science and religion; they are not incompatible in their views of the natural world.

If we trace the origins of modern science, we find that it was born and developed, not accidentally, in Christian countries. P. E. Hodgson, a British theorist in particle physics at Corpus Christi College, Oxford, observes in regard to Galileo's story:

> All this has obscured the most important feature of scientific investigation, namely, that it is a thoroughly Christian way of studying the world that was first developed within a Christian civilization, precisely because it presupposes beliefs about the natural world that are, as a coherent whole, only to be found in catholic theology.[5]

Similarly, at the 1992 conference sponsored by *La Croix*, the agnostic French philosopher, François Jacob, expounded the idea that scientific thinking flourished in the West due to the concepts, categories, and distinctions elaborated by medieval theology, beginning in the twelfth century. He thus echoed the thesis advanced earlier by the great American philosopher and mathematician, Alfred North Whitehead, who wrote in one of his works on the origin of science: "My explanation is that the faith in the possibility of science, generated antecedently to the development of modern scientific theory, is an unconscious derivative from medieval theology."[6]

In practical rather than theoretical terms, the direct influence of Christianity on the development of science is best exemplified by the work of the Society of Jesus, founded in 1534 by St. Ignatius of Loyola. As part of their mission to spread the Gospel to the ends of the earth, the Jesuits endeavored to acquire and disseminate a wealth of scientific information relevant to cosmology, which was needed for a deeper understanding of the Bible, and mathematics, the God-created language through which the natural world expresses itself to mankind.

As American historian John L. Heilbron has shown, the Jesuits were active world-wide as teachers and missionaries in the seventeenth century. Among them were great scientists—Fr. Christoph Scheiner (1575–1650), for example, who discovered the sunspots in 1611 and explained why the sun appears elliptical when approaching the horizon, and also Fr. Francesco Grimaldi, who discovered diffraction of light in 1665. Among their students, too, were great scientists, one of the most illustrious being Descartes. According to Heilbron, "A complete inventory of the Jesuit-trained savants would include most of the members of the Paris Academy of Science during the 17th and 18th centuries and the leading mathematicians of France, Italy, and southern Germany."[7]

The role of the Jesuits in science continues today. More recently, in 1987, on the occasion of the tercentenary of Newton's *Principia*, a book that literally opened up the ways of the firmament, Pope John Paul II invited a group of twenty-one eminent scholars of various religious backgrounds to his residence in Castel Gandolfo near Rome to explore topics of common interest for scientists, philosophers, and theologians. Fr. George Coyne, a Jesuit astrophysicist and director of the Vatican observatory, organized the conference. A cursory reading of the proceedings numbers at least four Jesuits among the twenty-one participants.

5. Awe and Excitement in Science and Religion

Many scientists, then, have been and are believers. The question then arises: what do science and religion have in common, so that realms previously thought to be mutually exclusive can now be seen as intimately linked? We may point to three elements common to both science and faith: the belief in things unseen, the awe and excitement of discovery, and the goal of service to others. First, the belief in things unseen. It is said of Einstein that he was

> a religious person . . . in the sense that he [had] no doubt of the significance of those super-personal goals which neither require nor are capable of rational foundation. His was not a life of prayer or worship. Yet he lived by a deep faith . . . that there are laws of Nature to be discovered. His lifelong pursuit was to discover them. His realism and optimism are illuminated by his remark: "Subtle is the Lord, but malicious He is not."[8]

Like Einstein, I believe that the laws of nature are an expression of God's revelation to humanity. His word is not only to be found in the Bible; God also speaks to us through the facts of nature. The book of nature is open in front of us, so that we can read into it. To explore the laws of the natural world is to read the word of God. As the Fathers of the Second Vatican Council affirmed, "God, who through the Word creates all things (cf. Jn.1:3) and keeps them in existence, gives people an enduring witness to Himself in created realities."[9]

We can sense God's presence in the beauty of a mathematical proof or derivation, in the harmony of a great synthesis, when many scattered, apparently unrelated phenomena are all brought together by a single formula, the signature of the One who is the principle of everything. Even when an experiment is not working out the way we expected, God is talking to us, telling us how nature works, giving us a different picture from the one we had preconceived. Scientific research is thus a continuous dialogue between God and humankind. If someone were to ask me, "Is faith a benefit to you as a scientist?" my answer would be: "Faith helps me to see my work as a scientist from God's perspective. I read in the book of nature written by God. In this way, I can establish a special relationship with God."

One aspect that links science and religion together and characterizes a scientist's spirituality is the feeling of excitement, the thrill that both scientists and believers experience when confronted with a new facet of the truth that lies beyond the boundary presently accepted as the ultimate limit of our knowledge. As John Polkinghorne, a British professor of theoretical particle physics at Cambridge University and now an Anglican priest, observes, "Part of the authentic experience of a scientist is the feeling of astonishment he or she experiences when contemplating the remarkable rational beauty of the physical world, as it unfolds in his/her research."[10]

The eminent physicist, Isidor Isaac Rabi (1898–1991), who was honored with the Nobel Prize in 1944, bears witness to the religious dimension of this experience of astonishment:

> When I discovered physics, I realized it transcended religion. It was the higher truth. It filled me with awe, put me in touch with a sense of original causes. Physics brought me close to God. That feeling stayed with me throughout my years in science. Whenever one of my students came to me with a scientific project, I asked only one question, "Will it bring you nearer to God?" They always understood what I meant.[11]

Rabi first learned how to come closer to God through awe-filled scientific discovery in the early thirties, when he himself was a graduate student studying under Victor W. Cohen, a professor of physics at Columbia University. The two men were conducting a series of experiments, through which they established the nuclear spin of sodium to be 3/2. Cohen, in a conversation with J. Ridgen, gives a very interesting account of the awe and excitement experienced while conducting this research with Rabi:

> After a long day at the laboratory, he should have been tired—but he was not. He walked with a light step across the campus . . . . He was going home to sleep, but he was not sleepy. He had just finished an experiment with the equipment that he and Rabi had recently redesigned. The results were definitive. Cohen looked in the faces of those other passengers . . . . He had the rarest of feelings. "I know something that none of you know," thought Cohen. "I am the only one in the world who knows that the nuclear spin of sodium is 3/2." With Cohen's definitive result . . . *Rabi moved nearer to God.* (p. 82)

The episode had a profound impact on Rabi's life, and on his world vision of science and religion. At the time Rabi himself had no particular religious affiliation, except for his background, which was strongly rooted in Orthodox Judaism. According to his own testimony, his upbringing in a household where the holy books of the

Bible were familiar readings gave him a definite spiritual formation that affected his attitude toward science:

> To choose physics in the first place requires a certain direction of interest. In my case it was something that goes to my background, and that is religious in origin. Not religion in a secular way, but religion as the inspirer of a way of looking at things. Choosing physics means, in some way, you're not going to choose trivialities. The whole idea of God, that's real class . . . real drama. When you're doing good physics, you are wrestling with the Champ. You have one life to do it, you don't want to waste it. (pp. 79–80)

Like Rabi, who moved "nearer to God" through scientific research and discovery, Xavier Le Pichon, a professor of oceanography and geophysics at the prestigious Collège de France, speaks of his amazing encounters with the God of nature. A member of the French National Academy of Sciences, he has been exploring the bottom of the oceans for the past thirty years. Those underwater explorations have, as he says, awakened his "capacity for adoration":

> I have often experienced this capacity for adoration during my scientific explorations. I think in particular of my first descent in a submarine in the Rift valley, in the middle of the Atlantic ocean, at a depth of ten thousand feet. . . . In our little boat, we are the first people to discover this scenery reminiscent of Genesis, the virgin crust, produced by the marriage between fire and Earth. I had an appointment with the Earth so that I could make an offering to God of the great cliffs of black lava which was twinkling at the light beams of the projectors of our submarine, in the middle of absolute night, in these icy waters, where some bright spots revealed the presence of strange animals.[12]

According to Le Pichon's own account, however, neither the quest for things unseen nor their awesome discovery is enough for a complete spirituality as a scientist. The element of loving service must be added. As he explains, "God has entrusted us with His creation, but it is an unfinished creation, in a way. . . . We must introduce love into this creation" (pp. 166–67). In other words, God invites us to be his collaborators. We are called by God to help him in his work and to complete it.

This fundamental insight of Le Pichon is the final result of a profound crisis of values that he experienced "after some ten years of hard work in [his] research, ten hours a day, seven days a week, ten years dedicated to the secrets of the Earth." Outside of the human "presence of those who suffer most," Le Pichon experienced the absence of God and found that "a feeling of tiredness was progressively invading [his] soul":

> Where was the feast? Where was His love? Where was His presence? Without presence, there is no love, and without love, there is no feast. Active work is no substitute for His presence. To work for the people and with other people does not necessarily imply to live with people, to be present to the people, to love the people. But how can we say that we love our neighbor if we are not even in the presence of those who suffer most, among those who live around us, just across the street, in front of our house? (p. 168)

In the midst of this spiritual turmoil and soul-searching, he went in 1973 to see Mother Teresa and spent two weeks among the destitute in Calcutta. "It was a little child," he writes, "close to death by starvation, who gave me an answer to my quest." The dying child, too weak to speak, gave to Le Pichon "a unique gift . . . of an infinite depth, the gift of his presence," which, in turn, opened Le Pichon's innermost self to God's presence:

> A path had been opened in my innermost self. He was there, with me; we were united in this presence, one to the other, a presence that was giving me, at the same time, God's presence, the presence of the Virgin Mary. . . . It was then, in front of this child, at the feet of the Virgin Mary, that I made a promise, never again to live as though the poor did not exist. (pp. 169–70)

Le Pichon came to understand that he should not abandon his work in science, but that his profession had now become part of a greater plan that God had unveiled for him. He returned to his university job, but at the same time he joined with his family a religious community, l'Arche, devoted to the assistance of the mentally handicapped.

From that time on, Le Pichon has been filled with the conviction that

> Science and technology are not only necessary; they are indeed the main tools needed to perfect this Creation entrusted to mankind by God. . . . To the extent we place the poor and the least ones at the center of our society, to the extent we ask them to inspire the civilization we are about to build up, science and technology will appear means offered to mankind in order to create a civilization of love, aiming toward their ultimate goal, God, who is merciful and tender, God, who is Love, who wanted us to be not only His servants, His collaborators, but also His friends. (pp. 171–73)

At the close of the historic Parisian conference sponsored by *La Croix*, Louis Leprince Ringuet, a member of both the French Academy and the Academy of Sciences, a highly distinguished scientist famous for his contributions to cosmic ray physics, made a passionate, personal act of faith as a scientist-believer. His words express my own experience of the great harmony between science and faith when he finds in "Christ's message . . . such a revolutionary wisdom in loving our neighbor, in going beyond ourselves" and in "the Christian attitude of hope" such strength for meeting the multiple "tests staking out our existence," that he can only affirm: "I find it so stimulating for my intellectual and spiritual progress—[the thought that] Christ is with us up to the end of times—briefly, I find in the Gospel message such a potential for going beyond ourselves, for joy and boldness, such a meaning in life, that for me this message has the seal of truth."[13]

Notes

1. Galileo Galilei, "Letter to the Grand Duchess Christina," trans. Stillman Drake, in *Discoveries and Opinions of Galileo* (New York: Doubleday, 1957), p. 186. The whole letter, which is quite long, deals with the issue of using biblical quotations in matters of science.

2. Quoted by Abraham Pais, *Niels Bohr's Times* (Oxford: Clarendon Press, 1991), p. 318.

3. Albert Einstein, *Letters to Solovine* (New York: Philosophical Library, 1987), p. 131.

4. Abraham Pais, *Subtle Is the Lord: The Science and the Life of Albert Einstein* (Oxford: Clarendon Press and New York: Oxford University Press, 1982), p. vi.

5. P. E. Hodgson, "Science and the Christian World View," in *Can Scientists Believe?* ed. Neville Mott (London: James and James, 1991), p. 71.

6. Alfred N. Whitehead, *Science and the Modern World*, Lowell Lectures (New York: Macmillan, 1925), p. 17.

7. John L. Heilbron, "Creativity and Big Science," *Physics Today* 45.11 (1992), p. 42.

8. Pais, *Subtle Is the Lord*, p. vi.

9. "Dogmatic Constitution on Divine Revelation" (*Dei Verbum*) in *The Documents of Vatican II*, ed. Walter M. Abbott, S.J., trans. Msgr. Joseph Gallagher (Boston: America Press, 1966), 1.3, p. 112.

10. John Polkinghorne, "Faith Conceptions of a Physicist," in *Le Savant et la Foi*, ed. Jean Delumeau (Paris: Champs and Flammarion, 1989), p. 230. All translations from this work are mine.

11. Quoted in John S. Ridgen, *Rabi, Scientist and Citizen* (New York: Basic Books, 1987), p. 73. The passages immediately following, cited parenthetically, are from the same source.

12. Xavier Le Pichon, "Everything That Is Mine Is Yours," in *Le Savant et la Foi*, p. 166. Subsequent citations from this same source are given parenthetically.

13. Quoted in " 'Science et Foi,' Conference Organized by the Newspaper *La Croix-l'Événement*" (Paris: Centurion, 1992), p. 188. I want to acknowledge in conclusion that this article would never have seen the light of day without the suggestions and the encouragement of my wife Adele, who, early in our married life, started to point out to my consideration many parallels between scientific knowledge and what we believe as Christians.

VALERIE MIKÉ

Spirituality and Contemporary American Medicine: A Postmodern Perspective

In late 1991, when his new book *Final Exit*—a manual of suicide techniques for the terminally ill—was being highly publicized in the mass media, Derek Humphry was interviewed by William Buckley on the television program "Firing Line."[1] In the course of the discussion Buckley asked the author to name some major figures in the history of philosophy whose views would support his own position concerning the problem of suicide. Appearing surprised, Humphry replied that he had never read a philosophy book in his life. Just the same, his book became a national bestseller and is still widely read today. Not long ago I happened to look for it in the county library of a New Jersey shore community where I was visiting. The on-line catalogue listed twenty-two copies of *Final Exit* and thirteen copies were checked out, including an audio cassette version.

The question of suicide for the seriously ill and the role of doctors in aiding suicidal patients is hotly debated in current biomedical ethics. The legalization of physician-assisted suicide is on the political agenda of a number of states. And Jack Kevorkian, the "Death Doctor" peddling his bizarre suicide gear, has attained celebrity status.

But there is another, less well known aspect of this complex and troubling issue. Fear of pain and suffering is what may drive some people to seek a way out by ending their own lives. A number of studies have shown, however, that there is widespread ignorance

among health care professionals about the effective use of modern
methods of pain control and the diagnosis and treatment of psychological distress.[2] Many patients thus do not receive adequate management of their pain and other symptoms. They are being wooed
instead by the siren call of self-proclaimed gurus of euthanasia.

The topic of this essay is spirituality and the American health
care system. The relationship between medicine and religion—the
concern with illness, suffering, and the great mysteries of life—is a
vast subject, as old as recorded history. But our focus here is on the
present, on spirituality for the postmodern era. It will suffice for
now to consider the term "postmodern" in a general sense, as reflecting the widespread feeling that something is very wrong with
modernity, with the conditions and worldview of modern existence, and that humanity can and must go beyond it.[3] I will be
more specific later, in the context of the material and concepts I
have presented. My overall objective is to offer some thoughts on
what I believe to be a crucial role for spirituality in the crisis facing
contemporary American medicine. The preoccupation with suicide
is just a symptom reflecting a host of underlying problems.

THE CRISIS IN AMERICAN MEDICINE

Let me emphasize that there is no intent here to question the
marvelous achievements of modern medicine, which has emerged
as a powerful combination of science and technology. For the first
time in history truly effective agents are available for the treatment of disease. Antibiotics and immunization have revolutionized
the practice of medicine. Success has also been attained in numerous other areas, such as diagnostic procedures, trauma medicine,
and the treatment of hypertension, diabetes, cancer and psychiatric disorders. A vigorous national biomedical research program
continues to make advances on many fronts. Test-tube babies, organ transplants, genetic engineering—all bear witness to human
creative genius. American medicine is considered the best in the
world, and people from many other countries come here for specialized treatment. Nevertheless, the problems are daunting.

First—and the subject of much public discourse—are the issues of cost and access. There is the spiraling cost of health care in
the United States, the highest per capita cost among developed
nations—more than twice the average for the others. Yet nearly
forty million Americans are without basic health insurance. Ex-

cept for South Africa, we are the only industrial nation in the world without universal health insurance for our citizens.

Despite the high expenditures, the United States ranks fifteenth in infant mortality and ninth for women and twelfth for men in life expectancy among twenty-two developed nations.[4] These statistics, and the American health care system as a whole, can only be understood in the broader context of national life. By this I mean the breakdown of the family, the central role of poverty, and what has been called the medicalization of social problems.[5] Included among these problems are violence, teenage pregnancy, and the various forms of substance abuse—the latter frequently the major factor in other serious medical conditions. Much of the health care dollar is spent on advanced-technology medicine, often in crisis-oriented care, which has very little impact on the general health of the population.

Less well publicized by far are problems related to the limitations of medical knowledge. Generally lacking in technological literacy, the public is not aware of the extent of medical uncertainty. The causes of most major diseases are still unknown, and for most there is as yet no cure. Market forces, supported by popular demand and a third-party payment system, are driving the diffusion of medical technology. New medical technologies are constantly being introduced that far surpass the boundaries of medical knowledge. According to a comprehensive report issued by the Institute of Medicine of the National Academy of Sciences, no more than 10–20% of medical procedures in use today have been evaluated in properly controlled trials.[6] A large number may be useless or perhaps harmful. There is also a great deal of geographic variation in medical practice. Studies have shown that even when results are definitively established, physicians tend to ignore them and prescribe instead treatments that are customary in their own communities. Many may lack sufficient technical knowledge to assess critically the medical literature.[7]

At the same time, an estimated 50% or more of complaints brought to doctors indicate not organic but functional disorders that may be of emotional origin. And the vast majority of medical conditions are self-limited; people get better even without treatment. There is also the powerful but little-understood placebo effect: Patients tend to respond to any kind of treatment. Indeed, until recently the history of medicine was essentially the history of the placebo effect.

Poorly informed, often anxious and confused, the public turns to medicine to seek relief for a wide variety of ills and symptoms. Medical services are in great demand, but when they fail, malpractice litigation is all too often the recourse of choice for the patient. Given a secular culture dominated by reductionist thought, limited in its ability to address the deeper questions of meaning and ultimate concern, people perhaps unconsciously expect medicine to provide relief from all the problems related to anxiety, suffering and death. Medical sociologist Renée Fox has referred to the American pursuit of organ transplantation as a kind of "ritualized optimism," the symbolic expression of our relentless drive for success and progress.[8] In other words, in the absence of other cultural options, life must be continued by the repair and replacement of failing bodily parts. And now, as the most recent development, the physician is being asked to assist in suicide, to assume the final role of liberator—by becoming executioner.

Faced with the explosion of health care costs, the uncontrolled growth of medical technology, much of it not properly evaluated, with overwhelming social problems, and the unreasonable expectations of the public, American medicine is in a state of unprecedented crisis. There is a concentrated effort now to develop programs of outcomes research, in order to better assess the results, or outcomes, of medical interventions. The need for health care reform is seen to be of utmost urgency. But given the enormous complexity of the system and the lack of consensus on specifics, reform will at best be a long-term undertaking. And in any case, the focus has so far been primarily on economic and management issues.

A SPIRITUAL AGENDA

We come now to the theme of these reflections. It is my belief that medicine can respond to the crisis and fulfill its true potential only in the context of a renewed spirituality. I mean by this a spirituality that respects the autonomy of temporal realities, but imbues them with meaning and value in light of the transcendent dimension of human life.

There has been increasing interest on the part of the public in holistic health and alternative forms of medicine, such as homeopathy, osteopathy and acupuncture, adopted from other cultures or recalled from our own past.[9] The book *Healing and the Mind*, based on the recent PBS series hosted by Bill Moyers, has become a national bestseller. The etiology of major alternative systems of medicine encompasses body-mind-spirit, reaching beyond the material world. Orthodox medicine, on the other hand, has been bounded by our present cultural horizon. Intense focus on the physical world has yielded the dazzling achievements of scientific medicine. But it has been at a price—that of ignoring other aspects of reality.

I would like to sketch a four-fold spiritual agenda that I believe is essential to the resolution of the crisis in medicine. This agenda addresses: (1) our intellectual worldview, (2) the role of the churches in health care, (3) ethics and the proper use of medicine, and (4) education and the nurturing of spirituality in children.

1. Needed: A Unified Vision for Humanity

The most important long-range goal must be the development of an integrated worldview—a new vision for humanity—based on a creative merging of the insights of diverse disciplines. The aim should be restoration of the balance that has been shifted by the pervasive spirit of scientism, with its offer of false absolutes. The challenge facing us has been described eloquently in a message issued a few years ago by Pope John Paul II. Especially noteworthy about the message is the strong support it expresses for the autonomous role of science in contributing to the achievement of a meaningful intellectual synthesis. Because of its relevance to our discussion, I will give a brief summary of some of the important points made in this document.

In 1987, on the occasion of the three hundredth anniversary of the publication of Newton's *Philosophiae Naturalis Principia Mathematica*, the Vatican sponsored a conference to examine the multiple relationships among theology, philosophy and the natural sciences. Pope John Paul II delivered an address to the participants, which was published as part of the conference proceedings.

In his message the pope described the Church and the Academy as two major institutions in world civilization, both of which have had great influence on the development of ideas and values and on the course of human action. He spoke of the mutual support provided by each in the past, as well as the times of needless conflict, and called for joint reflection now as we approach the close of this millennium. He referred to the world seemingly "in fragments, in disjointed pieces," which within the academic community is seen as the separation between truth and value, and the isolation of scientific, humanistic, and religious cultures, making common discourse difficult if not impossible.[10]

Addressing the relationship between religion and science, the pope called for increased openness and interchange that must develop and grow both in its depth and its scope. And in the process, he said, "we must overcome every regressive tendency to a unilateral reductionism, to fear, and to self-imposed isolation" (p. M7). He posed some crucial questions for consideration: "Is the community of world religions, including the Church, ready to enter into a more thoroughgoing dialogue with the scientific community, a dialogue in which the integrity of both religion and science is supported and the advance of each is fostered? Is the scientific community now prepared to open itself to Christianity, and indeed to all the great world religions, working with us all to build a culture that is more humane and in that way more divine" (pp. M7-M8)?

The pope commented on the necessarily close interaction between, and mutual interdependence of, science and religion in the human effort to "make sense of experience":

> Science develops best when its concepts and conclusions are integrated into the broader human culture and its concerns for ultimate meaning and value. . . . Science can purify religion from error and superstition; religion can purify science from idolatry and false absolutes. Each can draw the other into a wider world, a world in which both can flourish. . . . Only a dynamic relationship between theology and science can reveal those limits which support the integrity of either discipline, so that theology does not profess pseudo-science and science does not become an unconscious theology. Our knowledge of each other can lead us to be more authentically ourselves. No one can read the history of the past century and not realize that crisis is upon us both. The uses of science have on more than one occasion proven massively destructive, and the reflections on religion have too often been sterile. We need each other to be what we must be, what we are called to be. (pp. M13-M14)

The pope's words invite renewed dialogue and cooperation by the worldwide community of scholars. Stimulated by recent advances at the forefront of fundamental physics, there has in fact been a resurgence of interest among scientists to explore the limits of rational inquiry in the search for purpose and meaning in the universe. An example of this is the book by Paul Davies, *The Mind of God: The Scientific Basis for a Rational World.*[11]

When the time comes that will begin yielding the achievement of integrated cultures and a unified vision, there will be less pressure on medicine to provide what is clearly outside its scope and function. But such a vision may well be the fruit reserved for another generation.

2. The Role of the Churches in Health Care

The second item on my suggested spiritual agenda is an approach pertaining to the social order. Even in our present state of cultural fragmentation there are resources that can be better utilized. We can invoke our spiritual traditions to seek a solution to current problems of the health care system. A commitment to charity as well as social justice would seek the best possible health care for all.

The strong demand for medical care in this country has not produced a popular consensus to take care of the poor. Even Medicaid, the government health plan for the indigent, covers only half of those living under the poverty level, and in some states less than 20%.[12] One out of four children under six lives in poverty, and half of all black children under six, while 20% of pregnant white women, and nearly 40% of pregnant women who are black, do not receive prenatal care until after the first trimester. Infant mortality and morbidity are much higher and chronic diseases more prevalent among the poor. In terms of expenditures, the cost of high-technology medical care of a prematurely born infant, for example, can be enormous, and the child may be handicapped for life. Although there is today no direct way to reallocate funds, a reduction in teenage pregnancies and adequate prenatal care for all pregnant women would cost far less and would greatly alleviate this problem.

Given the bewildering spectrum of social ills facing the nation, how does one even begin to speak of solutions? Any answer, I believe, has to be based on education and motivation; the fostering of personal responsibility is essential.

How to motivate and provide values and moral support in today's cultural milieu is a difficult question, but one that offers a special challenge to the churches. There is an existing social network with a long tradition of facing such issues—that of church communities around the country. Two thirds of the American people belong to a church of some denomination.

Within the past few years, more than a dozen Christian church bodies as well as Jewish groups in the United States have produced statements on economic justice asserting the need to help the poor.[13] Enhancing the traditional concept of charity is that of justice—a sense that the poor have a right to essential services. These endorsements of ethical principles by the church groups are not specific in terms of policy directives, but they can serve to raise consciousness and to inspire church members to assume more responsibility for action.

The churches are also in the best position to provide the kind of counseling to the sick and dying that would help put the uses of medical technology and of spiritual resources into a balanced perspective. This of course requires that those involved in pastoral ministry be cognizant of the latest advances as well as the limitations of contemporary medicine.

It can even be argued that the churches have a responsibility to teach their members about health in areas where medicine and religion overlap, and that they can help focus attention on the need for prevention.[14] It has been pointed out that there is a special opportunity for the Church at this time to reclaim its traditional role in health and healing.[15] But, in contrast to the denial and extravagant promise of the holistic movement, there is a clear-cut need to acknowledge and offer sustaining interpretations of inevitable suffering.

3. Ethics and the Proper Use of Medicine

This brings us naturally to the third approach of our spiritual agenda. We see that the issues go beyond providing health care for the poor. A spirituality that promotes the full development of temporal realities would call for the best available health care for all—the best that medicine has to offer. This means not only high quality medical research, but also careful assessment of clinical innovations, with continuous education of health care professionals as well as the general public. It means constantly seeking to understand what today's medicine can and cannot do, and then using spiritual resources to deal with the whole situation—a situation that of necessity involves many uncertainties.

Thinking along these lines, I am now working on what I have called the "ethics of evidence," an approach to medical uncertainty to be incorporated into the evolving scope of biomedical ethics.[16] The primary motivation for this work has been the recognition that better scientific validation is needed for meaningful, ethically defensible action in many areas of health care, in both medical practice and public policy. Quite aside from the grantedly pressing fiscal situation, this factor must for ethical reasons be an integral part of any serious attempt at reforming the health care system.

The ethics of evidence pertains to standards for the creation, assessment, and communication of evidence. Its main tenet is twofold, comprising two distinct imperatives. The first imperative asserts the need to develop and disseminate the best possible scientific evidence as a basis for every phase of medical decision making. Complementing it, the second imperative addresses the need to come to terms with the ultimately irreducible nature of uncertainty. This dual tenet can be viewed as a newly formulated principle of biomedical ethics.

From the perspective of my own professional experience, the most critical feature of the first imperative—to develop and disseminate the best possible medical evidence—is its focus on scientific method. This imperative calls attention to the importance of gaining insight into the nature of medical evidence. Included here is the need for greater "numeracy" on the part of both health care professionals and the public—meaning facility with numbers and skill in quantitative reasoning. Especially relevant is the branch of mathematics dealing with the assessment of random variation in observable phenomena—the theory of probability and statistics— which is essential to the evaluation of the safety and effectiveness of medical procedures. Better understanding is needed of the power as well as the limitations of statistical methodology, and the often incomplete and ambiguous scientific evidence on which clinical decisions must be based. The goal must always be to obtain the best evidence possible at our current state of knowledge, and for the medical community to share what has been learned, and what remains uncertain, with the general public.

It can be shown that this first imperative of the ethics of evidence is supported by the three basic principles of contemporary bioethics, the principles of autonomy, beneficence, and justice. Briefly, the main considerations are as follows:

The principle of autonomy—or respect for persons—states that patients have the right to make their own decisions about their treatment, to give their informed consent. But it is hardly possible to give "informed" consent if the procedure in question has not been properly evaluated. The necessary information is just not available, and typically the patient is not even aware of the extent of medical uncertainty.

The principle of beneficence and nonmaleficence—help or at least do no harm—dates back to Hippocrates and is directly relevant to the ethics of evidence. It implicitly mandates the careful assessment of all medical interventions for their safety and effectiveness. According to this principle it is unethical to use powerful diagnostic and therapeutic procedures that have not been properly evaluated and may thus be useless or even harmful.

The principle of justice, generally applied in the bioethics context to the fair selection of research subjects, has broader implications; it can be interpreted to mean access to adequate health care for all. This principle supports the ethics of evidence in an indirect but very special way. If only those medical procedures were used that are safe and really effective, the resulting savings would help alleviate the fiscal crisis and provide medical coverage for the many millions of Americans now without health insurance. The approach of seeking and focusing on safe and effective procedures would at the same time yield better health care for all.

The first imperative of the ethics of evidence, firmly based on currently accepted principles of biomedical ethics, is thus well within the scope of secular humanism. The second imperative, on the other hand, extends beyond the secular to the realm of the spiritual.

If we demand at all times the best that medical science can provide, requesting full disclosure of what is known as well as what remains still unknown, then we have to openly confront the resulting uncertainty. Dealing with this uncertainty, with the anxiety, with the fear of suffering and death, requires recourse to cultural alternatives that in the past have provided humanity with hope and meaning. Understanding medical uncertainty is I believe essential for making progress toward the proper—that is, more limited and realistic—use of medicine. But our excessive faith in medical technology cannot be controlled in a vacuum, if nothing is offered in its place for coping with the deeper issues. A radical shift in focus is called for.

The essence of what I mean by the second imperative of the ethics of evidence—a coherent response to the uncertainty around us—finds poignant expression in the words of Blaise Pascal. A seminal thinker of the seventeenth century, Pascal is also considered the founder of probability theory, my own discipline. What he saw and felt as scientist at the dawning of the modern era has an authentic ring for us today:

> When I consider the short duration of my life, swallowed up in the eternity before and after, the little space which I fill, and even can see, engulfed in the infinite immensity of spaces of which I am ignorant, and which know me not, I am frightened, and am astonished at being here rather than there; for there is no reason why here rather than there, why now rather than then. . . . The eternal silence of these infinite spaces frightens me.[17]

But Pascal had his own impassioned response to this experience: "There are only two kinds of people one can call reasonable; those who serve God with all their heart because they know Him, and those who seek Him with all their heart because they do not know Him" (*Pensée* 194, p. 63).

What Pascal's response implies for us today is the need to search for meaning in the face of uncertainty and suffering. It implies the need to share the vision or insights we may have, or to join with others in the seeking. The search itself requires intellectual honesty and humility, an openness to all the evidence that may be offered, regardless of the source, to be judged by the highest standards of scholarship in every field.

To illustrate the ethics of evidence, we can return to the question of suicide for the seriously ill. The first imperative holds health care professionals responsible for the knowledge and skill needed to provide their patients with the most effective techniques of pain and symptom management. Even the basic principle of beneficence demands no less. The second imperative, on the other hand, calls on patient and community alike to draw on our cultural resources for solace and meaning. To be able to offer helpful advice and support to others in coping with life's great mysteries requires more compassion and wisdom and learning than was revealed, for example, by Derek Humphry, who—compounding his ignorance of medical advances—admits to never having read a philosophy book in his life.

In a recent review essay on a series of books concerned with suffering and pain, Arthur Frank refers in his title to "varieties of postmodern pain."[18] Four of the books address special topics,

namely, anorexia, infertility, chronic pain, and children dying of
cancer, each considered in the context of intensive medical interventions and of society's attitudes and response. Frank adopted the
term "postmodern pain" from the fifth book he reviewed, David
Morris' *The Culture of Pain*.[19] Morris bases his notion of postmodern
pain on the definition of postmodernism given by the philosopher
Jean-François Lyotard, as "the condition in which vast, overarch-
ing, general systems of explanation (he calls them 'metanarratives')
lose their power." Morris sees it as the most striking feature of contemporary suffering that it "cannot be enfolded within a single over-
arching metanarrative or system of explanation"—hence the expression "postmodern pain." While agreeing with this observation,
Frank notes that of the combination of explanations available to the
sufferer, none in itself is new. Chief among these are the metanarratives of medicine and religion.

The term "metanarrative"—just like "postmodern"—may
mean different things to different people. It is not my intention
here to interpret Morris or Frank or Lyotard or Morris' interpretation of Lyotard or Frank's interpretation of Morris. But there is at
least an analogy between my own dual concept of the ethics of
evidence and the postmodern distinction between metanarrative
and narrative. What I am suggesting as a replacement for the contemporary metanarrative of the physician as the ultimate liberator
from pain, death and life itself is a concrete and realistic medical
narrative. In confronting illness, there is the need for full awareness and thorough assessment of what medicine today has to
offer—the current medical narrative. The latter in turn needs to be
complemented by the spiritual metanarrative, which over the ages
has not only helped humanity to come to terms with suffering, but
in some inscrutable way has even led many to discern in its endur-
ance ever new depths of meaning and joy.

4. Education and the Ultimate Questions

The call for a comprehensive system of education, integrating a
broad spectrum of disciplines, is part of the fourth approach in our
spiritual agenda. A better understanding of technology, including
more attention to mathematics and the scientific method, should be
a major national goal. In addition to literacy, "numeracy" is increasingly becoming a prerequisite for meaningful citizenship in a democratic society. But there is also a need for greater awareness of our

rich heritage of responses to the sacred. Reasoned discourse in presenting the options of our spiritual traditions—of dealing with the age-old problems of suffering and death—is an important aspect of the process of communication and education. This is being done, for example, in the case of euthanasia, as well as other controversial issues in biomedical ethics.[20]

Also promising for the challenge of expanding spiritual horizons is current research on the role of imagination in ethics.[21] Drawing on insights from such fields as hermeneutic philosophy and cognitive psychology, this work examines the need to go beyond the discursive and logical in moral reasoning. It explores the function of story and symbol, of the virtue ethic, and of tradition which helps us to get in touch with the historical roots of our values. It is essential to follow up on these leads in preparing the young to respond effectively to the critical issues of our day.

Relevant here is a recent book entitled *The Spiritual Life of Children*, by the noted child psychiatrist Robert Coles. Coles has spent thirty years writing about the culture of children. His findings, obtained in field studies around the world, are based on his observations and on conversations carried out with thousands of children. But this final book has been almost like an afterthought.

After the publication of his five-volume work, *Children of Crisis*, it was suggested to him by Anna Freud, the daughter of Sigmund Freud and the founder of child psychoanalysis, that it would be of interest to go back over his material—the recorded interviews, children's drawings and other documents—to look for what he might have missed the first time around. But it was several years and two books later that memories began to emerge—a child's remark made, a picture drawn, a reverie shared, all in some way having a religious and spiritual theme. Undertaking now a systematic review of his material, he was surprised by what he uncovered—the many opportunities missed over the years, strong hints not picked up, lines of inquiry not pursued.

Coles had been trained in the traditional school of psychoanalytic orthodoxy, which considers religion as a universal obsessive neurosis. Writing now, he recalls: "The people I met in hospitals and clinics were all too often turned into a reductive putty by my mind."[22] And he continues: "Even today I recall with sadness and remorse some of the thoughts I had, the words I used, as I worked with children who had their own moral concerns, their philosophical interests, their religious convictions" (p. 10).

When he decided to do a prospective study of children with the

aim of focusing on the spiritual, he had great difficulty obtaining
foundation support; there was little interest in religion and even
puzzlement as to what he wanted to do with the subject. The research project reported in the book was carried out over a period of
several years in the United States, Central and South America, Europe, the Middle East, and Africa. It involved extended and repeated
conversations with hundreds of children, in the context of three
great world religions, Christianity, Islam and Judaism, as well as
secular settings. The author learned of children's pervasive interest
in God, in the sacred and the supernatural, in the ultimate meaning
of life. He observed children even from agnostic homes intensely
struggling with essentially religious and spiritual questions.

Discussing the rich and surprising findings of the study, Coles
points the way for others to follow, to further enhance these insights. In his words: "Others, too, might enjoy walking this road,
one that has been somewhat neglected, even shunned, by any number of us who are significantly secularistic and scientific in our
education. From such others we would, surely, learn more of what
it means to be a human being, possessed of language and consciousness. And from the religious we might well learn what a great
Teacher said of the spiritual life: 'Suffer little children to come
unto me, and forbid them not; for of such is the kingdom of God' "
(p. 39).

CONCLUSION

We have covered a wide range in these reflections, just barely
touching on some of the highlights. The suggestions of a spiritual
agenda are only a few of what could perhaps be made by others.
But these suggestions seem essential for responding to the needs of
contemporary medicine.

The position developed in this essay fits well into the conceptual framework described by David Ray Griffin as "constructive or
revisionary postmodernism." The latter entails the construction of
a postmodern worldview by a revision of modern premises and
premodern concepts, to bring about the integration of scientific,
ethical, religious, and esthetic intuitions. Constructive postmodern
thought does not reject science; it rejects scientism, the currently
widespread ideology in which nothing beyond the data of the modern natural sciences is granted relevance for a meaningful worldview. The balanced approach of constructive postmodernism calls

for preserving the unparalleled achievements of the modern world, in a rich synthesis of modern and traditional truths and values.

This vision of a creative intellectual synthesis was given powerful expression in the words of Pope John Paul II cited earlier. In the context of the present discussion, its attainment is in turn crucial for long-term resolution of the crisis in American medicine.

In an ideal world only those medical procedures are used that are really effective, and they are available to all. To this end there must be a more critical attitude toward medical technology on the part of both professionals and the public, with awareness of its intrinsic limitations. Other cultural resources must be used to help cope with life's uncertainties, with suffering and death. There is a central role in this for the churches and an immense challenge for education.

A renewed, deeper spirituality has much to contribute to the meaningful development and functioning of American medicine. The achievement of a balanced worldview needs to be sought as the highest priority. But here and now, committed to social justice as well as charity, such a spirituality must seek the best possible health care for all. It must also explore diverse means of education to nurture and further develop the natural sense of wonder and spirituality of the young.

A unified vision of the ultimate mysteries permits medicine to flourish—to fulfill its true potential of seeking greater insight into life processes and thereby the eradication of disease. And when medicine fails, as it must sooner or later fail in every life, spirituality has still more to offer. There is for example the joyous message of the Gospel—the hope of resurrection and eternal life, when in the end "death is swallowed up in victory" (1 Cor 15:54).

Notes

1. William F. Buckley, Jr., "The Right to Death: An Interview with Derek Humphry," *Firing Line*, PBS (October 20, 1991).

2. Kathleen M. Foley, "The Relationship of Pain and Symptom Management to Patient Requests for Physician-Assisted Suicide," *Journal of Pain and Symptom Management* 6 (1991): 289–97.

3. See David Ray Griffin, "Introduction to SUNY Series in Constructive Postmodern Thought," in *The Reenchantment of Science:*

Postmodern Proposals, ed. David Ray Griffin (Albany: State University of New York Press, 1988), pp. ix–xii.

4. Dorothy P. Rice, "Do We Get Full Value for our Health Dollar?" *Hospitals* 62.6 (1988):18.

5. See Robert H. Ebert, "A Twentieth Century Retrospective," in *Medicine and Society: Clinical Decisions and Societal Values*, ed. Eli Ginzberg (Boulder, CO: Westview Press, 1987), pp. 7–19.

6. For the Institute's report, see *Assessing Medical Technologies* (Washington, D.C.: National Academy Press, 1985).

7. See my "Understanding Uncertainties in Medical Evidence: Professional and Public Responsibilities," in *Acceptable Evidence: Science and Values in Risk Management*, ed. Deborah G. Mayo and Rachelle D. Hollander (New York: Oxford University Press, 1991), pp. 115–37.

8. See "Medical Uncertainty: An Interview with Renée C. Fox," *Second Opinion* 6 (1987): 90–105.

9. See Andrew Weil, *Health and Healing: Understanding Conventional and Alternative Medicine* (Boston: Houghton Mifflin, 1983).

10. John Paul II, "Message of His Holiness Pope John Paul II," in *Physics, Philosophy, and Theology: A Common Quest for Understanding*, ed. Robert J. Russell, William R. Stoeger and George V. Coyne (Notre Dame: University of Notre Dame Press, 1988), pp. M1-M14. Subsequent citations are given parenthetically by page.

11. Paul Davies, *The Mind of God: The Scientific Basis for a Rational World* (New York: Simon and Schuster, 1992).

12. Victor W. Sidel, "Medical Technology and the Poor," *Technology Review* 90 (May/June 1987): 24–25.

13. See Robert M. Brown and Sydney T. Brown, ed., *A Cry for Justice: The Churches and Synagogues Speak* (New York: Paulist, 1989).

14. Cf. William Foege, "The Vision of the Possible: What Churches Can Do," *Second Opinion* 13 (1990): 36–42.

15. Cf. Martin E. Marty, "The Tradition of the Church in Health and Healing," *Second Opinion* 13 (1990): 48–72.

16. See my "Toward an Ethics of Evidence—and Beyond: Observations on Technology and Illness," *Research in Philosophy & Technology* 9 (1989): 101–113; "Ethics, Evidence, and Uncertainty," *Controlled Clinical Trials* 11 (1990): 153–156; and "Quality of Life Research and the Ethics of Evidence," *Quality of Life Research* 1 (1992): 273–276.

17. Blaise Pascal, *Pensées: Thoughts on Religion and Other Subjects*, trans. William F. Trotter (New York: Washington Square Press, 1965), 205–06, p. 66.

18. Arthur W. Frank, "Varieties of Postmodern Pain: Recent Narratives of Witness and Response," *Second Opinion* 18.4 (1993): 128–39.

19. David B. Morris, *The Culture of Pain* (Berkeley and Los Angeles: University of California Press, 1991), pp. 282–83.

20. See Kevin O'Rourke, "Assisted Suicide: An Evaluation," *Journal of Pain and Symptom Management* 6 (1991): 317–24.

21. See Philip S. Keane, *Christian Ethics and Imagination* (New York: Paulist, 1984); Edith Wyschogrod, *Saints and Postmodernism: Revisioning Moral Philosophy* (Chicago: University of Chicago Press, 1990).

22. Robert Coles, *The Spiritual Life of Children* (Boston: Houghton Mifflin, 1990), p. 10. Subsequent citations are parenthetical.

ELENA LUGO

Reflections on Philosophy, Spirituality, and Mariology

The meaningful interrelationship of the concepts in our title—as cultural entities or as a dimension of human experience—is by no means evident. Inspired by the following expression of Sertillanges, I intend to explore a possible inner connection of the above concepts within the framework of philosophy's own present search for self-identity and role.

In *The Intellectual Life: Its Spirit, Conditions, and Methods*, Sertillanges offers words of special significance for our time:

> Do you want to do intellectual work? Begin by creating within you a zone of silence, a habit of recollection, a will to renunciation and detachment which puts you entirely at the disposal of the work, acquire that state of soul unburdened by desire and self-will which is the state of grace of the intellectual work.[1]

In what follows I would like to proceed deductively, but be open to intuition when I judge it pertinent to the complex subject, to demonstrate: first, how the self-questioning of philosophy regarding its identity and mission leads to a search of its existential roots; second, how these roots reveal an inherent spirituality; and finally, how the full meaning of that spirituality points in the direction of Christian thought, particularly toward a *Mariology*.

1. Present Quest of Philosophy for Its Identity and Mission

Here I intend a narrow perspective of modernism and post-modernism only and insofar as pertaining to a critical issue in and for some philosophers. Critics of philosophy, as an institution, claim that contemporary philosophy experiences a crisis rooted in its disillusionment with its modern project to become a science.[2] The modernist spirit as reflected in modern philosophy is well-known for its foundationalist project: the concerns with what we can know, how we should live, in what or whom we should hope or trust—indeed, all the basic epistemological, ethical, and religious issues—were dominated by the epistemological quest for certainty. This certainty was conceived according to the rigorous and precise criteria of the natural sciences and mathematics. The foundation was to be found in objective reality, as grasped and represented by human reason, applying the scientific method. Thus, philosophy rested on the modern assumptions about progress, universality, and regularity, as inspired and promoted through a scientific and correspondingly emerging technology, while neglecting the traditional quest for wisdom.

The disillusionment of philosophy regarding its modern foundationalist project is often expressed as *postmodernism*. As a philosophical critique of the modern spirit, postmodernism is characterized by (a) disenchantment with reason as the way to mirror reality; (b) acceptance or resignation regarding the failure to find a foundation for one's ideas, values, and beliefs; and (c) rejection of the great systems—philosophical, political, and religious—with universal and permanent principles. In other words, postmodernism opposes the modernist foundational project and invites us to give up the longing for the eternal, for certainty, and for objectivity. We live in an age of suspicion toward all totalizing ideologies and belief systems. By and large, postmodernism as an attitude, a way of thinking, expresses a loss of faith in the ability to legitimize or validate the great ideas of the Enlightenment: Reason, Objectivity, and Science.

In what follows I concentrate on postmodernism as a challenge for a traditionally conceived philosophical quest for wisdom. One may ask: how has postmodernism as a critique of the modern spirit challenged philosophy to search for a new identity and purpose? The challenge, as I envision it, is threefold: philosophy must respond to the challenge of *skepticism* in knowledge, of *fragmenta-*

tion of a world view, and of *aimlessness* as to the purpose of life. As
Mark Schwehn says,

> For the first time in postmodern history, the answers to
> all three modern questions (What can we know? How
> should we live? In what or whom should we hope?) seem,
> to a large number of intellectuals at least, to depend
> completely upon the answer to the prior question: Who
> are we?[3]

Rather than engage in a debate with Rorty and Castaneda on
the great divide—whether philosophy as a cultural creation is at
its end and having no further historical role to play a proper object
of study (Rorty), or if, on the contrary, philosophy in continuity
with its glorious history, as well as transcending history, is entering
a new phase of its systematic pursuit of an increased understanding of human nature and the world in which it is deployed
(Castaneda)—I would rather focus on the primordial question of
who is the one who in order to be must philosophize.

An existential focus stresses the inner life of human beings, the
search for meaning and significant relationships in a mysterious
universe. From this perspective, philosophy presupposes a *caring*
in the related modes of (1) self-discovery and reflection, (2) self-
searching and realization, and (3) self-questioning and surrender.
Both the modern enlightenment and the postmodern disillusion
entail philosophy as concerned with the original opening of man to
the world. Its primary function is not so much to establish an
objective science of being, as to elicit and strengthen that original
freedom of mind which is a distinguishing feature of human existence in the world.

On this occasion I am not concerned with the different kinds
of facts and meanings, nor with the distinctive modes of understanding and corresponding truths that philosophy as a primordial openness to otherness generates. I would rather focus on
the inner conditions of the philosopher as a free openness to
the world, the conditions for understanding of this world independently from subjectivism and for the communication of this
understanding to other free persons from whose criticism the
philosopher is disposed to learn.

The inner conditions viewed as sources of vitality—and indeed, the root of freedom for philosophy—constitute an existential
spirituality, not yet identifiable as religious. I now propose three

sets of conditions corresponding to caring as self-reflection, self-realization and self-surrender.

Self-reflection implies sensitivity to hidden assumptions and presuppositions in oneself and in the other; it entails a flexible imagination as a precaution against a premature fixation on one answer or exclusive perspective. Self-reflection is based on spontaneity or a free act which is voluntary and intentional and hopefully liberating from immediate biases and preferences. Thus, self-reflection turns out to be a form of self-discovery, and the equivalent to freedom-as-spontaneity. (Later on we hope to connect self-discovery/self-reflection by way of moral entailment with the spirit of humility, as well as with a spirituality of childlikeness toward God.)

Self-realization as a conquest of self entails a distance from subjective inclinations and an exercise of self-restraint in hindering communication, complementarity and criticism. One must confront the question of one's existence, the lived experience of the subject, and the pursuit of integrity with one's inner resources. For this task one may not be merely passive or receptive to what is given, but rather creative and innovative and open to alternatives and self-correction. Thus, self-realization takes the form of freedom in the mode of creativity. But this creativity might demand the spirit of self-denial, which in turn is suggestive of disinterested love in the Christian context.

Finally, intellectual life entails an inner possibility of *self-surrender* by being able to connect special perspectives and the ultimate horizon of the life-world, to broaden one's own perspective to encompass the whole, and to dare to wonder and cultivate reverence, acceptance and affirmation of what is and what can be in view of ideals. Freedom as freedom "for/toward," in fidelity to values and ideals that transcend the ego, is connected to self-surrender and thus hopefully also to the spirit of faith and specially to Christian Practical Belief in Divine Providence.

From the above we may conclude that the conditions for the philosophical life of inquiry—caring in free openness to reality—appear as a process of self-reflection, self-realization, and self-surrender. Or, in other words, the philosophical activity entails spontaneity, creativity and reverence of freedom as conditions for human openness to the whole of being.

Now the answer to the question before us is by no means obvious: do the conditions or existential roots of the philosophical activity reveal an inherent spirituality? The formulation in itself presupposes a certain definition of spirituality. We mean by *spirituality* a fundamental vital source and point of reference for our mind, will and heart, a basis of orientation or conscious direction of human activity and inquiry. Spirituality is the pursuit of meaning, of an intimation of purpose and sense of vital connection to one's ultimate environment—the dimension of depth in all of life's endeavors and institutions. In short, a spirituality functions as a principle of enlightenment, integration and finality without which our self-reflection, self-realization and self-surrender could become superficial, chaotic and aimless.

At this point we must add two more questions: is it conceivable, if not by strict deduction at least by intuition, to link philosophy as a principle of enlightenment, integration and finality to spirituality in the theological context; and furthermore, is it possible for spirituality in its secular, even religious, context to respond to the *skepticism, fragmentation* and *aimlessness* that afflict postmodern philosophy?

2. The Link between Philosophy and Spirituality

The self-reflection and spontaneity of the philosophical life is rooted in humility. Humility as defined by philosopher M. Mandelbaum is "that attitude in which one feels (one's) own self to be small when compared with other realms of being."[4] Two aspects of humility come together here:
1) it is relational. It has to do with how we stand in relation to other realms of being, and
2) it is an assessment of the universe and one's place in it. Thus, humility has an epistemological import, having to do with self-knowledge and knowledge of our circumstances. It has to do with discovery and acceptance of self. But it also has to do with reverence and solidarity toward other persons; with the conservation, preservation and transformation of nature, and with the acknowledgment, if not submission, toward the Transcendental.

Humility is therefore not simply an internal attitude, but a matter of special structure and solidarity. Its internal aspect is a world-transforming attitude that opens the heart to being able to receive and give love; its external aspect is a new social order.

Self-realization as creaturely self-conquest entails the spirit of self-denial. By self-denial I mean the capacity first to risk and then to give ourselves up, if necessary, for the sake of truth. All denial of part of ourselves is essential to the process of growing into the truth together. Truth as a goal of a community effort requires self-discipline.

As already implied in humility and self-denial, the spirit of faith animates the self-surrender and fidelity to Truth, Goodness and Beauty, which we have already developed as conditions for the intellectual/philosophical life. Each of us as scholars, teachers and students must acknowledge that we at the university cannot explore the larger issues of life without faith and human confidence in what we have received. All of us rely upon the work and the thought of others, and we cannot possibly think well in an atmosphere of mistrust. Practically speaking, it means that we typically believe in what we are questioning and at the same time question what we are believing.

3. Philosophy and a Catholic Spirituality

We might view humility, self-denial and faith as a spirituality which enlightens, integrates and orients the inner freedom of intellectual self-realization, conquest and surrender in response to the crises of our times. But are these virtues of secular spirituality in themselves an effective—that is, reliable, appealing and durable—means to cope with the challenges?

We turn our attention to this question of effectiveness. A secular spirituality might be the natural condition, basis and personal contribution for the empowerment of our spirituality through grace. I hope that what now follows is not a mere "leap of faith" in the sense of the Danish philosopher Kierkegaard. I will now seek to root humility in the Christian notion of *childlikeness* before God, to root self-denial in a *Christian Covenant of Love*, and to root faith in the *Practical Belief in Divine Providence*. I shall do this within the context of Fr. Joseph Kentenich's Marian and patrocentric spirituality, which developed in Schoenstatt as a lay spirituality specifically thought and lived by him and his followers as an effective *remedy* (not only a critical response) to the modern and postmodern crises of our times. Indeed, Kentenich inspired us to respond to the challenges of our time with joy and confidence.

It has been written about Kentenich: "With great compassion and knowledge he looked into the inner life of modern man and applied many of the revealed truths as a remedy for modern ills."[5] His critique of modernism and postmodernism as a sequel is brilliantly expressed in a succinct fashion by the concept of a mechanistic world view.

A mechanistic world view separates into distinct ontological units what in reality are aspects or dimensions of a complex whole or a structure's order of being. It isolates into self-sufficient units what functions in interdependence, and stresses the static in the structure of being, with detriment to the dynamic processes of life, of growth, of becoming in the world.

From a mechanistic perspective man can appear either as isolated from the rest of reality, as ontologically self-sufficient and ethically independent from objective values; or else as reduced to a disposable part of a collectivistic system. Mechanistic thinking has also contributed to a further reduction of man's whole interior structure to a single aspect of his person: be it the rational, or the irrational (emotive or biological). In any case, mechanistic thinking views man as an atom-like entity doomed to depersonalization, while all his bonds with self, others, nature and the Transcendental are severed. As an antidote to mechanistic thinking, Kentenich prepared a world view which also is an organic method of thinking and an organic way of living and loving; in it, mind, will and heart interlock so as to inspire us intellectually with a piety that encompasses critical thinking but places it in the service of love.

This organic perspective assumes that faith, revelation and the affirmation of belief constitute the theological foundation without which no full integration or reliable integrating perspective of reality is secured. The theological dimension secures, complements and elevates—as a functional analogue of the effect of grace on nature—the knowledge which reason by way of logical inquiry can and indeed must demonstrate. The theological dimension of an integral world view reveals the ultimate origin and finality of reality, and thus the source and purpose of human life, both individual and communal, and provides a transcendental justification in terms of Being for man's sense of the Good as a moral category.

From the vast richness of Kentenich's organically-conceived spirituality, we discover features which best enlighten, integrate, orient—that is, vitalize, secure, sustain and give direction to—the threefold spirit of the intellectual life: humility, self-denial and faith. In what follows I relate these three features—childlikeness, the Covenant of Love, and Practical Belief in Divine Providence—to the three conditions of the philosophical life.

Childlikeness is for Kentenich not a stage in one's psycho-social-physical growth once attained to be then abandoned. Nor is it to be confused with infantilism or childishness, which incidentally could lead to depression. Rather, it is an ontological mode of being proper to the created order. As Kentenich observes, "Childlikeness is an elemental and essential aspect of our human nature. Being human simply means being a child. Being human means having a drive towards childlikeness. Is this true? The deep philosophical foundation lies in our contingency as created beings. . . . No created being is self-sufficient" (p. 37).

Childlikeness—as humble openness toward, acceptance of, and dependence on a higher "You" that is more intimate to me than self—also secures self-denial and animates our faith. On the interrelatedness of childlikeness, faith, surrender and self-denial, Kentenich writes:

> I can be a child to the extent that I dedicate all wishes and movements of my heart entirely to the Heavenly Father. This self-surrender presupposes constant self-abandonment. . . . A childlike person abandons his ego entirely and surrenders himself completely to the Father. Childlikeness is a concentration of strength, an energetic, firm, heroic striving for being alone with God. That is to say, a childlike person sacrifices his own self out of love for God. (p. 81)

The new, childlike person in Kentenich's conception can serve as model for the philosopher. He or she is a Spirit-imbued person whose attachment to ideals stems principally from the point of view of inner freedom and thus transcends all forms of coercion to attain the autonomy of authenticity of being and of a life lived by inner convictions. The new person strives for self-realization, or the perfection of one's own nature, but within the order of supernatural grace which calls the person to become divinized to be the child of God. A person is perfect when one's life is marked by an ideal fundamental attitude, and when all one's noble natural and supernatural talents have unfolded harmoniously. (This definition recalls, of course, the familiar Thomistic dictum that grace presupposes nature; grace does not destroy nature, but elevates and perfects it.)

The new person is an instrument—free, conscious, loving—and in this existential mode—that is, as instrument—the humility of the child of God is also the exaltation of our human condition, joy, and peace—never a source of depression. Through childlikeness, the intellectual can engage in self-realization and view knowledge as inseparable from Love. In the words of Kentenich:

> We are capable of leaving the reins of our lives in God's hands only if we are convinced that He loves us more than we love ourselves. He is more concerned about our well-being than we ourselves are. The saints became holy from the moment they began to love. This is in keeping with the other truth that they began to love the moment they believed, knew and felt that they were loved. True greatness is completely independent of circumstances. It consists in the total, childlike self-surrender of my whole nature to God. True holiness does not consist of knowledge, but of my childlike self-surrender to the Heavenly Father, of completely centering on God. It consists of giving everything, my will and my heart, to the Father in childlike love. The child lives entirely in the Father's heart. (pp. 80–81)

One cannot consider childlikeness apart from love and the mutual relationship Kentenich described as a *Covenant of Love*. Love is the basic and central drive of the human soul. As the basic element, love animates all the spiritual functions of the person, leading one to personal integration and to union with the beloved "you." As central drive, love is connected with all the powers of the soul and therefore seizes, rules and coordinates all the person is and does. Love bridges the differences between people and unites them in great goals. As a strong fundamental power, it forms the individual persons in an original way, thus preserving their individuality, but also directing them toward the common good of the community.

Rights to self and duties to others, the private and the public are blended by the formative power of love. The self-realization of the new person integrated within the new community presupposes, as is by now evident, a *covenant* of love which is not only the *contractual bond* or the ethics of rights or merely the contact/compact bond advocated by the counter-balancing ethics of responsibility. Beyond the language of rights and duties is love, but a love that preserves the claims of rights and duties. In so doing, love secures the claims of justice and autonomy. The covenant of love thus fosters communal obligations which strive to secure a real, love-filled unity and do not rest on the mere accommodation of compromise and tolerance. The covenant of love harmonizes the polaric tensions of self-realization/self-renunciation, or of autonomy and surrender to a person. Thus, it counterbalances the modern and postmodern trend toward fragmentation. In essence, a covenant of love is an exchange of hearts—the core of one's personality—of interests, and of goods with a beloved person. The idea of the covenant answers man's innate aptitude and longing to be complemented by another in the unique dignity, being and value of this other person. This demands humility.

First of all, man as a spiritual being dependent on God needs the complementation of God for his perfection. God revealed himself as God of the covenant, and appointed man to enter the covenant and thus gain salvation. In our surrender to a personal God we gain our true self as desired by God from all eternity.

The covenant of love responds to man's fundamental power of soul and guards us against the loss of personality: God for us is not only the spiritual God, an incomprehensible idea, but a person who loves us and who expects our love in return. The covenant secures the worth of the individual person, the root of one's dignity and rights to autonomy. Renunciation of one's primitive nature and acceptance of God by way of love secures the realization of our redeemed nature.

But the covenant besides securing the experience of a personal God, of the personality of each one, also fosters the Christian community. It overcomes the loss of personality in one's fellowman. The other is not a number, not a replaceable object. God has entered into a covenant with each person in the community, thus elevating, complementing and securing their unique, personal ideals and values. Others are with us drawn into God's covenant of love with mankind, and therefore we are connected to one another and with one another and thus bear responsibility for one another. Renunciation of part of one's self for the sake of the good of the other also enhances the power over one's selfish nature, increases one's autonomy, and realizes one's true self in its relational or interpersonal dimension.

Thus the covenant of love is the grounds of self-denial in a free and creative interchange of goods, hearts and interests which secures a full conquest and realization of self, thus providing an ultimate security against the depersonalizing, dehumanizing, destructive forces in man's denial of his own dignity today and the fragmentation of community. We will refer in detail to this point later.

We now turn to the last aspect of Kentenich's spirituality,

which we have selected as specially significant for the intellectual life: Practical Belief In Divine Providence. Kentenich defines one particular aspect of Divine Providence in warm, existential terms:

> Simple faith in Divine Providence is childlikeness to the highest degree. If I am a simple child, then [I believe that] God loves me so tenderly that he governs my life by his special providence. . . . God has mapped out the plan of my life from all eternity and has provided for it. All I have to do is to say yes. . . . To the extent that we love God with childlike hearts, we are prompted in joyful readiness to do or omit all that the Father wants and in the way He wants it. (pp. 94–95)

On the part of God, this providential relationship implies two acts: first, there is an act of the mind. God made a plan and included in this plan everything that is happening today. Secondly, it also includes an act of the will. God wants every happening in life to serve the execution of his plan.

On our part, this relationship also implies acts of the mind, will and heart. The mind recognizes that everything has been foreseen and that, as Kentenich liked to affirm, "God's goodness is the source of everything" (cf. p. 72). This prompts a secure human response to the happenings of life in the belief: God's fatherly will stands behind everything. I know that I am loved. My life's destiny is not blindly tossed about; it is personally directed by God the Father, a personal God who speaks a personal yes to my destiny and to my personality with its originality. This fundamental security inspires, in turn, an active cooperation with God's will.

How well can Kentenich's spirituality of childlikeness, Covenant of Love and Belief in Divine Providence enlighten the philosopher in our response to contemporary skepticism, fragmentation and aimlessness? We now make the answer more explicit, for the preceding discussion already indicated our line of thought. According to Kentenich, childlikeness entails an attitude of awe and reverence to counterbalance the skepticism of postmodernism and the arrogance of modernism, and thus presents a challenge to the self-sufficiency of many of us.

As Kentenich observes, "A child's first conscious act is reverent admiration for all he sees and absorbs" (p. 99). In this humility the path toward certainty is opened: "Awe, a reverent perception of creation, is the characteristic quality of a childlike person" (ibid).

Thus, the childlike philosopher is able to resist the destructive skepticism of modern man.

The humility of the childlike person may reveal the intellectual arrogance of the modernistic quest for absolute certainty by way of the priority of reason over all other human faculties. It restores the wonder, expectation and trust toward reality so much in question in postmodernism by helping to discover anew a point of spontaneous interaction with the universe. Humility does not mean uncritical acceptance, but an attitude of childlikeness that, in practical terms, entails the presumption of wisdom and authority in the other person and spontaneous respect toward the sources of truth.

Moreover, humility, properly understood, is the antidote for its own caricature or misconstrued version as depression. To adopt the *scala* of St. Bernard, humility is the first of three steps of truth: it gives us truth about self—even as charity offers us truth about others, and contemplation, truth about God—and thus restores our embeddedness in a universe of nurture and care.[6]

The covenant of love as the basis for the freedom of creative self-conquest and self-realization presupposes the spirit of self-denial. We also see it as a counterbalance to the self-affirming self-sufficiency of man in the modernistic tendency to rely almost exclusively on natural science as the criterion for knowledge and on technology as the model for the practical control and design of the world.

Self-denial does not entail either a fatalistic resignation to outside control or the futility of the search for foundation, unity, ideas, values and beliefs. It includes, to be sure, a search for *foundation*—but a foundation not in the mundane reality modern science/technology proposes, nor in the human subject as the individual autonomous designer of one's own scheme and scale of values. Self-denial is an aid to transcend not only the individualism and subjectivism of postmodernism, but also the narrow conception of reality in modernism, through openness and an affirmation of divine reality as the ultimate ground for being. It contributes to unity and coherence in world view and thus counters the fragmentation of postmodernism. Moreover, self-denial is not the self-destruction or rejection of our own nature, which is often the depressing outcome of postmodernist skepticism. Self-denial is a means to a self-affirmation at a higher order.

What we have stated about the covenant of love may also incidentally respond to the postmodernist concern with community—

academic ones in particular—in view of its role as a source of truth in terms of consensus. In *To Know As We Are Known* (1983), Parker Palmer insists that both knowledge and truth are communal terms. Knowledge is not the result of the isolated individual's efforts to mirror the world; it is instead a form of responsible relationship, even a "means to relationship" with others. Knowing becomes a reunion of separated beings whose primary bond is not logic but love; truth is the name of this "community of relatedness."[7] But we cannot, as Palmer and Rorty do, place philosophy in the social context of possible discourses and conversations, while presupposing no disciplinary matrix which unites the speakers with hope for agreement, not on the basis of the discovery of an antecedently existing common ground, as "persons whose paths through life have fallen together, united by civility rather than by a common goal, much less a common ground" (ibid.).

My point is: we need a common goal, a common ground. It seems our covenant of love contributes toward this ground. For Kentenich the power of love works through structural principles which give form to the community, helps to harmonize the rights of individuals with their duties to the community, and animates all forms of responsibility. The structural principles secure an objective basis for the interplay of love between those in authority and their followers and vice versa, and of love among equals. Thus, to ask about the meaning of truth is to raise questions about context, boundaries, language, and about the virtues that collectively define the shape and substance of a particular community of inquirers whose primary intention is to discover the truth.

A covenant of love animating a federative structured community is indeed relevant. We must remember that the quality of the individual's thought and the quality of the community's thinking are mutually dependent upon one another. The tension existing between the free personality or autonomous person and the community is extremely valuable. Strong personalities inject the community with new life and innovative ideas and protect it from superficiality and any disregard for the uniqueness of the person. The community in turn ensures that the individual persons offer their talents and capacities at the service of the common good and do not develop one-sidely in isolation and dissipation of talent. Thus, one of the most valuable life forces of an ideal state is to be found in the tension between the person and the community.

The tension between the person and the community/family is ultimately harmonized by the power of love. The heart of the community is the power of love, and as such it can be called the principle of unity which in turn is complemented by the principle of creative tension; for indeed, love fosters the growth of life among diverse and individual persons who retain their individuality precisely by contrasting and enriching it in complementary contact with others who must also be respected in their own individuality if one is to retain one's own. Thus, as Kentenich understood it, the principle of unity singles out the central role of the covenant of love which forms a community, and the principle of creative tension preserves and increases the vitality of the community. It is precisely these two last principles which contribute the most to the integration of man as community with God and the rest of creation. A perfect community presupposes, then, perfect personalities who are united in love and who strive toward a common ideal recognized as an objective good.

Kentenich's teaching on a Practical Belief in Divine Providence counteracts the aimlessness of modern life. Modernistic thinking is rooted in natural faith in progress and in universality and regularity as accomplishments of natural reason. In postmodern times, as we have indicated, not even this faith in reason is prevalent—hence the near despair before the quest for foundation-reliable meaning and the age of suspicion. Faith is placed in the power of criticism, revision, deconstruction. And as we all know, once you do not have faith or belief in some objective-reliable ideal, then you believe in anything for the most superficial, transitory motives—hence fanaticism, cults, etc.

4. A Mariological Conclusion

We now turn to Mary as a model for the Intellectual Person. I believe this Mariological reference to be a proper and *effective* way to conclude our response to the challenges of modernism and postmodernism. That is, when we recognize in the person of Mary the clearly defined features of self-discovery, conquest and surrender with their corresponding spirit as already indicated, we are moved toward contemplation. The invitation to contemplate complements our inquiry.

We contemplate Mary's *Being*, the fullness of her person as the new person, under the designation of "the Immaculate Conception." In the image of the *Immaculata* we have discovered the fully integrated person, the microcosmos who in creaturely dependence and openness to God restores the order of reality within the person and in relation to the rest of creation. In such a fully integrated person the mind is clear, the judgment is prudent, the will is imperturbable and decisive, and the emotions are refined and ordered to the perfection of the whole. All the mental and spiritual faculties cooperate when such a person enters into communication with the social, cultural and physical surroundings with which personal and vital bonds are established.[8]

As the Immaculate being, Mary is the Model for any lay spirituality, but specifically for us in Schoenstatt. In the image of the Immaculata, we can clearly see that she, as the one made whole by God, is the sensitive human being who forms an entity in herself, but who is not closed off in herself; on the contrary, she is unfeignedly open to others.

In Mary we recognize the whole person to be an integrated person and, through the Covenant of Love with her, we find a means to resemble the Immaculata, and thus strive for a religious ethics of love in terms of which the polarization of rights and duties, private and public, individual and community can find a harmony of complementarity. In the Immaculata, the intellectual contemplates the inner freedom of spontaneity, the integration of personality, and a childlike, animated, practical belief in Divine Providence.

Since Mary is the most perfect child of the Father, the permanent helpmate of the Son for the salvation of the soul, as well as the temple for the indwelling of the Holy Spirit, she embodies all the virtues of the "new person" in Christ. She is the perfect Christian. She, as the Immaculata, embodies the perfect harmony of spirit and matter, of reason and emotions, of justice and love, and clears the path toward Truth, both intuitive and discursive. Her will is in harmony with God's will. She models the Beauty of inner order and relatedness to the whole.

From Mary's being as Immaculata, as the manifestation of Truth, Goodness and Beauty, we may derive—via the contemplation which crowns our reflection—a Marian mentality that may form the spirit of the intellectual. We now choose only these aspects of Marian mentality judged pertinent to our theme.

THE HANDMAID OF THE LORD: A RESPONSE TO SKEPTICISM

Mary is the embodiment of childlikeness, heroic humility and self-discovery as a child of God. Reflecting on the picture of Mary as the Handmaid at the hour of the Annunciation, Kentenich observed, " 'Ecce ancilla Domini Fiat. . . . ' (Lk 1:38). These words convey the infinitely simple, childlike self-surrender of the whole nature to the eternal God's will. Perfect humility, perfect simplicity! Childlikeness, most heroic childlikeness!" (p. 58). Mary is spontaneous, intelligent, fully dignified in her instrumentality. "The entire life of Our Lady is an actualization of God's will, a constant and absolute surrender to the wish and will of the Father" (ibid.).

In Mary the intellectual learns to transcend the self-sufficiency of a critical spirit with no discernment of what or how experience may be questioned, as well as the anxiety and pessimism of the skeptic. Neither the self-sufficient nor the anxious appreciates the primacy of affirmation of the intuitive openness to what presents itself with clarity before a pure heart.

THE SORROWFUL MOTHER: A RESPONSE TO FRAGMENTATION

Mary is the embodiment of self-conquest, self-denial and the creativity of giving of self freely in and through love. Here, in the image of the Sorrowful Mother standing beneath the Cross of Christ, the intellectual learns to appreciate the value of self-discipline: the renunciation of everything in the self and outside of it that distracts, denies, distorts or can in any way hinder our search for Truth, Goodness and Beauty, particularly as they are perfectly exemplified in Incarnate Wisdom. The great intellectual, saint and philosopher Edith Stein spoke of the new perspective on reality which the acceptance of the Cross entails.

The Mater Dolorosa shows us how full dedication and commitment to a task is an interplay of enlightened mortification and purification, as well as the experience of conquest, of self-realization in creative freedom toward all that surrounds us. She accompanies us in our painful search, in our doubts, in our lonely and confusing journey, when we struggle to grasp the depth or the height of our object of inquiry and find ourselves unable to communicate it or secure through it benefits.

THE ASSUMPTA: A RESPONSE TO AIMLESSNESS

Mary's self-surrender and freedom of unconditional fidelity reaches the goal of our faith, that is, participation in the Divine. Mary Assumed into heaven teaches us to value the true role of the physical in the plan of creation, the symbolic significance of the bodily impulses which should not distract us from our search for the goods of the Spirit, and the hope for the full integration of body and soul in heaven. The Assumpta inspires hope in the midst of our doubts, mistakes, limitations before the complexity and magnitude of our search.

In Mary we have the personal, Immaculate mode of being which embodies the response and indeed the remedy we as intellectuals in the Catholic tradition may contemplate and imitate by allowing her to form us. She enlightens, integrates and directs our spirituality in an effective manner in our critical times, enhancing our contribution as academics to Church, society and humanity.

As *Ancilla Domini*, she overcomes the skepticism of postmodernism, as well as the intellectual self-sufficiency and critical mode of modernism. In her Fiat we rediscover our true spontaneity and freedom as children of God who in humility remain open, receptive, willing to be enriched, complemented and enlightened. In her we rediscover our childlikeness before the Father, as Kentenich demonstrated. We discover the truth of ourself in a *Fiat* ("Let it be done unto me") which is the condition of our creative mode of self-realization.

As *Mater Dolorosa*, she overcomes the dispersion, fragmentation and decenteredness of postmodernism, even as she remains outside the closed system of totalizing modernist ideologies. In her we reconquer our entire person of mind, will and heart. In her we learn to view and to have a new strength to conquer life, and particularly to accept the cross of personality, of community life, and of professional tasks. Because of her unity of Being as the Immaculata, she preserves our equanimity and creative freedom before the challenges and trials of our lives as persons and intellectuals. She shows us that the piety of the intellectual must emanate, serve and culminate in love, indeed, in a covenant of love with God, others and creation.

Finally, as *Assumpta*, she overcomes the aimlessness and lack of foundation affecting postmodern man, and also moderates the illusion of progressivism, regularity and universality which inspired the modernistic man. In self-surrender, in fidelity as maximum freedom, she mediates for us a vision of Divine Providence, revealing God to be the authentic and ultimate aim of all we think, do and love in co-responsibility. A living God is the unshakable foundation of our ideas about reality and of the values which animate our involvement with the world. Mary makes our *faith* a living experience that encompasses all our faculties, not just the intellect, and is effectively vital in all circumstances of our existence. It is a living faith within daily experience that establishes the grounds for, sets the boundaries of, and gives direction to our inquiries, transcending the narrow limits of modernistic radicalism, but also protecting us against the arbitrariness of believing just anything.

By way of summary, then, we discover in Mary the spontaneity of the child, humble, in awe before the wonders of God's creation, and learn from her intellectual reverence. We conquer and realize with Mary, in the inner creativity and freedom which only love sustains, a full personality as a point of reference that gives us meaning for understanding the world, and learn intellectual creativity as a source of search for objectivity and truth. We surrender in-with-for Mary in fidelity to the Divine Plan of the Father-God's love, Wisdom, and Power—a surrender that enriches our faith, bringing it to a new level of certainty, as a new unifying factor in our lives, as a new goal for our endeavors. Finally, as the culmination of our freedom to participate in a new order of ideals, we learn intellectual joy, peace and the pure love of Truth. In her person we understand all that grace can or may do in our nature as it transfigures us. She brings into interaction the humility of the child of God the Father and the self-denial of the Co-redemptrix or permanent companion of the Son, even as she exemplifies the living Faith of one who is vessel of the Holy Spirit. In her the challenge of skepticism is overcome by way of reverence, fragmentation by way of creative love, and aimlessness by way of fidelity.

Notes

1. A. D. Sertillanges, O.P., *The Intellectual Life: Its Spirit, Conditions, and Methods* (Westminster, MD: The Newman Press, 1959), p. viii.

2. See Richard Rorty and Hector Castaneda, *The Institution of Philosophy*, ed. M. Henri, A. Cohen, and M. Dasal (Illinois: Open Court, 1988).

3. Mark Schwehn, "Religion and My Life of Learning," *First Things* (September 1990), p. 34.

4. Maurice Mandelbaum, *The Phenomenology of Moral Experience* (Baltimore: The Johns Hopkins Press, 1969), p. 162.

5. I quote from the preface to *God My Father*, trans. and privately published by the Schoenstatt Sisters of Mary (Waukesha, Wiscon-

sin, 1977, repr. 1992). Subsequent citations of this edition of apho-risms, taken from the writings of Fr. Kentenich, are parenthetical by page.

6.   See St. Bernard, "The Steps of Humility and Pride," trans. M. Ambrose Conway, O.S.C.O., in *Treatises II*, Vol. 5 of *The Works of St. Bernard of Clairvaux* (Washington, D.C.: Cistercian Publications, 1974).

7.   Parker Palmer, *To Know As We Are Known: A Spirituality of Education* (San Francisco: Harper and Row, 1983), as quoted by Schwenn, p. 40.

8.   See Sr. M. Ludowika, "Mary Immaculate: Blueprint of the New Man," a talk delivered at the 1977 October Conference in Schoenstatt, Germany.

Contributors

ANN W. ASTELL received her Ph.D. from the University of Wisconsin-Madison. A medievalist, she is Associate Professor of English at Purdue University. Her publications include *The Song of Songs in the Middle Ages* (1990) and *Job, Boethius, and Epic Truth* (1994), both from Cornell University Press. Astell is a member of the Secular Institute of the Schoenstatt Sisters of Mary.

GÜNTHER M. BOLL is a native of Germany, born in Frankfurt/ Main. A founding member of the Secular Institute of the Schoenstatt Fathers, he is editor of the theological journal *Regnum*, a lecturer on spiritual theology, and a recognized leader in the International Schoenstatt Movement.

TOM W. BOYD received his Ph.D. in Religion from Vanderbilt University. He is Associate Professor of Philosophy and Kingfisher Chair in the Philosophy of Religion and Ethics at the University of Oklahoma. In the spring of 1988 he was Rockwell Visiting Scholar in Religion at the University of Houston. His academic publications have focused on values—religious, ethical, social and personal growth values. His current interests are the dialogue among world religions and the dialogue between science and religion.

ROBERTO COLELLA, Professor of Physics at Purdue University, received his doctorate at the University of Milan, Italy, in 1958. He has worked as a research scientist at the Joint Nuclear Research Center of Euratom in Ispra, Italy, and as a postdoctoral research associate at Cornell University. His research interests are in the fields of experimental x-ray diffraction physics, thermal vibrations, charge densities, interferometry, diffraction in perfect crystals and, most currently, quasicrystals.

MARY GERHART is Professor of Religious Studies at Hobart and William Smith Colleges. Her advanced degrees are from the University of Missouri (M.A., English) and the University of Chicago (M.A., Theology and Literature, and Ph.D., Religion and Literature). She is the author of more than sixty-five articles and six books, the most recent among them, *Genre Choices, Gender Questions* (University of Oklahoma Press, 1992). Her interests range over hermeneutics, the theory of metaphor, feminist studies, postmodern philosophy and theology, and the thought of Paul Ricoeur.

PHILIBERT HOEBING, O.F.M., received his M.A. at the Franciscan Institute at St. Bonaventure University. An Associate Professor of Philosophy at Quincy University, he specializes in teaching bioethics, environmental ethics, and Franciscan philosophy.

ELENA LUGO received her Ph.D. from Georgetown University. She is Professor of Philosophy and Director of the Center for the Philosophy and History of Science and Technology at the University of Puerto Rico-Mayagüez. Well-known for her work in biomedical ethics, she is the author of numerous articles and five books, *Medical Ethics* (1985), *Ethics in Engineering* (1985), *Philosophy and Psychology* (1980), *Psychiatry and Ethics* (1980), and *Existential Perspectives in Religion* (1978). She is a member of the Secular Institute of the Schoenstatt Sisters of Mary.

MARY WALSH MEANY is Associate Professor and former Chair of Religious Studies at Siena College. Her research has focused on Franciscan spirituality, the *Vita Christi* tradition, and various women mystics, especially Catherine of Siena, Julian of Norwich, and Angela of Foligno.

VALERIE MIKÉ, a native of Budapest, Hungary, has a Ph.D. in mathematics from New York University. She is Clinical Professor of Biostatistics in Public Health at Cornell University Medical College and former Head of the Biostatistics Department at the Sloan-Kettering Institute for Cancer Research. Her most recent publications and current research focus on ethical and value issues pertaining to uncertainty in science and technology.

DONALD W. MITCHELL is Professor of Asian and Comparative Philosophy in the Department of Philosophy at Purdue University and Director of the Religious Studies Program there. He is on the executive board of the Society for Buddhist-Christian Studies and is associate editor of its journal, *Buddhist-Christian Studies*, published by the University of Hawaii Press. Mitchell, who received his Ph.D. from the University of Hawaii, is author of *Spirituality and Emptiness: The Dynamics of Spiritual Life in Buddhism and Christianity* (Paulist Press, 1991), as well as numerous articles in the Buddhist-Christian dialogue.

ANN L. PIRRUCCELLO is Assistant Professor of Philosophy at the University of San Diego. She received her Ph.D. from Purdue University. Her current work focuses on Simone Weil and other twentieth-century continental philosophers.

JOHANN ROTEN, S.M., a native of Switzerland, is Director of the International Marian Research Institute at the University of Dayton. An internationally known retreat master, he holds a doctorate in the Social Sciences from the University of Fribourg and a S.T.D. from the Marianum in Rome. Among his many publications is a book on Hans Urs von Balthasar's theological anthropology.

THOMAS RYBA holds a Ph.D. in the History and Literature of Religion from Northwestern University. He is the author of many articles and a book, *The Essence of Phenomenology and Its Meaning for the Scientific Study of Religion* (1991). He is Adjunct Professor of Theology at the University of Notre Dame, Adjunct Professor of Philosophy at Purdue University, and Theologian-in-Residence at the St. Thomas Aquinas Center at Purdue.

ALDO TASSI, Professor of Philosophy at Loyola College in Maryland, received his Ph.D. from Fordham University. He is the author of *The Political Philosophy of the American Revolution* (University Press of America, 1978), as well as numerous articles on political philosophy, metaphysics, philosophy of language, the concept of the self, and theater. A playwright, he is currently writing a book that attempts to "engage Being through the theatre, insofar as the latter can be viewed as the 'enactment of Being.' "